MATRIMONIAL CONVEYANCING

AUSTRALIA
Law Book Co
Sydney

CANADA AND USA
Carswell
Toronto

HONG KONG
Sweet & Maxwell Asia

NEW ZEALAND
Brookers
Wellington

SINGAPORE and MALAYSIA
Sweet & Maxwell Asia
Singapore and Kuala Lumpur

MATRIMONIAL CONVEYANCING

NINTH EDITION

Stephen Harker

LONDON
SWEET & MAXWELL
2006

First Edition	1981 (by William M. Hartley)
Second Edition	1985 (by William M. Hartley)
Third Edition	1988 (by William M. Hartley)
Fourth Edition	1991 (by William M. Hartley)
Fifth Edition	1993 (by William M. Hartley)
Sixth Edition	1987 (by William M. Hartley)
Seventh Edition	2000 (by Stephen Harker)
Eighth Edition	2003 (by Stephen Harker)
Ninth Edition	2006 (by Stephen Harker)

Published in 2006 by Sweet & Maxwell Limited
of 100 Avenue Road, Swiss Cottage, London, NW3 3PF
www.sweetandmaxwell.co.uk
Typeset by LBJ Typesetting Ltd of Kingsclere
Printed and bound in Great Britain by Ashford Colour Press

No natural forests were destroyed to make this product; only farmed timber was used and re-planted.

British Library Cataloguing in Publication Data

A CIP catalogue record for this book is available from the British Library

ISBN-10 0-421-95040-4
ISBN-13 978-0-421-95040-5

All rights reserved.
Crown Copyright material is reproduced with the permission of the Controller of HMSO and the Queen's Printer for Scotland.

No part of this publication may be reproduced or transmitted, in any form, or by any means, or sorted in any retrieval system of any nature, without prior written permission, except for permitted fair dealing under the Copyright, Designs and Patents Act 1988, or in accordance with the terms of a licence issued by the Copyright Licensing Agency in respect of photocopying and/or reprographic reproduction. Precedent material included in this publication may be used as a guide for drafting of legal documents specifically for particular clients, though no liability is accepted for by the publishers or authors in relation to their use. Such documents may be provided to clients for their own use and to the solicitors acting for other parties to the transaction subject to acknowledgment of the course of the precedent. Precedents may not otherwise be distributed to other parties. Application for permission for other use of copyright material including permission to reproduce extracts in other published works shall be made to the publishers. Full acknowledgement of author, publisher and source must be given.

©
Sweet & Maxwell
2006

Acknowledgment

© Crown copyright. Land Registry Forms are reproduced by kind permission of Land Registry.

Preface

This book has been a valuable source of reference in many family practitioners offices over the years since the first edition. As a conveyancing partner in a largely family practice I can certainly vouch for the book's usefulness in guiding family practitioners through the various procedures and forms needed to transfer interests in and ownership of the former family home.

There have been a number of changes in the law and the requirements of HM Land Registry since I took over the editorship of this book in 2000. I hope that this edition continues to provide the guidance to family practitioners referred to in the previous paragraph.

The object of the book has not changed over the years and that is to provide the busy practitioner with an easy reference to precedents which can be utilised and adapted to meet the particular situations he or she is dealing with.

In most divorces it is still the family home which comprises the biggest asset of the parties and therefore it is still a keenly fought issue. There are often emotional as well as legal issues which make it a key part of any proceedings. The precedents have been updated to reflect changes brought about by the Land Registration Act 2002, the Finance Act 2003, the Civil Partnership Act 2004 and the Tax and Civil Partnership Regulations 2005 so that they remain relevant to family practitioners and their conveyancing colleagues.

My thanks go to Sweet & Maxwell for their continued support and patience. I hope the book continues to provide practical and relevant assistance in many solicitors offices.

The law is stated as at May 1, 2006.

Stephen Harker   London, April 2006

Contents

	Page
Acknowledgment	v
Preface	vii
Table of Cases	xv
Table of Statutes	xix
Table of Statutory Instruments	xxiii

1 General Principles
1. The scope of this book — 1
2. The effect of the Land Registration Act 2002 (the 2002 Act) — 2
3. The effect of the Civil Partnerships Act 2004 (the CPA) — 3
4. The advantage of a court order — 4
5. Covenants for title — 4
6. Property subject to a mortgage — 7
7. Practice of HM Land Registry — 9
8. Tax — 17
9. Council tax — 17
10. Insolvency — 17
11. Former council houses — 19
12. Execution of documents — 19
13. Legal service commission statutory charge — 20
14. Community legal service funding and conveyancing costs — 21

2 The Tax Aspects
1. Capital gains tax — 23
2. Inheritance tax — 26
3. Stamp duty land tax — 27

3 Home in Sole Name of One Party Transfer to Other
1. Notice of home rights — 33
2. Protection of the transferee's position before lodging of transfer for registration — 51
3. Procedure — 60
4. Covenants for title — 62
5. Where the property is subject to a mortgage — 62
6. Steps to be taken following completion of the transfer — 64

Precedents
1. Transfer of entirety to other party. No mortgage. By court order (form TR1) — 70

2	Assignment of leasehold property to other party. No mortgage. By court order (form TR1)	73
3	Transfer of entirety to other party by order of the court. Property subject to mortgage. Transferee (with mortgagee's agreement) assuming liability. Transferor released (form TR1)	76
4	Transfer of entirety to other party by order of the court. Mortgage. Transferor remaining liable. Transferee indemnifying (form TR1)	79
5	Transfer of entirety to other party. Sale. Property subject to first and second mortgages. Transferee assuming liability for the first and transferor released. Transferor remaining liable on second (form TR1)	82
6	Consent to transfer subject to mortgage by occupier	86

4 House in Joint Names Transfer to Sole Name

1	Severance	89
2	Procedure	90
3	Form of transfer	91
4	Covenants for title	93
5	Where the property is subject to a mortgage	93
6	Steps to be taken following the completion of the transfer	94

Precedents

7, 8 & 9	Notice of severance by one party to the other severing joint tenancy	96
	(Precedent 7—Unregistered land)	96
	(Precedent 8—Unregistered land)	96
	(Precedent 9—Registered land)	96
10	Transfer by one party as joint tenant to the other joint tenant. No mortgage. By order of court (form TR1)	97
11	Transfer by one joint tenant to the other joint tenant. Sale. No mortgage (form TR1)	99
12	Transfer by one joint tenant to the other joint tenant by order of court. Mortgage. Transferor released (form TR1)	101
13	Leasehold—assignment by one joint tenant to the other joint tenant by order of the court. Mortgage. Transferor released (form TR1)	104
14	Transfer by one joint tenant to the other joint tenant. Sale. Mortgage. Transfer released (form TR1)	107
15	Leasehold assignment by one joint tenant to the other joint tenant. By agreement subject to mortgage. Transferor released (form TR1)	110
16	Transfer by one joint tenant to the other joint tenant by order of the court. Transferor not released but transferee indemnifying. Mortgage not a party (form TR1)	113

	17	Transfer by one party to the other. Sale of transferor's share in the family home held by them as tenants in common in equal shares. No mortgage (form TR1)	116
	18	Transfer by one party to the other by order of the court of transferor's share in family home held by them as tenants in common. No mortgage (form TR1)	119
	19	Release of transferor from mortgage by mortgagee at date subsequent to transfer to transferee subject to the mortgage	122
5	**Transfer of Ex-partner's Interest to New Partner**		
	1	Procedure	124
	2	Covenants for title	125
	3	Form of transfer	126
	4	Where the property is subject to a mortgage	126
	5	Advice to be given to parties taking as joint tenants or tenants in common	127
	6	Steps to be taken following the completion of the transfer	128
Precedents			
	20	Transfer on sale by one joint tenant to stranger (new partner). Remaining joint tenant and stranger becoming joint tenants. No mortgage (form TR1)	130
	21	Transfer on sale by one party of share in family home (held by self and other party as tenants in common in equal shares) to new partner. Transferees holding as tenants in common. No mortgage (form TR1)	133
	22	Transfer on sale by one party of share in family home. Original parties joint tenants. Transferee and new partner taking as tenants in common. Mortgage. Transferee and new partner responsible. Transferor released (form TR1)	136
	23	One party to receive whole property (in sole name of other party) by court order, but requests transfer to self and new partner as joint tenants. No mortgage (form TR1)	139
	24	House in joint names of the parties. One party entitled to sole interest by court order. Transfer to that party and new partner. Mortgage. Transferor released (form TR1)	142
	25	House in sole name of one party. Transferee entitled to 50 per cent by court order. Sale of other 50 per cent to new partner. Transferee and new partner to hold as joint tenants (form TR1)	145
6	**House to be held on Certain Terms and Conditions**		
	1	Comment of the Mesher order	150
	2	Procedure	152

3	Covenants for title	153
4	Tax considerations	153
5	Form of transfer	155
6	Trusts of Land and Appointment of Trustees Act 1996	157
7	Contents of the declaration of trust	158
8	Where the property is subject to a mortgage	158
9	Steps to be taken following the completion of the transfer and declaration of trust	159

Precedents

26 Transfer of family home (in sole name of one party) to both parties to hold on terms of court order (form TR1) 161

27 & 28 Transfer on family home (in sole name of one party) to independent trustees to hold on terms agreed between the parties (form TR1) 164–169
(Precedent 28—Declaration of trust) 164
Family home (parties joint tenants) to be held on terms of court order. Occupying party to repair and insure 167
(Precedent 29—Registered land) 169
(Precedent 30—Registered land) 169
(Precedent 31—Declaration of trust—Registered and unregistered land) 169

32 Family home (parties joint tenants) subject to mortgage, to be held on terms of court order. Non-occupying party responsible for mortgage (interest only) 170

33 & 34 Family home held by both parties as joint tenants to be held following court order or agreement by independent trustees for one party to reside until specified event, non-residing party to be responsible for major repairs (and receive credit) and both parties covenanting with the trustees 172
(Precedent 34—Declaration of trust) 175

7 Deferred Charges and Adjustment Between Both Parties of their Interests

1	Conduct of the conveyancing	178
2	Covenants for title	179
3	Tax considerations	179
4	Form of transfer	180
5	Where the property is subject to a mortgage	181
6	Steps to be taken following the completion of the transfer	182

Precedents

35 Assignment by one party (tenant in common) of part of undivided share in sale proceeds of family home to other party (co-tenant in common) following court order. No sale until happening of specified event 184

36 Family home in one party's name. Transfer to other subject to payment. Court order (form TR1) 185

37 & 38	Family home in joint names of parties as joint tenants. Transfer of whole to one party by court order. Other party to have charge. Not to be called in until fixed date. Interest payable meantime. Leasehold (form TR1)	187
	(Precedent 38—Legal Charge)	189
39 & 40	Family home in sole name of one party. Court order. Transfer to other party subject to existing charge. Deferred charge (2nd mortgage) in favour of transferor for specific amount not to be enforced until certain events. No interest chargeable until happening of events	191
	(Precedent 40—Notice of second charge to first mortgagee)	193
41	Family home in sole name of one party (following court order) subject to existing charge. Deferred charge in favour of other party for percentage of sale proceeds on specified events. No interest chargeable meantime	194
42	Family home held by both parties and one party's mother as to two thirds for the both parties as joint tenants and one third for the mother. Transfer by order of court of one party's interest to the other (form TR1)	197

8 Reluctance by Transferring Party to Execute Transfer or Mortgage

1	Execution of the transfer or mortgage by the court	199
2	Vesting orders	202
3	The lack of title documents	203

Precedents

43	Affidavit of petitioner's solicitors where transferor fails to execute transfer. Mortgage	204
44	Affidavit by process server as to delivery of engrossed transfer to respondent and service of court order	206
45	Attestation clause on transfer to be executed by the court	207

9 Life Policy Collateral to the Mortgage on the Home

1	Introduction	209
2	Procedure	210
3	The different policies	210
4	Covenants contained in the assignment	211
5	Payment of premiums	212
6	Steps to be taken following the completion of the assignment	212

Precedents

46	Policy on life of one party to be assigned to other party by order of the court	213
47	Policy on life of one party charged to bank or building society to be assigned to other party (subject to charge) by order of court	214

	48	Notice of assignment to assurance company given on behalf of assignee	214
	49	Policy on lives of both parties charged to bank or building society. Benefit of policy (subject to charge) by order of court to be assigned to one party. Assignee to pay premiums	215
	50	Policy on life of husband written under MWPA 1882 for benefit of wife. Husband as trustee. Benefit to be held for Assignor	216
	51	Deed of appointment of new trustees where MWPA policy on life of husband held for benefit of wife by husband and another who now retires	216
	52	Notice of assignment on appointment of new trustees of a policy of assurance	217

10 The Insolvent Transferor

1	Introduction	219
2	Insurance	219
3	The effect of the transferor's insolvency on the ownership of the family home	220
6	Steps to be taken following completion of the transfer from the insolvent party's trustee	222

Precedents

53	Declaration of solvency at time of transfer to solvent party	222
54	Transfer of insolvent party's share of former jointly owned property (held as Beneficial Joint Tenants) to solvent party's sister who has provided the purchase price, the property being subject to mortgage (form TR1)	224

11 Transfer to Surviving Party form Deceased Party's Estate

1	Avoiding further claims against the one party during his or her lifetime	227
2	Avoiding a claim against the deceased's estate after his or her death	228
3	Transfer to the surviving party following proceedings under Inheritance (Provision for Family and Dependants) Act 1975	229

Precedents

55	Transfer of house in deceased's sole name to surviving party (or former spouse or civil partner, not remarried or having entered into a new civil partnership) following court order under Inheritance (Provision for Family and Dependants) Act 1975. No mortgage	232
56	Appointment of new trustee of transfer, one of two tenants in common having died	235

Index 239

Table of Cases

(*References are to paragraph numbers*)

Abbott (Bankrupt No.8 of 1980), Re sub nom:Trustee of the Property of the Bankrupt v Abbott [1983] Ch. 45; [1982] 3 W.L.R. 86; [1982] 3 All E.R. 181; 126 S.J. 345 1–18
Ahmed v Kendrick [1988] 2 F.L.R. 22; (1988) 56 P. & C.R. 120; *Times*, November 12, 1987; *Independent*, November 9, 1987 4–03
Aspden v Hildesley [1982] 1 W.L.R. 264; [1982] 2 All E.R. 53; [1982] S.T.C. 206; 55 T.C. 609; [1981] T.R. 479; *Times*, December 1, 1981 2–06
Austin-Fell v Austin-Fell [1990] Fam. 172; [1990] 3 W.L.R. 33; [1990] 2 All E.R. 455; [1989] 2 F.L.R. 497; [1990] F.C.R. 743; [1989] Fam. Law 437; (1989) 139 N.L.J. 1113 10–01

Barnett v Hassett [1981] 1 W.L.R. 1385; [1982] 1 All E.R. 80; 125 S.J. 376... 3–05
Barton v Morris [1985] 1 W.L.R. 1257; [1985] 2 All E.R. 1032; (1986) 51 P. & C.R. 84; (1986) 83 L.S.G. 118; *Times*, May 1, 1985 4–02
Booth v Ellard [1980] 1 W.L.R. 1443; [1980] 3 All E.R. 569; [1980] S.T.C. 555; 53 T.C. 393; [1980] T.R. 203; 124 S.J. 465 .... 6–05, 6–07
Browne (formerly Pritchard) v Pritchard [1975] 1 W.L.R. 1366; [1975] 3 All E.R. 721; 119 S.J. 679 7–01
Burgess v Rawnsley [1975] Ch. 429; [1975] 3 W.L.R. 99; [1975] 3 All E.R. 142; (1975) 30 P. & C.R. 221; 119 S.J. 406 4–03
Butler v Mountview Estates Ltd [1951] 2 K.B. 563; [1951] 1 All E.R. 693; [1951] 1 T.L.R. 524 1–09

Carlton v Goodman sub nom: Goodman v Carlton [2002] EWCA Civ 545; [2002] 2 F.L.R. 259; [2002] Fam. Law 595; (2002) 99(22) L.S.G. 36; [2002] N.P.C. 61; *Independent*, May 17, 2002 .... 4–02, 5–09
Chelsea & Waltham Green Building Society v Armstrong [1951] Ch. 853; [1951] 2 All E.R. 250; [1951] 2 T.L.R. 313 3–12
Clutton v Clutton [1991] 1 W.L.R. 359; [1991] 1 All E.R. 340; [1991] 1 F.L.R. 242; [1991] F.C.R. 265; [1991] Fam. Law 304; (1990) 134 S.J. 1682; *Independent*, October 30, 1990 .... 6–01, 7–01
Copeland v Houlton sub nom: 26 Clarendon Villas, Hove (Trusts Affecting), Re [1955] 1 W.L.R. 1072; [1955] 3 All E.R. 178; 99 S.J. 708 1–23
Crossley v City of Glasgow Life Assurance Co (1876–77) L.R. 4 Ch. D. 421   9–09
Crosthwaite v Crosthwaite [1989] 2 F.L.R. 86; [1989] Fam. Law 315; *Independent*, January 30, 1989 6–02

Deane v Hall (1828) 3 Russ 1 7–05
Dinch v Dinch [1987] 1 W.L.R. 252; [1987] 1 All E.R. 818; [1987] 2 F.L.R. 162; [1987] Fam. Law 267; (1987) 84 L.S.G. 1142; (1987) 131 S.J. 296   1–05
Draper's Conveyance, Re sub nom: Nihan v Porter [1969] 1 Ch. 486; [1968] 2 W.L.R. 166; [1967] 3 All E.R. 853; (1968) 19 P. & C.R. 71; 204 E.G. 693; 111 S.J. 867 4–03

88, Berkeley Road, NW9, Re sub nom: Rickwood v Turnsek [1971] Ch. 648; [1971] 2 W.L.R. 307; [1971] 1 All E.R. 254; (1971) 22 P. & C.R. 188; (1970) 115 S.J. 34 4–03

Fender v St John Mildmay sub nom: Fender v Mildmay [1938] A.C. 1 6–06

TABLE OF CASES

First National Securities Ltd v Hegerty [1985] Q.B. 850; [1984] 3 W.L.R. 769; [1984] 3 All E.R. 641; (1984) 48 P. & C.R. 200; [1984] Fam. Law 316; (1984) 81 L.S.G. 2543; (1984) 128 S.J. 499 4–03
Flint (A Bankrupt), Re [1993] Ch. 319; [1993] 2 W.L.R. 537; [1993] 1 F.L.R. 763; (1992) 136 S.J.L.B. 221;
Times, July 16, 1992 3–07

Goodman v Gallant [1986] Fam. 106; [1986] 2 W.L.R. 236; [1986] 1 All E.R. 311; [1986] 1 F.L.R. 513; (1986) 52 P. & C.R. 180; [1986] Fam. Law 59; (1985) 135 N.L.J. 1231; (1985) 129 S.J. 891 .... 4–02, 5–09, 10–05
Gorman (A Bankrupt), Re [1990] 1 W.L.R. 616; [1990] 1 All E.R. 717; [1990] 2 F.L.R. 284; (1990) 87(19) L.S.G. 41 .... 4–03, 10–05

Harris v Goddard [1983] 1 W.L.R. 1203; [1983] 3 All E.R. 242; (1983) 46 P. & C.R. 417; [1984] Fam. Law 242; (1983) 80 L.S.G. 2517; (1983) 133 N.L.J. 958; (1983) 127 S.J. 617 4–03
Harvey v Harvey [1987] 1 F.L.R. 67; [1987] Fam. Law 17 6–02
Harwood v Harwood [1991] 2 F.L.R. 274; [1992] F.C.R. 1; [1991] Fam. Law 418 .... 4–02, 5–09
Holmes v H Kennard & Son (1985) 49 P. & C.R. 202; (1985) 82 L.S.G. 363; (1984) 128 S.J. 854; *Times*, November 30, 1984 3–05
Hyman v Hyman Joined Cases: Hughes v Hughes [1929] A.C. 601 11–01

Jones (DI) v Jones (FI) sub nom: Jones v Jones [1972] 1 W.L.R. 1269; [1972] 3 All E.R. 289; 116 S.J. 745 8–03
Jones v Maynard [1951] Ch. 572; [1951] 1 All E.R. 802; [1951] 1 T.L.R. 700; 95 S.J. 442 4–02

Knibb v Knibb [1987] 2 F.L.R. 396; [1987] Fam. Law 346; (1987) 84 L.S.G. 1058; (1987) 131 S.J. 692 7–01
Kumar (A Bankrupt), Re sub nom: Lewis v Kumar [1993] 1 W.L.R. 224; [1993] 2 All E.R. 700; [1993] B.C.L.C. 548; [1993] 2 F.L.R. 382; [1993] Fam. Law 470 1–18

L v L [1962] P. 101; [1961] 3 W.L.R. 1182; [1961] 3 All E.R. 834; 105 S.J. 930 11–02
Lewis v Rook [1992] 1 W.L.R. 662; [1992] S.T.C. 171; 64 T.C. 567; [1992] S.T.I. 206; [1992] E.G.C.S. 21; (1992) 89(14) L.S.G. 32; (1992) 136 S.J.L.B. 83; [1992] N.P.C. 23; *Times*, February 28, 1992; *Independent*, March 16, 1992 (C.S.); *Financial Times*, March 3, 1992 2–04

M (Deceased), Re [1968] P. 174 11–01
Marren v Ingles [1980] 1 W.L.R. 983; [1980] 3 All E.R. 95; [1980] S.T.C. 500; 54 T.C. 76; [1980] T.R. 335; 124 S.J. 562 7–04
Martin (BH) v Martin (D) [1978] Fam. 12; [1977] 3 W.L.R. 101; [1977] 3 All E.R. 762; (1977) 7 Fam. Law 175; 121 S.J. 335 6–01
Mesher v Mesher [1980] 1 All E.R. 126 (Note) *Times*, February 13, 1973 ... 6–01
Midland Bank Plc v Cooke [1995] 4 All E.R. 562; [1997] 6 Bank. L.R. 147; [1995] 2 F.L.R. 915; [1996] 1 F.C.R. 442; (1995) 27 H.L.R. 733; [1995] Fam. Law 675; (1995) 145 N.L.J. 1543; (1995) 139 S.J.L.B. 194; [1995] N.P.C. 116; *Times*, July 13, 1995; *Independent*, July 26, 1995 4–02
Minton v Minton [1979] A.C. 593; [1979] 2 W.L.R. 31; [1979] 1 All E.R. 79; 122 S.J. 843 11–02
Moody v Stevenson sub nom: Moody (Deceased), Re [1992] Ch. 486; [1992] 2 W.L.R. 640; [1992] 2 All E.R. 524; [1992] 1 F.L.R. 494; [1992] F.C.R. 107; [1992] Fam. Law 284; (1991) 135 S.J.L.B. 84; *Times*, July 30, 1991; *Independent*, September 17, 1991; *Independent*, August 5, 1991 (C.S.); Guardian, August 21, 1991 11–04

TABLE OF CASES

Mortimer v de Mortimer-Griffin [1986] 2 F.L.R. 315; [1986] Fam. Law 305 6–01
Mullard v Mullard (1982) 12 Fam. Law 63; 126 S.J. 98................. 10–01

Nielson-Jones v Fedden [1975] Ch. 222; [1974] 3 W.L.R. 583; [1974] 3 All E.R. 38; 118 S.J. 776 4–03

Omielan v Omielan [1996] 2 F.L.R. 306; [1996] 3 F.C.R. 329; [1996] Fam. Law 608; *Times*, July 30, 1996 6–01

Palmer (Gavin) (Deceased) (A Debtor), Re sub nom: Gavin Hilary Palmer Estate Trustee v Palmer [1994] Ch. 316; [1994] 3 W.L.R. 420; [1994] 3 All E.R. 835; [1994] 2 F.L.R. 609; [1995] 1 F.C.R. 320; [1994] Fam. Law 566; [1994] E.G.C.S. 52; (1994) 138 S.J.L.B. 72; [1994] N.P.C. 41; (1994) 68 P. & C.R. D13; *Times,* March 30, 1994; *Independent,* April 6, 1994 10–05
Perez-Adamson v Perez Rivas [1987] Fam. 89; [1987] 3 W.L.R. 500; [1987] 3 All E.R. 20; [1987] 2 F.L.R. 472; (1988) 55 P. & C.R. 5; [1987] Fam. Law 416; (1987) 137 N.L.J. 409; (1987) 131 S.J. 939 3–07
Pettitt v Pettitt sub nom:P v P [1970] A.C. 777; [1969] 2 W.L.R. 966; [1969] 2 All E.R. 385; (1969) 20 P. & C.R. 991; 113 S.J. 344 10–05
Popat v Popat [1991] 2 F.L.R. 163; [1991] Fam. Law 100................. 7–01

R. v Porter [1990] 1 W.L.R. 1260; [1990] 3 All E.R. 784; (1991) 92 Cr. App. R. 126; (1990–91) 12 Cr. App. R. (S.) 377; (1991) 155 J.P. 62; [1991] Crim. L.R. 217; (1990) 154 J.P.N. 722; (1990) 134 S.J. 1122 4–02
R. v Rushmoor BC Ex p. Barrett [1989] Q.B. 60; CA (Civ Div); affirming [1987] Q.B. 275; [1986] 3 W.L.R. 998; [1987] 1 All E.R. 353; [1987] 1 F.L.R. 246; (1986) 18 H.L.R. 534; 85 L.G.R. 225; [1987] Fam. Law 91; (1987) 151 L.G. Rev. 171 1–20

S v S (Legal Aid Taxation) [1991] Fam. Law 271....................... 1–23
Savage v Norton [1908] 1 Ch. 290 8–02
Springette v Defoe [1992] 2 F.L.R. 388; [1992] 2 F.C.R. 561; (1992) 24 H.L.R. 552; (1993) 65 P. & C.R. 1; [1992] Fam. Law 489; [1992] N.P.C. 34; *Independent,* March 24, 1992; *Guardian,* April 29, 1992 4–02

Turner (A Bankrupt), Re sub nom: Trustee of the Property of the Bankrupt v Turner; Trustee Ex p. v Turner [1974] 1 W.L.R. 1556; [1975] 1 All E.R. 5; 118 S.J. 84 10–05

Whittingham v Whittingham [1979] Fam. 9; [1978] 2 W.L.R. 936; [1978] 3 All E.R. 805; (1978) 36 P. & C.R. 164; (1978) 8 Fam. Law 171; 122 S.J. 247 3–07
Williams & Glyn's Bank Ltd v Boland Joined Cases: Williams & Glyn's Bank Ltd v Brown [1981] A.C. 487; [1980] 3 W.L.R. 138; [1980] 2 All E.R. 408; (1980) 40 P. & C.R. 451; 124 S.J. 443 .... 1–11, 3–12, 4–11, 5–08, 6–12, 7–08
Wilson v Wilson (Matrimonial Home) [1963] 1 W.L.R. 601; [1963] 2 All E.R. 447; 107 S.J. 314 5–09

Table of Statutes

(References are to paragraph numbers)

Year	Statute	Paragraph
1837	Wills Act (7 Will. 4 & 1 Vict. c.26)	
	s.18A	11–01
1867	Policies of Assurance Act (30 & 31 Vict. c.144)	
	s.1	9–04
	s.3	9–09
1882	Married Women's Property Act (45 & 46 Vict. c.75)	9–05, 11–02
	s.11	9–05
	s.17	4–03
1891	Stamp Act 1891 (54 & 55 Vict. c.39)	
	s.57	2–10, 2–13
1925	Trustee Act (15 & 16 Geo. 5 c.19)	8–03
	ss.3–4	6–10
	s.6	6–10
	s.19	6–10
	s.19(1)(b)	6–10, 6–11
	s.20	6–10
	s.21(5)	6–10
	ss 31–32	6–11
	s.36	6–08, 6–09, 6–10, 7–05, 9–05, 11–04
	s.39	7–07
	s.44	8–03
	s.44(vi)	8–03
	s.63A	8–03
	Law of Property Act (15 & 16 Geo. 5 c.20)	11–04
	s.3(2)	4–03
	s.27	4–03, 6–08, 7–05, 10–05
	s.30	10–05
	s.36(2)	4–07
	s.52(1)	1–21, 8–03
	s.52(2)(f)	8–03
	s.72(4)	4–07
	s.76(1)	3–12
	s.77(1)(c)	1–10
	s.77(1)(C)	1–10
	s.136	9–03
	Land Registration Act (15 & 16 Geo. 5 c.21)	1–03, 1–14
	s.123	1–14
1925	Administration of Estates Act (15 & 16 Geo. 5 c.23)	
	s.394	4–02
1961	Trustee Investments Act (9 & 10 Eliz.2 c.62)	6–11
1963	Law of Property (Joint Tenants) Act (c.63)	
	s.1	4–03
	s.1(1)	6–02
1967	Matrimonial Homes Act (c.75)	3–02
1972	Land Charges Act (c.61)	3–03
	s.5	3–07
1973	Matrimonial Causes Act (c.18)	1–05, 9–01, 11–02
	Pt II	1–04
	s.19	8–03
	s.22A	2–09
	s.23A	2–09
	s.24	1–20, 3–07, 3–08
	s.24(1)(b)	7–01
	s.24(1)(d)	8–03
	s.24(3)	2–07
	s.24A	2–09
1975	Inheritance (Provision for Family and Dependants) Act (c.63)	4–02, 11–02, 11–04
	s.1(1)	11–03
	s.1(1)(b)	11–03
	s.1(1)(e)	11–03
	s.2	11–03
	s.2(1)(c)	11–04
	s.15	11–03
	s.15(1)	11–03
1979	Charging Orders Act (c.53)	10–01
1981	Matrimonial Homes and Property Act (c.24)	1–01
	Supreme Court Act (c.54)	
	s.39	8–02, 8–03
1983	Matrimonial Homes Act (c.19)	1–01, 3–02, 10–04
1984	County Courts Act (c.28)	
	s.38	8–02, 8–03
	s.148(1)	8–03
	Sch.2, Pt I	8–03

1984	Matrimonial and Family Proceedings Act (c.42) 1–01, 11–02		1990	Courts and Legal Services Act (c.41)	
				s.3	8–02
	Finance Act (c.43)			s.125(2)	1–21
	s.72(1) 9–01, 9–07			Sch.17(2)	1–21
	Inheritance Tax Act			Sch.20	1–21
	(c.51)	6–06	1991	Child Support Act (c.48) ..	1–01
	s.3	6–06	1992	Taxation of Chargeable Gains Act (c.12)	
	s.3A	2–07			
	s.10 .... 6–06, 7–04			s.2(1)	2–02
	s.10(1)	2–07		s.2(2)	2–06
	s.11 .... 2–07, 6–06			s.3	2–06
	s.18(1)	2–07		s.22	7–04
	s.48(1)	6–07		s.58 .... 2–03, 2–06	
	s.53(2)–(3)	6–07		s.73	6–07
	s.199	2–07		s.165	2–06
	s.199(2)	2–07		ss 222–224	2–05
	s.270	2–07		s.222 .... 2–04, 6–07	
1985	Companies Act (c.6)			s.222(5)	2–05
	s.36A	1–21		s.222(5)(a)–(b)	2–05
	Housing Act (c.68) 1–20, 11–04			s.223	2–04
				s.225 .... 2–05, 6–07	
	ss.155–156	1–20		s.226(a)	6–07
	s.160(1)(c)	1–20		s.251	7–04
1986	Finance Act (c.41) .. 2–07, 2–13			s.286(2)	2–07
	Sch.19, Pt I, para I	2–07	1992	Local Government Finance Act (c.14) ...	1–16
	Insolvency Act (c.45) 1–18, 10–04			s.6(2)–(3)	1–16
				s.9	1–16
	s.283(3)	10–05		s.11	1–16
	s.306	10–04	1994	Insolvency Act (No. 2) Act (c.12)	1–19
	s.335A	10–05			
	s.336	3–05	1994	Law of Property (Miscellaneous Provisions) Act (c.36) 1–06, 1–08, 3–10, 4–09, 5–05	
	s.336(2) 3–05, 10–04				
	s.336(3)	3–05			
	s.339 ...... 1–17, 5–01, 10–05			s.1(1)	1–06
	s.339(3)(c)	1–18		s.1(4)	9–06
	s.341	1–17		s.2(1)(a)–(b)	1–07
	s.341(2A)	1–19		s.3(3)	11–04
1988	Income and Corporation Taxes Act (c.1)			s.4(1)(a)–(b)	1–09
				s.5(1)–(3)	7–03
	s.282	2–03		s.6(1)–(2)	1–06
	s.552	9–09		s.8(1)	1–06
	Housing Act (c.50)	11–04		s.21(1)	4–03
1989	Finance Act (c.26)		1995	Pensions Act 1995 (c.26)	1–01
	s.124	2–06		Landlord and Tenant (Covenants) Act (c.30)	1–10
	Law of Property (Miscellaneous Provisions) Act (c.34)				
				s.16	1–10
	s.1	1–21	1995	Law Reform (Succession) Act (c.41) ... 11–01, 11–03	
	s.1(3)	1–21			
	s.1(5)	1–21	1996	Family Law Act (c.27) ... 1–01, 3–02, 3–03, 3–05, 3–15, 10–04	
	Companies Act (c.40)				
	s.130(2)	1–21			
	Children Act (c.41)			Pt IV	1–04
	s.6	11–01		s.3(1)–(2)	3–02

1996 Family Law Act—*cont.*
s.30 3–02
s.30(2)(a)–(b) 3–02
s.32 .... 3–05, 6–02
s.33(3)(b) 3–02
ss.34–35 10–4
s.66(1) 11–03
Sch.4 para. (1)(a) 3–05, 6–02
Sch.4 para. (1)(b) 3–05
Sch.4 para. 2 3–05
Sch.4 para. 3(1)–(2) 3–05
Sch.8, Pt I,
  para. 27(1) 11–03
Sch.8, Pt I,
  para. 27(5)–(6) 11–03
Trusts of Land and
  Appointment of
  Trustees Act (c.47) .. 6–10,
            7–05, 10–05
s.14 10–05
Sch.2 para. (4) ... 4–03, 4–07
Housing Act (c.52) 1–20,
            11–04
1997 Land Registration Act
  (c.2) 1–14
1999 Access to Justice Act (c.22)
s.9 1–23
s.10(7) 1–22
2002 Land Registration Act
  (c.9) 1–01, 1–03, 1–14,
       3–17, 4–02, 4–14, 5–02,
       6–09, 8–03, 8–06, 10–05
s.4 1–14

2002 Land Registration Act—
  cont.
s.19 3–07
s.34 3–08
s.40 .... 4–04, 4–08
s.44 .... 6–09, 7–06, 11–05
s.49 7–10
Sch.12 para 20 1–10
2003 Land Registration Act
  (c.9) 1–01
s.86 10–03
Finance Act (c.14) 2–08
s.48 2–10
Sch.3 ...... 2–09, 2–10, 2–11,
       2–12, 2–13, 3–14, 4–11,
       5–01, 5–10, 6–13, 7–09,
            11–06
Sch.3 para. (3)(a)–(b) .. 2–09
Sch.3 para. (3)(c)(i) 2–09
Sch.3 para. (3)(d) 2–09
Sch.4 para. (8) ... 2–10, 2–13
2004 Finance Act (c.12) 6–07
Civil Partnership Act
  (c.33) ... 1–01, 1–04, 2–01,
       2–07, 3–02, 3–03, 3–05,
       3–14, 6–02, 10–04, 11–03
s.82 .... 3–02, 3–05
Sch.9 paras 1(1) 3–02
Sch.9 paras 1(3) 3–02
Sch.9 paras 2(1)–(3) 3–02
Sch.9 paras 4(1) 3–02
Sch.9 paras 4(4) 3–02
Sch.9 paras 15(1)–(2) ... 3–05
Sch.9 paras 15(4)–(5) ... 3–05

Table of Statutory Instruments

(References are to paragraph numbers)

1925	Land Registration Rules (SR & O 1925/1093)		1–03
	r.247		1–19
1990	Land Charges Fees Rules (SI 1990/327)		3–15
1991	Family Proceedings Rules (SI 1991/1247)		
	r.2.59(4)		3–12
	r.59(2)		1–11
	r.59(4)		1–11
1993	Land Registration (Official Searches) Rules (SI 1993/3276)		4–05
	r.3		3–09
2000	Community Legal Service (Financial) Regulations (SI 2000/516)		
	Pt III, reg. 44		1–22
	Pt III, reg. 52		1–22
	Pt III, reg. 52(2)		1–
	Pt III, reg. 53		1–22
2001	Community Legal Service (Finance) (Amendment No. 3) Regulations (SI 2001/3663)		1–22
2003	Land Registration (Official Searches) Rules (SI 2003/???)		
	rr. 147–160		3–08
	Land Registration Fees Order (SI 2003/165)		3–07, 3–08
	Land Registration Rules (SI 2003/1417)		1–01, 1–03, 1–08, 1–21, 5–07
2003	Land Registration Rules—*cont.*		
	r.8(2)		1–19
	r.10		3–09
	r.64		3–12, 3–13, 4–11
	r.67(5)		1–08
	r.68		1–08
	r.82		3–07
	r.82(1)		3–04
	r.91		11–05
	r.92		4–04, 6–09, 7–06
	r.94		6–09
	r.206		1–12
	r.212		1–12
	Sch.1		1–12, 1–21
	Sch.4		4–04
	Sch.9		1–21
	Sch.12 Form A		4–08
2004	Land Registration Fee Order (SI 2004/595)		1–03, 1–12, 3–09, 3–15, 4–04, 4–08, 4–14, 5–13, 6–16, 7–12, 10–08
	scale 1		1–14, 3–17, 4–14, 5–13, 7–12, 10–08
	scale 2		1–14, 3–17, 4–11, 4–14, 5–13, 6–16, 7–12, 11–06
2005	Land Registration (Amendment) (No. 2) Rules (SI 2005/1982)		
	r.12(2)		3–04
	Tax and Civil Partnership Regulations (SI 2005/3229)		2–01

Chapter 1

General Principles

In most modern day situations involving relationship breakdown the family **1–01**
home is the main capital asset owned by the parties either jointly or by one of them. As such this is the asset most likely to be contested in negotiations or proceedings between the parties.

The importance of the family home is highly significant and this has been recognised increasingly by the legislature over the last 20 years and since the first edition of this book was published in 1981. During that time Parliament has passed the Matrimonial Homes and Property Act 1981, the Matrimonial Homes Act 1983, the Matrimonial and Family Proceedings Act 1984, the Family Law Act 1996 and the Civil Partnership Act 2004. In so far as the conveyancing aspects of relationship breakdown are concerned the Land Registration Act 2002 and the corresponding Land Registration Rules 2003 have had an impact together with the Finance Act 2003 which was responsible for the introduction of Stamp Duty Land Tax. These are described in more detail later in this Chapter and throughout the book.

Home ownership continues to be extremely popular in the United Kingdom and therefore orders and arrangements concerning the family home continue to be very relevant in the current climate. As stated in previous editions this relevancy is especially highlighted at a time when the prospect of a "clean break" (which could be encouraged by the transfer of the family home into the sole name of one party or the other) has become somewhat eroded by the provisions of the Child Support Act 1991 and the earmarking of pensions pursuant to the Pensions Act 1995.

1 The scope of this book

The first edition of this book assumed a conveyance or transfer of the **1–02**
family home following a court order or agreement in matrimonial proceedings. Whilst this edition still primarily addresses that situation it is also equally relevant to all forms of relationship breakdown which involve the conveyance of the family home.

In its treatment of conveyancing, surrounding relationship breakdown this book is not concerned with the merits of the parties respective claims nor with the proceedings in connection with those claims. It deals with the necessary conveyancing following the making of a court order or agreement between the parties relating to the family home and with the disentangling of life policies should that be necessary. This book is not confined to the needs of the conveyancing practitioner indeed it is written so that the family practitioner is aware of the different types of conveyance which may be ordered by the court or agreed between the parties and the points which should be taken into account at that time, the protective measures that might be taken before the conveyance is concluded and the documentation that may be required in dealing with life policies.

In the precedents which follow no assumptions have been made as to which party is transferring to the other and they are simply referred to as Transferor and Transferee and not husband and wife as in previous editions.

This chapter touches on various points and may usefully serve as a reminder of items to be considered outside the drafting of the property transfer itself.

2 The effect of the Land Registration Act 2002 (the 2002 Act)

1–03 This Act came into force on October 13, 2003 together with the corresponding Land Registration Rules 2003. The 2002 Act is being introduced in stages over a period of time. It was heralded as the greatest change to the system of land registration in England and Wales since the introduction of the 1925 legislation. Indeed the 2002 Act repealed the Land Registration Act 1925 in its entirety and the 2003 rules replaced the Land Registration Rules 1925. It is the purpose of the 2002 Act and associated rules to bring about a system of electronic conveyancing thereby increasing speed and the need for paper documentation. It is hoped that the new system will be fully operational in a relatively short period of time but clearly there are interim measures to operate a dual electronic and paper system, which are discussed further below.

In order to facilitate the move towards a system of electronic conveyancing there have been a number of changes to the law. Voluntary first registration is being encouraged by a series of reduced fees as set out in the Land Registration Fee Order 2006. Compulsory registration has been enlarged and includes all transactions envisaged by this book. Cautions and inhibitions have been abolished (except cautions against first registration which remain) and the only way to protect an interest now is by way of notice or restriction. Most situations previously covered by cautions now fall within the definition of a unilateral notice, which operates in a similar way. In both cases an entry can be made in the register without the consent of the registered proprietor although notice of the application will be served on the registered proprietor in each case giving him or her the chance to apply to have the notice removed or object to the restriction.

It is the philosophy of the 2002 Act that the register should provide as complete a picture of the title to the property in question as is possible. This is so that almost all details of the legal estate can be obtained on line at any one time. HM Land Registry now have a very effective website and a subscription service known as Land Registry Direct and most documents on the register can be viewed and copied in printed form within moments. Clearly, the whole notion of overriding interests calls this into question and, as a result, the 2002 Act has greatly reduced the number of such interests and those which do remain are limited in time. In the final analysis there will be only six overriding interests; persons in actual occupation where the occupation is apparent; leases of three years or less (currently the 2002 Act states seven years or less but it is widely expected to be reduced to three years shortly); legal easements that have arisen by prescription, implied grant or reservation; customary or public rights; local land charges and some mineral rights. As previously stated the main change to be brought about by the 2002 Act is the introduction of compulsory electronic conveyancing. Over the last 10 years or so the Land Registry have spent considerable time and effort computerising the register and this is available to most practitioners through Land Registry Direct as stated above. This system will be widened so that applications and changes to the register can be made by the solicitor acting for the parties concerned. All transfers and other dispositions in land will be submitted to the Land Registry in electronic form by computer and will be executed by the secure system envisaged thereby abolishing the need for any paper as with the present system. On completion of an average conveyancing transaction the electronic mechanism will execute the transfer, register the transaction and arrange the transfer of funds simultaneously. There will be no gaps as with the present system between completion and registration. All Land Registry forms will ultimately become electronic forms completed on computer and submitted in the same manner. Compulsory electronic conveyancing will take some time to introduce and the registrar has the power to issue notices and instructions at appropriate times so that practitioners are not taken by surprise. It is thought that it will take several years before the full introduction of a non-paper system. In the interim paper applications will continue to be accepted at HM Land Registry and this edition has been produced on that basis.

3 The Effect of the Civil Partnerships Act 2004 (the CPA)

The CPA 2004 came into force on December 5, 2005 and it enables single sex partners to obtain legal recognition of their relationship by entering into a civil partnership. This kind of legal union is to be distinct from marriage however the requirements for entering into and ending a civil partnership are largely based on those relating to marriage. In so far as property rights are concerned and the ability of the courts to make property adjustment orders these are modelled on those set out in Part II of the Matrimonial Causes Act 1973. 1–04

In relation to family home rights, occupation orders and transfer of tenancies Part IV of the Family Law Act 1996 is to be amended to give registered civil partners the same rights as spouses.

As far as this book is concerned the precedents contained in the following pages are drafted so as to apply with equal relevancy to orders and agreements made on the dissolution of a marriage or registered civil partnership.

4 The advantage of a court order

1–05 Although agreement may be reached between the parties as to the future of the family home, it is strongly advised that such agreement be embodied in a "consent order" of the court; if the court does not have the power directly to make an order under the Matrimonial Causes Act 1973 (for instance in relation to repairs to property held subject to certain conditions and in relation to payment of premiums of life assurance policies) the same effect can be achieved by formulating the obligations of each party as undertakings given to the court. Indeed, because of the court's limited power, the policy of ultimate caution must be for the terms of any conveyancing documentation to be agreed between the respective solicitors before the consent order is applied for.

Such an order has inheritance tax advantages (if dissolution of the marriage has taken place), the advantage being that a return to court can be made to force execution of a property transfer and, as any financial provision can be expressed in the order to be in full and final settlement of the wife's claims (see Ch.11), it is less likely to be upset than an agreement between the parties not carried into a "consent order" (see for instance *Dinch v Dinch* [1987] 1 W.L.R. 252 where the court refused to make a further order on the grounds that the consent order had conclusively determined the rights of the parties in the matrimonial home). A court order avoids the repayment of the discount on the transfer of a former council house (see further this chapter) and it is only by court order (with the agreement of the parties) that future claims against the estate of one party to the former marriage can be barred out.

5 Covenants for title

(a) Freehold

1–06 The Law of Property (Miscellaneous Provisions) Act 1994 implies two statutory covenants for title, these are:

- full title guarantee;
- limited title guarantee.

Before these two forms are examined, further points should be noted:

(a) covenants are only implied if the key statutory words are used. The law does not entitle the transferee to any covenant for title; covenants for title may be excluded altogether by not using the key statutory words;

(b) the covenants can be restricted or extended by agreement between the parties (s.8(1)) (e.g. liability can be avoided by expressly making the disposition subject to a revealed matter s.6(1));

(c) the covenants will be implied even if there is no consideration provided the statutory words are used (s.1(1));

(d) the transferor's capacity (i.e. whether as a sole owner or as trustee because a joint owner) is irrelevant; it is up to the parties to agree what level of title guarantee is given;

(e) if the transferee knows of something affecting the property transferred, then notwithstanding the title guarantee the transferee takes subject to it (s.6(2)); and

(f) the Act applies to any disposition of real or personal property.

It is appropriate to consider the two forms of title guarantee:

1 Full title guarantee 1–07
The use of such words implies that:

(a) the covenantor (i.e. transferor) has the right (along with anyone else joining in the property transfer) to dispose of the property being transferred (s.2(1)(a));

(b) the covenantor will do all he or she reasonably can at his or her own expense to vest the title of the property being transferred in the transferee (s.2(1)(b)). This means in registered land transfers that the transferor will do all he or she can to ensure that the transferee is registered with at least the same class of title he or she had before the transfer. In the case of land to be registered, it means that the transferor will give all reasonable assistance to ensure the transferee's right to be registered as proprietor; and

(c) the property is free from all charges, incumbrances and third party rights (except those which he or she does not and would not reasonably be expected to know about).

2 Limited title guarantee 1–08
The transferor with "limited title guarantee" gives the previous covenants (a) and (b) but in place of (c) covenants that since the last disposition for value he or she has not:

(a) created a subsisting charge or incumbrance or subsisting third party right relating to the property;

(b) suffered it to be subject to such a charge or incumbrance or to be affected by such a third party right; and

(c) nor is he or she aware that anyone else has done so.

One is led to the view that where the one party is receiving a transfer of the family home from the other the transferee should insist on receiving the full title guarantee covenant; the transferee is usually receiving the property in exchange for giving up other rights (e.g. any future right to maintenance) and is therefore entitled to insist on the best form of title guarantee available to a purchaser.

Where the transferee is already a joint owner the transferor may say that the transferee should accordingly know about all charges, incumbrances and third party rights affecting the property so that only limited title guarantee is applicable. It is difficult to counter this argument so solicitors acting for the transferee may have to accept limited title guarantee covenants. It will be necessary to look at the circumstances: if the transferee is charging the property so as to be able to pay the transferor something for his or her interest, the mortgagee may require that the transferee receives "full title guarantee". In practical terms, therefore, whatever the academic arguments, the transferor will have no alternative but to transfer with full title guarantee. To avoid a dispute at the conveyancing stage, it is probably appropriate that the court order specifies the level of title guarantee to be given.

For registered land, no reference to the implied covenants are to be entered on the register, whether the implied covenants are modified or not (Land Registration Rules 2003, r.67(5)) but if the implied covenants are limited or extended they must refer to the relevant section of the 1994 Act (Land Registration Rules 2003, r.68) (see below). Should any questions arise however, the Registrar has a discretion (under Land Registration Rules 2003) to allow inspection of a filed transfer and it is understood that such discretion would be exercised if any difficulty could be resolved by production of the filed transfer.

(b) Leasehold

1–09 (a) *Implied covenants on an assignment/transfer by assignor/transferor* An assignment/transfer with full title guarantee implies (a), (b) and (c) above with further implied covenants:

(d) the lease is still subsisting (s.4(1)(a)); and

(e) there is no subsisting breach of the lease conditions or tenants covenants and the lease is not [in consequence] subject to forfeiture (s.4(1)(b)).

As in freehold land, limited title guarantee limits the covenant in relation to incumbrances (see above).

As both full title guarantee and limited title guarantee covenants imply that the tenant's covenants have been complied with (s.4(1)(b) (i.e. as to maintenance, repair and decoration) specific thought will have to be given to a limitation of liability on the part of the transferor, who may have been absent from the property for some time. While the transferee is likely to be aware of the state and condition of the property, it is prudent to exclude the transferor's liability for it (see Precedent 2 and p.62) (see generally *Butler v Mountview Estates* [1951] 2 K.B. 563). For example:

"The covenant by the Transferor implied by section 4(1)(b) of the Law of Property (Miscellaneous Provisions) Act 1994 by reason of him transferring with full title guarantee shall be limited so as not to extend to any breach of the terms of the registered lease on the part of the transferor relating to the condition of the property."

(b) *Implied covenants in favour of assignor/transferor* LPA 1925, s.77(1)(C) continues to apply to leasehold land and implies on behalf of the assignee that he or she will pay the rent, observe and perform the covenants and conditions in the lease and indemnify the assignor in respect thereof. Similar covenants are implied in the case of registered land by LRA 2002, Sch.12, para.20.

1–10

A distinction must be drawn here between "new tenancies"—being tenancies granted on or after January 1, 1996, and "old tenancies" granted before that date.

For old tenancies, the original tenant remained liable on the covenants under the lease even after he or she had assigned his or her interest but did have the assignee's implied covenant to perform those covenants and for indemnity (LPA, 1925, s.77(1)(c)). In unregistered land, the covenants were implied only where there was valuable consideration; as the definition of consideration in matrimonial conveyancing is a "grey area", these covenants will have to be expressly incorporated into any assignment (see Precedent 3). The covenants remain implied in the case of registered land whether or not the transfer is made for valuable consideration (LRA 2002, Sch.12, para.20).

Provisions of the Landlord and Tenant (Covenants) Act 1995 provide that on any assignment of a new tenancy, the assignor is released from liability for future breaches of the covenants contained in the lease with the result that the assignor no longer needs the protection of the assignee's implied covenant to perform those covenants and for indemnity. The landlord may in certain circumstances require the assigning tenant to enter into an authorised guarantee agreement (s.16) guaranteeing the performance of the covenants by the assignor's immediate successor. This is unlikely in the case of the family home.

6 Property subject to a mortgage

In many cases a mortgage will affect the property, and depending upon the terms of the court order or agreement the requirements of the mortgagee must be observed.

1–11

An application for a property adjustment order requires the applicant to identify the land, specify whether the property concerned is registered or unregistered (and, if the former, its title number), and give particulars (as far as known to the applicant) of the mortgage (for example the mortgage account number and the full names of the mortgagor(s)) (Family Proceedings Rules 1991 (as amended), r.2.59(2). A copy of the prescribed Form A shall be sent to the mortgagee (r.2.59(4)).

It is, of course, not legally necessary for a mortagee to be joined in a transfer of the equity in the property; however, without the title documents a property transfer of an unregistered title subject to a mortgage from one party to the other cannot be safely undertaken due to the requirements for compulsory registration described later in this book. No such problems prevent such a transfer where registered title is involved since official copies of the title can be obtained and the transfer once executed by the parties can be lodged at HM Land Registry. In almost all cases now there is a restriction on the proprietorship register requiring the consent of the mortgagee to such transfer. In other words practitioners should bear in mind when agreeing transfers of property that it will be necessary to gain the approval of the mortgagee to any such proposal if implementation is to be successful.

More commonly, however, one party to the original mortgage is to be released or another party added, and in these cases it is always necessary for the mortgagee concerned to be a party to the document. The terms of the mortgage may in any event require that the mortgagee be joined as a party to any document affecting the property subject to the charge in its favour, and if the title to the property is registered, as stated above, there is likely be a restriction to this effect on the proprietorship register. In practice, therefore, where a mortgage affects the property the mortgagee will be a party to the property transfer.

It used to be the practice that mortgagees had standard clauses which they would require the solicitor to incorporate in the property transfer of the charged property. This practice has largely, but not exclusively, been abolished and the drafting is invariably left to the mortgagees solicitor. All solicitors involved in transfers of equity of this kind should write, at the outset, to the mortgagee seeking consent for the property to be transferred subject to the charge (but with the transferor being released) and asking for details of any special conditions or requirements which they may have. In this way the practitioner will be armed with all the necessary information at the beginning thus avoiding irritating problems later.

Particular attention should be paid to the rights of occupiers as a result of the case of *Williams & Glynn's Bank Ltd v Boland* [1981] A.C. 487. This case and those which followed it highlighted the consequences for a mortgagee when a person other than the borrower lives at the mortgaged property. It confirmed such a person could have legal rights in the property which take precedence over those of the mortgagee. Most mortgagees now enquire of the borrower within the mortgage application whether any adult other than the borrower will be occupying the property at the time of or following completion of the mortgage. However a solicitor should also make enquiries of the borrower to ascertain if there will be any occupiers as this is required under the standing instructions of mortgagees set out in the CML Lenders Handbook (a copy of which is available at *www.cml.org.uk*).

If there are any adult occupiers at the time of the transfer of equity then these should be notified to the mortgagee and their standard "consent to a transfer by an occupier" should be sent to the occupier or occupiers for signature. This is a form whereby the occupier acknowledges that they live at the property, are aware of the legal charge and consent to its creation whilst at the same time postponing any rights they may have to those of the mortgagee under the mortgage. Almost all mortgagees have issued standard forms of consent for completion in these circumstances and many require the occupier to take it to an independent solicitor who must witness their signature and confirm that he or she has explained the legal issues behind the document to the signatory. A precedent of such a form is incorporated at Precedent 6.

If the mortgage is additionally secured by the assignment of a life policy, then the future of that policy must be dealt with. If the family home is to be transferred to the sole name of one party the mortgagee may be content to re-assign a life policy on the life of the transferor back to him or her, the mortgage on the property reverting to a repayment mortgage. Alternatively the benefit of the policy may pass to the transferee, subject to charge. This is dealt with more fully in Ch.9. Practitioners should note that the practice of assigning life policies to mortgagees is now largely redundant but there are still many policies assigned to lenders where the mortgage was taken out some years ago.

7 Practice of HM Land Registry

(a) Forms

Rule 206 of the Land Registration Rules 2003 specifies that the forms set out in Sch.1 to those Rules shall be used where appropriate to the particular transaction concerned. 1–12

Where no form is prescribed for a transaction, or a prescribed form cannot be conveniently adapted, r.212 provides that the instrument shall be in such form as the registrar may direct or allow. It will be appreciated that this rule gives the registrar a wide discretion. The forms set out in this book follow the prescribed forms required by the Rules and will therefore be acceptable to HM Land Registry. All Land Registry Forms are now easily available on the HM Land Registry website (*www.landregistry.gov.uk*) and these can be completed and printed off with ease.

All applications to HM Land Registry must be accompanied by the appropriate application form which in the majority of cases will be Form AP1 or in the case of first registration Form FR1 (copies of Forms AP1 and FR1 are set out on the following pages).

Details of the fees payable are set out where appropriate but the reader should bear in mind that fees change from time to time. The current fees are set out in full in the Land Registration Fee Order 2006.

(b) Description of property

Most of the transactions envisaged by this book relate to a transfer of an existing family home, so the description can be taken from the Property Register (or the last conveyance if unregistered). 1–13

In those few cases where part of the land is being conveyed or transferred (possibly on the division of the larger family home) practitioners are reminded that metric units of measurement should be used in the documentation and all plans should so far as possible be based on Ordnance Survey Plans with a scale of 1/1250.

(c) Compulsory First Registration

1–14 With the advent of the Land Registration Act 2002 the scope of unregistered transactions which require an application for first registration has been further extended so that all the transfers envisaged by this book now fall within the rules.

The system of land registration in this country was first introduced at the turn of the last century but it was not until December 1, 1990 that the final order was made making all parts of the United Kingdom subject to compulsory first registration. However, the types of disposition which triggered a requirement for first registration were such that they only included sales and the grants of a long leases.

On April 1, 1998 the Land Registration Act 1997 came onto force and this substituted various provisions of the Land Registration Act 1925 widening the scope of "qualifying" conveyances so as to include (amongst others) conveyances of unregistered land for valuable or other consideration, by way of gift or in pursuance of an order of any court (Land Registration Act 1925, s.123).

As stated above the requirements have now been further widened by the Land Registration Act 2002, s.4. The author believes that all family property transfers fall within this definition and this book has been prepared solely on the basis that whenever the practitioner is dealing with an unregistered title that such dealing will result in an application for first registration.

All the precedents are drawn on forms acceptable to HM Land Registry although it is only fair to say that on an application for first registration they will accept an unregistered conveyance in place of a Form TR1. The authors enquiries of the Land Registry do tend to indicate that they prefer transfers inducing first registration to be on Form TR 1 (or as appropriate) rather than in the old fashioned conveyance style. It is recommended that Form TR1 should invariably be used. As stated all the precedents are in the new form and can be adopted and used when an application for first registration will be necessary.

One of the unfortunate consequences of the new rules is that the party receiving the property as a result of the divorce proceedings will not benefit from the reduced land registry scale 2 fees if the transaction is one requiring first registration. All applications for first registration must be accompanied by the appropriate unregistered title deeds, the transfer, an application in form FR1 and a fee based on scale 1 of HM Land Registry Fees Order 2006 (or as appropriate).

**Application to
change the register**

Land Registry

If you need more room than is provided for in a panel, use continuation sheet CS and attach to this form.

1.	**Administrative area and postcode** *if known*
2.	**Title number(s)**

3. If you have already made this application by **outline application**, insert reference number: _____

4. **This application affects** *Place "X" in the appropriate box.*
   ☐ the **whole** of the title(s) *Go to panel 5.*
   ☐ **part** of the title(s) *Give a brief description of the property affected.*

5. **Application, priority and fees** *A fee calculator for all types of applications can be found on Land Registry's website at www.landregistry.gov.uk/fees*

Nature of applications numbered in priority order	Value £	Fees paid £
1.		

   TOTAL £

   FOR OFFICIAL USE ONLY
   Record of fees paid

   Particulars of under/over payments

   Fee payment method: *Place "X" in the appropriate box.*
   I wish to pay the appropriate fee payable under the current Land Registration Fee Order:
   ☐ by cheque or postal order, amount £_____ made payable to "Land Registry".
   ☐ by Direct Debit under an authorised agreement with Land Registry.

   Fees debited £

   Reference number

6. **Documents lodged with this form** *Number the documents in sequence; copies should also be numbered and listed as separate documents. Alternatively you may prefer to use Form DL. If you supply the original document and a certified copy, we shall assume that you request the return of the original; if a certified copy is not supplied, we may retain the original document and it may be destroyed.*

7. **The applicant is:** *Please provide the full name(s) of the person(s) applying to change the register. Where a conveyancer lodges the application, the applicant is the client, not the conveyancer.*

8. **The application has been lodged by:**
   Land Registry Key No. (if appropriate)
   Name (if different from the applicant)
   Address/DX No.

   Reference
   Email
   Telephone No.   Fax No.

   FOR OFFICIAL USE ONLY
   Codes
   Dealing
   Status

9.	**Where you would like us to deal with someone else** *We shall deal only with the applicant, or the person lodging the application if different, unless you place "X" against one or more of the statements below and give the necessary details.*

☐ Send title information document to the person shown below

☐ Raise any requisitions or queries with the person shown below

☐ Return original documents lodged with this form (see note in panel 6) to the person shown below
If this applies only to certain documents, please specify.

Name
Address/DX No.

Reference
Email

Telephone No.	Fax No.

10.	**Where you would like us to notify someone else that we have completed the registration of this application** *Place "X" in the box and provide the name and address of the person to whom notification should be sent.*

☐ Send notification of completion to the person shown below

Name
Address/DX No.

Reference
Email

11.	**Address(es) for service of the proprietor(s) of the registered estate(s). The address(es) will be entered in the register and used for correspondence and the service of notice.** *Place "X" in the appropriate box(es). You may give up to three addresses for service **one** of which **must** be a postal address but does not have to be within the UK. The other addresses can be any combination of a postal address, a box number at a UK document exchange or an electronic address.*

☐ Enter the address(es) from the transfer/assent/lease

☐ Enter the address(es), including postcode, as follows:

☐ Retain the address(es) currently in the register for the title(s)

12.	**Disclosable overriding interests** *Place "X" in the appropriate box.*

☐ This is not an application to register a registrable disposition or it is but no disclosable overriding interests affect the registered estate(s) *Section 27 of the Land Registration Act 2002 lists the registrable dispositions. Rule 57 of the Land Registration Rules 2003 sets out the disclosable overriding interests. Use Form DI to tell us about any disclosable overriding interests that affect the registered estate(s) identified in panel 2.*

☐ Form DI accompanies this application

The registrar may enter a notice of a disclosed interest in the register of title.

GENERAL PRINCIPLES 13

13. Information in respect of any new charge *Do not give this information if a Land Registry MD reference is printed on the charge, unless the charge has been transferred.*
Full name and address (including postcode) for service of notices and correspondence of the person to be registered as proprietor of each charge. *You may give up to three addresses for service **one** of which **must** be a postal address but does not have to be within the UK. The other addresses can be any combination of a postal address, a box number at a UK document exchange or an electronic address. For a company include company's registered number, if any. For Scottish companies use an SC prefix and for limited liability partnerships use an OC prefix before the registered number, if any. For foreign companies give territory in which incorporated.*

Unless otherwise arranged with Land Registry headquarters, we require a certified copy of the chargee's constitution (in English or Welsh) if it is a body corporate but is not a company registered in England and Wales or Scotland under the Companies Acts.

14. Signature of applicant or their conveyancer _____ Date _____

Crown copyright (ref: LR/SC50) 7/05

First registration application

Land Registry

FR1

If you need more room than is provided for in a panel, use continuation sheet CS and attach to this form.

1.	**Administrative area and postcode** *if known*
2.	**Address or other description of the estate to be registered**
	On registering a rentcharge, profit a prendre in gross, or franchise, show the address as follows:- "Rentcharge, franchise etc, over 2 The Grove, Anytown, Northshire NE2 9OO".

3. **Extent to be registered** *Place "X" in the appropriate box and complete as necessary.*

   ☐ The land is clearly identified on the plan to the _____
   Enter nature and date of deed.

   ☐ The land is clearly identified on the attached plan and shown _____
   Enter reference e.g. "edged red".

   ☐ The description in panel 2 is sufficient to enable the land to be clearly identified on the Ordnance Survey map

   When registering a rentcharge, profit a prendre in gross or franchise, the land to be identified is the land affected by that estate, or to which it relates.

4. **Application, priority and fees** *A fee calculator for all types of applications can be found on Land Registry's website at www.landregistry.gov.uk/fees*

   Nature of applications
   in priority order   Value/premium £   Fees paid £
   1. First registration of the estate
   2.
   3.
   4.
                                  TOTAL £

   Fee payment method: *Place "X" in the appropriate box.*
   I wish to pay the appropriate fee payable under the current Land Registration Fee Order:

   ☐ by cheque or postal order, amount £ _____ made payable to "Land Registry".

   ☐ by Direct Debit under an authorised agreement with Land Registry.

   FOR OFFICIAL USE ONLY
   Record of fees paid

   Particulars of under/over payments

   Fees debited £

   Reference number

5. **The title applied for is** *Place "X" in the appropriate box.*
   ☐ absolute freehold   ☐ absolute leasehold   ☐ good leasehold   ☐ possessory freehold
   ☐ possessory leasehold

6. **Documents lodged with this form** *List the documents on Form DL. We shall assume that you request the return of these documents. But we shall only assume that you request the return of a statutory declaration, subsisting lease, subsisting charge or the latest document of title (for example, any conveyance to the applicant) if you supply a certified copy of the document. If certified copies of such documents are not supplied, we may retain the originals of such documents and they may be destroyed.*

7. **The applicant is:** *Please provide the full name of the person applying to be registered as the proprietor.*

   Application lodged by:
   Land Registry Key No.(if appropriate)
   Name (if different from the applicant)
   Address/DX No.

   Reference
   E-mail
   Telephone No.   Fax No.

   FOR OFFICIAL USE ONLY
   Status codes

8.	**Where you would like us to deal with someone else** *We shall deal only with the applicant, or the person lodging the application if different, unless you place "X" against one or more of the statements below and give the necessary details.*

☐ Send title information document to the person shown below

☐ Raise any requisitions or queries with the person shown below

☐ Return original documents lodged with this form (see note in panel 6) to the person shown below
If this applies only to certain documents, please specify.

Name
Address/DX No.

Reference
E-mail

Telephone No.	Fax No.

9.	**Address(es) for service of every owner of the estate. The address(es) will be entered in the register and used for correspondence and the service of notice.** *In this and panel 10, you may give up to three addresses for service **one** of which **must** be a postal address but does not have to be within the UK. The other addresses can be any combination of a postal address, a box number at a UK document exchange or an electronic address. For a company include the company's registered number, if any. For Scottish companies, use an SC prefix, and for limited liability partnerships, use an OC prefix before the registered number if any. For foreign companies give territory in which incorporated.*

Unless otherwise arranged with Land Registry headquarters, we require a certified copy of the owner's constitution (in English or Welsh) if it is a body corporate but is not a company registered in England or Wales or Scotland under the Companies Acts.

10.	**Information in respect of a chargee or mortgagee** *Do not give this information if a Land Registry MD reference is printed on the charge, unless the charge has been transferred.*

Full name and address (including postcode) for service of notices and correspondence of the person entitled to be registered as proprietor of each charge. *You may give up to three addresses for service; see panel 9 as to the details you should include.*

Unless otherwise arranged with Land Registry headquarters, we require a certified copy of the chargee's constitution (in English or Welsh) if it is a body corporate but is not a company registered in England and Wales or Scotland under the Companies Acts.

11.	**Where the applicants are joint proprietors** *Place "X" in the appropriate box*

☐ The applicants are holding the property on trust for themselves as joint tenants

☐ The applicants are holding the property on trust for themselves as tenants in common in equal shares

☐ The applicants are holding the property *(complete as necessary)*

12.	**Disclosable overriding interests** *Place "X" in the appropriate box.*

☐ No disclosable overriding interests affect the estate

☐ Form DI accompanies this application

Rule 28 of the Land Registration Rules 2003 sets out the disclosable overriding interests that you must tell us about. You must use Form DI to tell us about any disclosable overriding interests that affect the estate.

The registrar may enter a notice of a disclosed interest in the register of title.

13. The title is based on the title documents listed in Form DL which are all those that are in the possession or control of the applicant.
    Place "X" in the appropriate box. If applicable complete the second statement; include any interests disclosed only by searches other than local land charges. Any interests disclosed by searches which do not affect the estate being registered should be certified.

    ☐ All rights, interests and claims affecting the estate known to the applicant are disclosed in the title documents and Form DI if accompanying this application. There is no-one in adverse possession of the property or any part of it.

    ☐ In addition to the rights, interests and claims affecting the estate disclosed in the title documents or Form DI if accompanying this application, the applicant only knows of the following:

14. *Place "X" in this box if you are NOT able to give this certificate.* ☐

    We have fully examined the applicant's title to the estate, including any appurtenant rights, or are satisfied that it has been fully examined by a conveyancer in the usual way prior to this application.

15. We have authority to lodge this application and request the registrar to complete the registration.

16. Signature of applicant
    or their conveyancer _____ Date _____

    Note: Failure to complete the form with proper care may deprive the applicant of protection under the Land Registration Act if, as a result, a mistake is made in the register.

    © Crown copyright (ref: LR/HQ/CD-ROM) 6/03

8 Tax

It is a fact of modern legal practice that the tax aspects of every transaction should be considered. This book does not claim to treat this topic exhaustively but focuses attention on the major heads of charge as a reminder of the possible tax consequences of transactions covered in this book (see Ch.2).   **1–15**

Each case will of course depend on its facts; regard should be had to any possible tax consequences before the court order or agreement between the parties is finalised.

9 Council Tax

This was introduced by the Local Government Finance Act 1992.   **1–16**

Since April 2, 1993 all dwellings are subject to the Council Tax and the full amount is payable where there are two or more adult residents. The liable person will normally be the resident who owns the property (s.6(2)); joint owners are jointly and severally liable (s.6(3)) as is the resident partner of a liable person (s.9).

If there is only one adult resident, a discount of 25 per cent can be claimed (s.11); it is important therefore that if the parties cease to live together each of them should notify the local authority that separation has taken place so as to end joint liability and for the remaining resident party to claim the discount (if applicable).

10 Insolvency

Practitioners will be aware that transactions at an undervalue can be put aside (Insolvency Act 1986, s.339) if the transferor is adjudged bankrupt within two years of the transaction or if he becomes bankrupt within five years of the transaction and was insolvent at that time or was insolvent by reason of it (s.341).   **1–17**

There are two potential problems which are dealt with below.

(a) *the possibility that the property transfer to the transferee may be set aside on grounds of undervalue in the event of the transferor's insolvency.*

It is difficult to say whether or not a transfer of a house pursuant, for instance, to a "clean break" is "less in money or money's worth than the value in money or money's worth of the consideration provided" (s.339(3)(c)) so there is always a risk that a property transfer following the court order or agreement may be attacked by a transferor's trustee in bankruptcy and the transferee cannot be absolutely safe until the five year period has expired. There is nothing in the Act to confer immunity on a property transfer carried out to comply with a court order (see *Re Kumar (a bankrupt)* [1993] 1 W.L.R. 224 where the court found the conveyance from   **1–18** joint names to the wife alone embodied in a court-approved consent order to be a transaction at an undervalue), but the existence of the wife's right to financial relief against her husband may provide sufficient value to prevent the transaction being at an undervalue within the context of the Insolvency Act 1986 (see Rayden and Jackson on *Divorce and Family Matters*, 18 edn., Vol.1(1), para.19.23).

In *Re Abbott* (*a bankrupt*) [1983] Ch. 45 (a case decided before the Insolvency Act 1986) a wife's petition for divorce sought an order transferring the jointly owned matrimonial home to her. Agreement was reached and a consent order subsequently made to the effect that the house should be sold and that the husband should pay the wife a lump sum of £9,000 from his share of the proceeds of sale. On the husband's bankruptcy within two years of the consent order, the Trustee sought to recover £9,000 from the wife, that sum being the amount in excess of the value of her half share in the house. The Court held that she was a purchaser for valuable consideration, the consideration being the withdrawal of a bona fide claim to a property adjustment order.

It is clear that just because a transfer is ordered by a court this does not confer upon it immunity from being held to be a transaction at an undervalue or which conferred a preference thereby leaving it open to scrutiny by a bankrupts trustee.

(b) the difficulty the transferee may have in selling the property on the grounds that it was transferred, or the transferor's interest in it was transferred at an undervalue.

1–19 Apart from the argument that there was no undervalue (see above) the Insolvency (No.2) Act 1994 protects a purchaser from the transferee (with two exceptions) so long as the purchaser buys in good faith and for open market value.

The two exceptions (see Insolvency Act 1986, s.342(2A) as inserted) relate to a buyer who is an associate of the undervalue transferor or transferee or a buyer who has knowledge of an undervalue transaction and that the original undervalue transferor is actually or about to be the subject of insolvency proceedings. In general therefore it is not felt that there will be difficulty but the transferee should always be advised to obtain a declaration of solvency from the transferor for use on a later transfer (*see* Ch.10).

Prior to April 1, 2000 neither of these issues had been a problem so far as land already registered at HM Land Registry is concerned as the consideration was not shown on the registered title. However, since the substitution of the Land Registration Rules 1925, r.247 as from April 1, 2000 the Registrar will on each change of ownership register either the price paid for the property or the value declared in the land registry application (now embodied in the Land Registration Rules 2003, r.8(2)). However, the Chief Land Registrar will not enter any note of the possibility that a transaction may be set aside in the event of a transferor's insolvency when registering a transfer with the result that a subsequent purchaser acting in good faith will not be affected or prejudiced by it (Ruoff and Roper, *Registered Conveyancing* looseleaf, Sweet & Maxwell, paras 34–015 and 34–016).

In the light of the above a prospective purchaser may be hesitant to proceed without adequate insurance protection (if obtainable). (See further Ch.10).

11 Former council houses

Many people have purchased the houses in which they live from the Local Authority, New Town Development or Social Landlords Corporations since the Housing Act 1985 came into force as widened by the provisions of the Housing Act 1996. The disposal of such dwelling-house within three years (Housing Act 1985, s.155 (as amended)) from the date of purchase "triggers" repayment of the discount on the proportion still outstanding by reference to the number of years since purchase but s.160(1)(c) of the Act, specifically exempts from the repayment provisions disposals in pursuance of an order under the Matrimonial Causes Act 1973, s.24, where continued occupation is envisaged (see *R. v Rushmoor BC Ex p. Barrett* [1987] 1 All E.R. 353).

1–20

Thus an order of the court that a former council house, New Town Development House or a house acquired from a Social Landlord be transferred to one party of the marriage will not necessitate at the time of the transfer repayment of the discount or any part of it allowable at the time of purchase.

Liability to repay the discount is secured by the registration of a notice at HM Land Registry (Housing Act 1985, s.156) and any transfer will of course be subject to such notice.

12 Execution of documents

A transfer of land or of any interest in it must be made by deed (LPA 1925, s.52(1)).

1–21

The Law of Property (Miscellaneous Provisions) Act 1989, s.1 specifies that if an instrument is to be a deed, this must be clear on the face of it and it must be validly executed; the individual must sign the deed in the presence of a witness who attests the signature (s.1(3)). Further, the deed must be delivered as a deed by the person executing it or by a person authorised to do so on his behalf; a purchaser or transferee may presume that a solicitor or licensed conveyancer is so authorised (s.1(5) as amended by Courts and Legal Services Act 1990, s.125(2) Schs 17 & 20). The Companies Act 1985, s.36A (as inserted the Companies Act 1989, s.130(2)) contains corresponding provisions relating to the execution of deeds by companies registered under the Companies Acts.

Form TR1 (Transfer of whole of registered titles) prescribed by Land Registration Rules 2003 and set out in Sch.1 incorporates the above requirements so that forms of registered dispositions are correctly executed and the acceptable forms of execution are set out in Sch.9 of the same Rules.

13 Legal Service Commission statutory charge

1–22 Under the Access to Justice Act 1999, s.10(7), if services have been funded by the Commission for an individual as part of Community Legal Service (formerly known as legal aid) funds expended by the Commission on behalf of the individual (except to the extent that they are recoverable from the other party) will constitute a first legal charge on any property recovered or preserved by that individual.

Periodical payments of maintenance escape the statutory charge as does the first £3,000 of any money or the value of any property recovered by virtue of matrimonial proceedings (The Community Legal Services (Finance) Regulations 2000, Pt III, reg.44 as amended by the Community Legal Services (Finance) (amendment No. 3) Regulations 2001 (SI 2001/3663)). In other words if a lump sum is recovered over £3,000 the statutory charge will apply to the balance and the Commission can seek immediate repayment of its deficiency from that.

If, however, the court order specifies that the lump sum is to be used for the purpose of purchasing a home for the assisted person or their dependants enforcement of the charge can be postponed. Similarly, if the property recovered or preserved is to be used as a home for the assisted person or their dependants enforcement of the charge can also be postponed (in both cases see The Community Legal Services (Financial) Regulations 2000 (SI 2000/516), Pt III, reg.52). In each case the Commission will, as soon as possible, register a charge on the former family home or the home bought with the lump sum.

The Commission will apply to register a statutory charge or alternatively apply to register a restriction which will state as follows; "no disposition of the registered estate is to be completed by registration without a certificate signed by the applicant for registration or his conveyancer that written notice of the disposition was sent by post to the LSC Land Charge Department at 85 Gray's Inn Road, London WC1X 8TX". Once the restriction is registered the statutory charge will be protected as against any purchaser.

At the present time if a statutory charge is registered it will attract interest on the balance outstanding to the Commission at the rate of 8 per cent per annum until March 31, 2002 and since then at a rate of 1 per cent above the Bank of England base rate (The Community Legal Services (Financial) Regulations 2001 (SI 2001/516 Pt III, reg.53 as amended by the Community Legal Services (Financial) (amended No. 3) 2001 (SI 2001/3663).

Normally the charge will be repaid when the property is sold but the Commission has a discretion to transfer the charge to a substitute property in certain circumstances (The Community Legal Services (Financial) Regulations 2000, reg.52(2)).

The Commission have a standard form of charge document which needs to be signed by the chargor. Correspondence relating to redemption or transfer of statutory charges should be addressed to the Legal Services Commission, Accounts Department, 85 Gray's Inn Road, London WC1X

8TX but practitioners are advised to check by telephoning the Commission for guidance on 020 7759 0000. All correspondence should of course quote the full name and address of the assisted person, the Community Legal Service reference number and the title number of the property.

14 Community Legal Service Funding and conveyancing costs

It is believed that following the cases of *Copeland v Houlton* [1955] 3 All E.R. 178 and *S v S* (Legal Aid Taxation) (1991) Fam. Law. 271, the cost of conveyancing work necessary to give effect to the terms of a court order in family proceedings will continue to be covered by a certificate issued under the Funding Code (approved by the Access to Justice Act 1999, s.9). This should apply equally to work necessary to implement consent orders. However, practitioners should always check with the Commission if there is any doubt as to what work is covered before undertaking it.

1–23

Chapter 2

The Tax Aspects

The Civil Partnership Act 2004 referred to in Ch.1 came in to force on December 5, 2005 as did the Tax and Civil Partnership Regulations 2005. The latter bring about tax parity between civil partners as defined in CPA 2004 and married couples. All references in this chapter therefore apply equally to civil partners and married couples. 2–01

The practitioner acting for the transferor should consider the tax effect of any transfer of the family home, or interest in it to the other party to the marriage or registered civil partnership, and upon whom the burden of any taxation is to fall.

In all circumstances relating to tax matters it must be appreciated that each set of facts is to be looked at separately. The contents of this chapter cannot describe the tax position on each transfer; they can only draw attention to the possible heads of charge and reliefs available in respect of each of them.

1 Capital gains tax

Prima facie if a disposal of the former family home or an interest in it occurs, there is a charge to capital gains tax. It is important therefore to have a look at the reliefs and exemptions that may be available. 2–02

The rate of tax on chargeable gains is that which results from adding the gain to the individual's total income. The gain may be taxed at the basic rate of income tax or at the higher rate. A non-resident is not liable to capital gains tax (Taxation of Chargeable Gains Act 1992 (TCGA 1992), s.2(1)).

(a) Parties living together

There is no charge to capital gains tax on a transfer of assets between husband and wife or civil partners provided that they have been living together in the year of assessment in which the transfer takes place (TCGA 1992, s.58). This continues to apply notwithstanding the introduction of independent taxation from April 6, 1990. Usually a husband and wife are regarded as living together if they are not separated under a court order or a deed of separation or separated in such circumstances as are likely to prove permanent (Income and Corporation Taxes Act 1988, s.282). HM Revenue & Customs (HMRC) treat the separation as likely to be permanent if the parties have been living apart for one year. 2–03

In many cases the parties will be living apart at the time of the court order, or at a time when agreement is reached between them concerning the former family home, in circumstances that are likely to prove permanent. Indeed the parties may in any event no longer be husband and wife or civil partners. Prima facie, therefore, a charge to capital gains tax will arise on any transfer by the parties of the former family home or of their shares or interest in it.

(b) Only or main residence

2–04   Relief from any liability to capital gains tax on any transfer should be available in most cases because the former family home will have been the only or main residence of both the parties. The Taxation of Chargeable Gains Act 1992, s.222 provides that gains accruing on the disposal of, or an interest in, a dwelling-house which is or has been an individual's only or main residence (together with garden or grounds of up to half a hectare in extent or other extent appropriate for the reasonable enjoyment of the residence according to the size and character of the dwelling house) throughout the period of ownership (but disregarding the last 36 months of that period (TCGA 1992, s.223) are exempt from capital gains tax. As to the inclusion of other properties (e.g. a gardener's cottage) within the exemption see *Lewis v Rook* [1992] W.L.R. 662.

It is clear therefore that a sale of the former family home within 36 months of the non-resident party leaving it, or a transfer of his or her interest in it to the resident party within that period, will not incur any charge to capital gains tax.

It will be otherwise if a sale or transfer takes place when the non-resident party left the home at least 36 months ago or has acquired another residence. In this case, only a proportion of the gain will be exempt by reference to the period of actual occupation and to the last 36 months of ownership. The balance will be subject to capital gains tax. As an example, if there is a gain on the sale of a property owned equally for 15 years, occupied for the first 10 years by both parties and for the last five years by only the resident party, there is complete exemption on the one-half share occupied by the resident party throughout, and a chargeable gain to the extent of two-fifteenths of the gain on the other half (the chargeable years being the five years after occupation had ceased less the 36 months). This brings us to consideration of the extra-statutory concession.

(c) Extra-statutory concession D6

2–05   This concession happily can exempt the whole gain resulting from the disposal from a charge to capital gains tax even if the conveyance or transfer to the resident party takes place 36 months after the non-resident party has left the former family home. It is quoted in full:

> "6 *Private residence exception: separated couples*
>
> Where a married couple separate or are divorced and one partner ceases to occupy the matrimonial home and subsequently as part of a

financial settlement disposes of the home, or an interest in it, to the other partner the home may be regarded for the purposes of ss.222 to 224 of TCGA 1992 as continuing to be a residence of the transferring partner from the date his or her occupation ceases until the date of transfer, provided that it has throughout this period been the other partner's only or main residence. Thus, where a husband leaves the matrimonial home while still owning it, the usual capital gains tax exemption or relief for a taxpayer's only or main residence would be given on the subsequent transfer to the wife, provided she has continued to live in the house and the husband has not elected that some other house should be treated for capital gains tax purposes as his main residence for this period."

The wording of the concession would seem to suggest that if one party moves out of the family home and makes no election that that party's new home is his or her main residence then he or she need do nothing further, since on any subsequent transfer of the former family home to the other party the principal private dwelling-house exemption will be available (provided he or she has continued to live there).

HMRC are of the view that a taxpayer's home (even if a rented flat) can be his or her main residence even if he does not own it. If a taxpayer has two residences he or she can elect which of them is to be treated as his or her main residence (s.222(5)) for the purpose of the exemption and notwithstanding the terms of the above concession the non-resident party can avoid difficulty if he or she makes a positive election.

If the non-resident party elects that his or her "new" home is to be treated as his or her main residence, then the disposal to the resident party of the former family home (or his or her interest in it) will give rise to a charge to capital gains tax; this will be on the gain accruing in respect of the period from when the family home ceased to be his or her main residence until the date of the court order or date of agreement between the parties. Section 222(5)(a) contains a time-limit of two years during which the election as to main residence can be made and if an election is not made within the period the question of which is the main residence is determined by the Inspector of Taxes, subject to the usual right of appeal. By making a positive election the non-resident party avoids the Inspector making a determination under s.222(5)(b) as to which is his or her main residence and avoids the necessity for an appeal and having to claim the benefit of the concession. In practice a great deal of discretion is exercised by HMRC with regard to this section, but to avoid an unexpected tax liability in relation to the transfer of the former family home the non-resident party is well advised to consider making his or her election within the two-year period.

A cautionary note should be added: a separated wife may be in possession of the former family home and wish to move house. If she does so and the husband purchases the replacement house for her, and she occupies it on the same terms, a subsequent transfer to her of that house will not be within the terms of the concession because that house will never have been a family home. A charge to capital gains tax could therefore arise unless the provisions of the TCGA 1992, s.225 apply.

Please note that the author's reading of the special concession is that it only applies to married parties or separated married parties and not to civil partners.

(d) Other reliefs

2–06 The above has been concerned with the only or main residence or one party's interest in it being transferred absolutely to the other. A transfer of other real property, such as a holiday home, will give rise to a capital gains liability if at the time of the transfer, as is more than likely, the parties are separated in such circumstances as are likely to prove permanent or are separated under a court order (see, for example, *Aspden v Hildesley* [1982] 1 W.L.R. 264 where a transfer of property which had never been the husband's main residence was made to the wife six years after the parties separated).

Transfers of assets between separated parties remain exempt from capital gains tax provided the asset is transferred to the other party before the end of the fiscal year after the date of separation. Thereafter the liability described in the previous paragraph will render all transfers liable to capital gains tax. The Law Society and other pressure groups are currently lobbying HMRC to amend TCGA 1992, s.58 to extend this period in view of the complexity of asset ownership in modern times. At present the cut off time remains April 5 following the date of separation.

Assuming that a capital gains tax liability is likely to arise, prima facie this will fall upon the conveying party or transferor; this potential liability should be taken into account, but regard should be had to other reliefs:

(i) *"Hold-over" relief*—Since the restriction of this relief by the Finance Act 1989, s.124 it is only likely to be available in business property transfer situations (such as a guest house or nursing home) (see TCGA 1992, s.165). The potential liability would pass to the transferee; to agree to elect for "hold over" will not necessarily be to the transferee's advantage.

(ii) *Annual exemption*—This is £8,800 in the tax year 2006/07 (TCGA 1992, s.3).

(iii) *Taper relief*—Taper relief is applied to gains chargeable to capital gains tax under TCGA 1992, s.2(2) in so far as individuals and trustees are concerned. The amount of the relief will depend on the amount of the gain and the number of years the family home has been owned.

The potential liability where the former family home is settled upon certain trusts is considered in Ch.6.

2 Inheritance tax

2–07 If both parties are domiciled in the United Kingdom, any transfer of assets between them is exempt from any charge to inheritance tax (Inheritance Tax Act 1984, s.18(1)). Further, a disposition between separated parties will rank as a transfer between spouses or civil partners; so that the exemption is still available, as there is no requirement (in contrast to the capital gains tax legislation) that the parties shall be living together.

Thus, as long as the marriage or civil partnership between the parties (assuming them both to be domiciled in the UK) is not dissolved, transfers of property between them will not incur a liability to inheritance tax. The marriage or civil partnership is not finally dissolved until the decree is made absolute or an equivalent order is made; thus, transfers of property in the period before the final decree or order incur no inheritance tax liability.

Once the marriage or civil partnership is dissolved, prima facie there is a charge to inheritance tax on a transfer of property between former partners unless the disposition is *not* intended to confer gratuitous benefit on either person and is made between persons not connected with each other (Inheritance Tax Act 1984, s.10(1)). A former husband and wife or former civil partners are not "connected persons" (see TCGA 1992, s.286(2), and the Inheritance Tax Act 1984, s.270).

It will be recalled that all transfers of property ordered by the court take effect only after the final decree or order (Matrimonial Causes Act 1973, s.24(3) as amended by CPA 2004), at which time the exemption relating to a transfer between former partners is not applicable. In most cases, however, a transfer of property between former spouses will fall within the provisions of s.10(1) mentioned above. The Inland Revenue as it was then known issued a Press Statement (see *Orange Tax Handbook* 1992/93, Butterworths, IHT Statements of Practice, E12) to this effect:

> "Transfer of money or property pursuant to an Order of the Court in consequence of a Decree of Divorce or nullity of marriage will in general be regarded as exempt from Inheritance Tax as transactions at arm's length which are not intended to confer any gratuitous benefit."

This statement of practice is now obsolete (JR 1311994 see Butterworth's *Orange Tax Handbook* 1996/97) as the Revenue now regard the statement of practice to be taken into its normal instructions, but it is worth quoting so that practitioners know what the normal instructions are.

It would appear therefore that if it can be shown that a transfer of property takes place to satisfy the claim of a former spouse or civil partner (*i.e.* that there is no gratuitous benefit intended) there should be no charge on the transfer to inheritance tax. Similarly if the house is transferred upon certain terms and conditions (*see* Ch.6) the Inheritance Tax Act 1984, s.11 should relieve the transfer from charge (*see* p.110) on the basis that it is for the maintenance of the other party. The safest course, must be either to complete the transfer (if by agreement) before the marriage or civil partnership is dissolved or to have the transfer made the subject of a court order and so usually fall within the provisions of s.10(1).

A sale by one former spouse or civil partner to the other of property or an interest therein should incur no inheritance tax liability if at full value, but if a sale takes place at an under value on the basis that a benefit is intended this is a transfer of value for inheritance tax purposes. Following the Finance Act 1986 this would be a potentially exempt transfer and only subject to a charge to inheritance tax if the transferor dies within seven years of the date of the transfer (Finance Act 1986, Sch.19, Pt I, para.I inserting Inheritance Tax Act 1984, s.3(A)).

In the event of the death of the transferor's former spouse or civil partner within the seven year period, the liability to inheritance tax falls upon the transferee (Inheritance Tax Act 1984, s.199) although if not paid within 12 months the transferor's personal representatives can be liable (s.199(2)). The transferor should take an indemnity from the transferee to protect his or her estate in the event of such liability arising.

3 Stamp duty land tax

2–08 Stamp Duty Land Tax (SDLT) was introduced by the Finance Act 2003 and came into force on December 1, 2003 after the last edition of this book was published. SDLT is not a charge on documents as with the old Stamp Duty but is chargeable on land transactions. All such transactions are to be notified to HMRC within 30 days of the effective date of the transaction which, for the purposes of this book, will usually be the date of completion. As stated below most transfers resulting from the breakdown of a marriage or civil partnership will be exempt from SDLT but the transferee will be required to complete a self-certification form to the effect that the transaction is not chargeable to SDLT and this must be sent to H M Land Registry with the application for registration. In cases where there is no exemption then an SDLT return must be completed by the transferee and sent to HMRC with a cheque for any SDLT payable. Upon receipt of the return and if there are no errors HMRC will issue a certificate and return it to the transferee's solicitor who will send the certificate to HMRC with the application for registration.

According to the Government the reasons for introducing SDLT were threefold; namely fairness, e-business and modernisation. Stamp Duty has been steadily increased by this Government since it came to office in the late 1990s and there were many avoidance devices in operation as a result. By introducing SDLT all transactions have been brought under the ambit of SDLT and avoidance is now less of an issue. Under the old system documents were physically stamped with duty and this is cumbersome and does not sit well with the move towards e-conveyancing and the paperless transaction. Other taxes have been brought up to date in recent years and it was felt that as with them SDLT should apply to the substance of the transaction and not the paper work associated with it.

On completion of any land transaction, as stated above, it is necessary for the transferee to complete an SDLT return. In most normal circumstances this will be a form known as SDLT 1. This form is proscribed by law and consists of boxes to be completed. These are then read by computer and processed automatically. Form SDLT 1 and supplemental forms SDLT 2 to SDLT 4 can be found on HMRC website at *www.hmrc.gov.uk*. In most situations involving breakdown of a marriage or civil partnership the self certification form SDLT 60 will be required and this can be found on the HMRC website as stated.

(a) Tax reliefs

Schedule 3 to the Finance Act 2003 provides that in general on divorce or the termination of a civil partnership there will be no liability to SDLT on the resultant property transfers. In particular the exemption will apply when the property transfer is made: 2–09

(i) under a court order on divorce or judicial separation, or nullifying a marriage (or the equivalent) (Sch.3(3)(a) and (b)); or

(ii) "in pursuance of an order of a court made at any time under section 22A, 23A or 24A of the Matrimonial Causes Act 1973" (Sch.3(3)(c)(i)); or

(iii) ". . .in pursuance of an agreement of the parties made in contemplation or otherwise in connection with the dissolution or annulment of the marriage, their judicial separation or the making of a separation order in respect of them" (Sch.3(3)(d)).

It is difficult to imagine any circumstances now where an inter spouse or civil partnership transfer of the kind envisaged by this book would give rise to a charge to SDLT even where the property is being transferred subject to an existing mortgage with the transferee taking over responsibility for it.

(b) Assuming the mortgage debt

In the past practitioners have had considerable difficulty where the transferee took over property subject to a mortgage liability as prima facie, this raised a liability to stamp duty under s.57 of the Stamp Act 1891 according to the value of the debt assumed by the transferee. Under the new regime, as stated above, there will be no liability to SDLT where a property is transferred subject to a mortgage in the circumstances described in Sch.3 of the Finance Act 2003. However, where land subject to a mortgage is transferred between parties by way of gift or in any event for no consideration special rules apply and there will be a charge to SDLT based on the value of the mortgage debt transferred to the transferee (Finance Act 2003, s.48 and Sch.4(8)). 2–10

In more specific terms where the consideration for the transfer of property comprises the satisfaction or release of a debt or the assumption by the transferee of an existing debt the amount of the debt satisfied, released or assumed is regarded as the consideration for the transfer and chargeable to SDLT.

Where therefore a property is transferred subject to a mortgage with the transferor being released the amount of chargeable consideration is the amount outstanding under the mortgage at the time. If only part of the debt is assumed by the transferee then it is the part of the debt released which forms the chargeable consideration for the transfer and on which SDLT will be charged.

In situations where there is no marriage or civil partnership and no other reliefs are available the debt released will be added to any consideration to arrive at the sum on which SDLT will be charged. The chargeable sum will not exceed the market value of the property even if the debt satisfied, released or assumed is greater than this.

(c) The charge

2–11 If the conveyance or transfer does not fall within the provisions of Sch.3 to the Finance Act 2003, one is thrown back on the usual Stamp Duty Land Tax charges which on a *conveyance or transfer on sale* are as follows:

consideration not exceeding £125,000	Nil
over £125,000 but not exceeding £250,000	1%
over £250,000 but not exceeding £500,000	3%
over £500,000	4%

(d) The hybrid situation

2–12 It is sometimes agreed between the parties to a marriage or indeed a civil partnership that the family home (or an interest in it) be transferred to one ex-partner and a third party (e.g. a new husband—*see* Ch.5). This is, in essence, a truncation of two separate transactions (a transfer to the transferee followed by his or her subsequent transfer to herself and the third party). These transactions could not fall within Sch.3 to the Finance Act 2003 and could therefore give rise to a charge to SDLT. Form SDLT 1 should be completed carefully and be submitted to HMRC with or without a cheque for the duty having calculated whether any tax is payable.

(e) Examples

2–13 Set out below are various categories of transfers and how they should be dealt with for stamp duty land tax purposes:

(i) Transfer pursuant to court order--no monetary consideration

(e.g. Precedents 1, 4 and 10)

Provided the transferee completes the self-certification form SDLT 60 and submits this to HM Land Registry with the application for registration then no SDLT is payable.

(ii) Transfer by the one party to the other, by agreement (i.e. not pursuant to court order)—no monetary consideration
Provided this meets the requirements of Sch.3 to the Finance Act 2003 (see above) and provided the self-certificate SDLT 60 referred to above accompanies the application for registration no SDLT is payable.

(iii) Transfer pursuant to court order or by agreement—transferee paying some consideration to transferor

(e.g. Precedent 36)

If by order of the court (or by agreement) and within the provisions of Sch.3 to the Finance Act 2003 (above), then provided the self-certificate SDLT 60 referred to above accompanies the application for registration no SDLT is payable.

(iv) Transfer pursuant to court order with transferor being released from the mortgage (transferee assuming liability)

(e.g. Precedents 3 and 12)

It was this type of conveyance which caused the most difficulty prior to the passing of the Finance Act 1985 because the Stamp Act 1891, s.57 triggered a charge to stamp duty under the old regime. Happily, such a conveyance falls within the provisions of Sch.3 to the Finance Act 2003 and there will be no charge to SDLT provided the appropriate self-certificate SDLT 60 accompanies the application for registration.

(v) Transfer by one party to the other (or a third party) for consideration (no element of gift)

(e.g. Precedents 5, 11 and 20 to 22)

Such a conveyance if not falling within the provisions of Sch.3 (above) (i.e. not made in connection with the divorce etc.) and not containing an element of gift requires the completion of SDLT 1 which must be submitted to HMRC with a cheque for the appropriate sum. Obviously there will be no cheque required in a situation where the consideration does not exceed £125,000 but the return must be submitted in any event.

It must not be forgotten that if either party or a third party is assuming the mortgage debt, so that the transferor is released, the amount of the debt assumed in addition to the cash consideration will be subject to SDLT (Finance Act 2003, Sch.4, para.8).

(vi) Transfer by one party to the other, with element of gift—no monetary consideration

This is the situation most likely to effect parties who are not married or subject to a registered civil partnership although in reality one would expect there to be some form of consideration. However, where there is no consideration in money or money's worth this is effectively a gift inter vivos and no SDLT is chargeable provided the application for registration is accompanied by self-certificate SDLT 60 properly completed.

(vii) Transfer to trustees (by Court order or by agreement) with no consideration

(e.g. Precedents 26 and 27)

Such a conveyance or transfer falls within the provisions of Sch.3 (above) as it is a conveyance or transfer for no consideration, an SDLT 60 is applicable.

Chapter 3

Home in Sole Name of One Party Transfer to Other

This chapter deals with the situation where the family home is in the sole name of one party, with the home being either free from any mortgage charge or subject to a mortgage debt. The court may order the proprietor to convey or transfer the home to the other party absolutely in the following manner: **3–01**

> "It is ordered that the Respondent shall transfer with full title guarantee to the Petitioner absolutely within 28 days from the date of this Order the property at 1 Blackacre Drive, Blackacre."

Chapter 6 deals with those cases where the home is in one party's sole name and that party is ordered to make a conveyance upon certain terms or settle the family home upon certain trusts.

The protection of the transferee's position prior to the court order and the risk of the transferor dealing with the property in the period between the court order and completion of the lodgment of the transfer to the transferee at HM Land Registry should first be mentioned as a reminder to practitioners.

1 Notice of Home Rights

No book relating to family home conveyancing would be complete without mention of the Notice of Home Rights (still largely referred to by reference to its unregistered equivalent as a Class F Land Charge). Although the registration of the notice precedes the situation covered in this book, and is thus more within the ambit of the practitioner advising in the initial stages of proceedings to end a marriage or civil partnership than the conveyancer, a reminder of the requirements and consequences of registration is relevant. **3–02**

It should be recalled that a right of occupation may already be postponed to the interest of a mortgagee.

The Family Law Act 1996 as amended by the Civil Partnership Act 2004 (CPA 2004) makes detailed provision for the protection of home rights by way of registration. These largely repeat the protection previously afforded by the Matrimonial Homes Act 1967 and the Matrimonial Homes Act 1983.

The Family Law Act 1996, s.31(1) and (2) (as amended by CPA 2004, s.82; Sch.9, paras 2(1), 2(2) and 2(3)) state that where one party to a marriage or civil partnership has a beneficial interest in the family home, then the other party's right of occupation is a charge on that estate or interest. Home Rights are defined in ss.30(2)(a) and (b) (as amended by CPA 2004, s.82; Sch.9, paras 1(1) and 1(3)) and grant to the party with no beneficial interest in the family home the following rights.

1. If in occupation, a right not to be evicted or excluded from the house or any part of it by the other party except by an order of the court pursuant to s.30 (as amended by CPA 2004).

2. If not in occupation, with the leave of the court, a right to enter into and occupy the house (s.33(3)(b) (as amended by CPA 2004, s.82; Sch.9, paras 4(1) and 4(4).

It is essential that home rights are registered in the appropriate way otherwise they will not be protected.

(a) Unregistered Land

3–03 All transfers of unregistered land covered by this book will now be subject to compulsory first registration as previously described but it will still be necessary to protect the right of occupation by way of a Class F Land Charge at HM Land Charges Registry where the family home is unregistered before any order or agreement for its transfer is implemented (Land Charges Act 1972 and Family Law Act 1996 as amended by CPA 2004).

In order to be effective the registration must be submitted to HM Land Charges Registry on form K2 (no fee payable) and it is vital that the owning party's full and correct name is entered on the form. A copy of form K2 is reproduced on the following page.

Unless the position is known it will be necessary to establish that the property is unregistered, as form K2 contains a certificate to the effect that the property is not registered at HM Land Registry. Traditionally this is done by submitting an application for an official search of the Index Map (Form SIM—no fee—a copy of the form appears after the copy of form K2 referred to above). The result will state whether or not the property is registered and provide the title number where appropriate.

A useful alternative to the above is to apply for official copies of the registered title at HM Land Registry (Form OC 1—fee £4 or £8 if the filed plan is also requested—a copy of the form appears after the copy form SIM referred to above). The title number should be left blank and the address details filled in. In box 7 one is asked to state whether the freehold, leasehold or other title is required, if this is not known simply tick both the leasehold and freehold boxes. if the land is unregistered the application will be returned, but if is registered the receipt of official copies entries gives the opportunity to check the charges register for mortgages.

HOME IN SOLE NAME OF ONE PARTY TRANSFER TO OTHER 35

Important: Please read the notes overleaf before completing the form

Form K2

**Land Charges Act 1972
(Family Law Act 1996)**

Application for registration of a Land Charge of Class F

Application is hereby made for the registration of a Land Charge of Class F in respect of the following particulars

Fee panel
If the fee is to be debited to your credit account put a cross (X) in this box

(See Note 1 overleaf)

1. Is there any subsisting registration of rights of occupation under the Matrimonial Homes Act 1967 or 1983 or matrimonial home rights under the Family Law Act 1996 which affects a dwellinghouse other than that referred to in this application?
Yes/No *(delete as applicable)*

2. If "Yes"
   (a) Give address of such dwellinghouse _____

   (b) If the subsisting registration was made:
   (i) under the **Land Charges Act** 1925 or 1972 OR (ii) under the **Land Registration Acts** 1925 to 1986
   give the Official reference number and date of registration.   give Title number under which the dwellinghouse is registered

(See Notes 2 and 3 overleaf)

LC _____ Date _____ Title No _____

Particulars to be registered

Enter full name and address *(See Note 4 overleaf)*	**Person entitled to benefit of the charge**
Complete if applicable *(See Note 5 overleaf)*	**Particulars of court order** By an order of the _____ Court dated _____ and made under s.33(5) of the Family Law Act 1996 or by virtue of s.2(4) of the Matrimonial Homes Act 1983 it was directed that
	F If application is made pursuant to a Priority Notice please state its official reference number
(See Note 6 overleaf)	**Particulars of dwellinghouse** County District Known as
Only one individual or body to be entered *(See Note 7 overleaf)*	**Particulars of estate owner** Forename(s) **Surname** Title, Trade or Profession Address
(See Note 8 overleaf)	**Key number**

For official use only

1	2	3
*C		
4	5	6

Solicitor's name and address
(See Note 9 overleaf)
If no Solicitor is acting enter applicant's name and address
(See Note 10 overleaf)

I/We certify that the dwellinghouse in this application is not registered at the Land Registry.

Signature of solicitor or applicant   Date
(See Notes 11 and 12 overleaf)

MATRIMONIAL CONVEYANCING

Explanatory Notes

The following notes are supplied for assistance in making the application overleaf. Detailed information for the making of all kinds of applications to the Land Charges Department is contained in a booklet entitled "Computerised Land Charges Department: a practical guide for solicitors" which is obtainable on application at the address shown below.

Fee payable	1.	Fees must be paid by credit account or by cheque or postal order made payable to "HM Land Registry" (see the "guide" referred to above)
Form completion	2.	Please complete the form in block letters (handwritten or typewritten) using black ink not liable to smear. No covering letter is required and no plan or other supporting documentation should be sent with the application.
Particulars of subsisting registration	3.	Under s.32 of, and paragraph 2 of Schedule 4 to, the Family Law Act 1996 a charge in respect of matrimonial home rights under the Act may be registered against one dwellinghouse only at any one time and the Chief Land Registrar will thus be bound to cancel any previous registration.
Person entitled to the benefit of the charge	4.	Please give the full name and address of the person whose matrimonial home rights under s.30(2) of the Family Law Act 1996 is sought to protect by registration.
Court order	5.	Insert details of any direction given by the Court that the Applicant's matrimonial home rights should not be brought to an end by the death of his/her spouse or the termination of the marriage otherwise than by death. Please state the name of the Court making the order and the date of the order.
County	6.	Enter as "County" the appropriate name as set out in the Appendix to Land Charges Practice Leaflet No. 3. As stated therein, if the land referred to in the application lies within the Greater London area, then "Greater London" should be stated as the county name.
Estate owner	7.	Please give the full name, address and description of the estate owner as defined in the Law of Property Act 1925 against whom registration is to be effected. Enter forename(s) and surname on separate lines.
Key number	8.	If you have been allocated a key number, please take care to enter this in the space provided overleaf, whether or not you are paying fees through your credit account.
Name and address	9.	The full name and address of the applicant to be inserted.
Solicitor's reference	10.	Any reference should be limited to 25 characters (including oblique strokes and punctuation).
Signature and certificate	11.	An application will be rejected if it is not signed or if the certificate that it does not affect registered land has been deleted. However, in a case of extreme urgency where it is not practicable for the applicant first to ascertain whether or not the land is registered, the Department will accept an application with the certificate deleted provided that it is accompanied by a letter to the following effect. The letter must certify that the applicant has applied for an official search of the index map at the appropriate district land registry. It must also contain an undertaking that he will apply to cancel this registration if the result of search shows that the title to the land is registered.
Despatch of form	12.	When completed, this application form should be despatched to the address shown below which is printed in a position to fit within a standard window envelope.

The Superintendent
Land Charges Department
Registration Section
Plumer House, Tailyour Road,
Crownhill, PLYMOUTH PL6 5HY
DX 8249 PLYMOUTH (3)

Crown copyright (ref: LR/HQ) 7/01

HOME IN SOLE NAME OF ONE PARTY TRANSFER TO OTHER 37

Application for an official search of the index map

Land Registry

SIM

Land Registry _____ Office

If you need more room than is provided for in a panel, use continuation sheet CS and attach to this form.

1.	**Administrative area**
2.	**Property to be searched** Postal number or description
	Name of road
	Name of locality
	Town
	Postcode
	Ordnance Survey map reference (if known)
	Known title number(s)

3. **Payment of fee** *Place "X" in the appropriate box.*

   ☐ The Land Registry fee of £ _____ accompanies this application.

   ☐ Debit the Credit Account mentioned in panel 4 with the appropriate fee payable under the current Land Registration Fee Order.

   For official use only
   Impression of fees

4. **The application has been lodged by:**
   Land Registry Key No. (if appropriate)
   Name
   Address/DX No.

   Reference
   E-mail
   Telephone No.   Fax No.

5.	If the result of search is to be sent to anyone other than the applicant in panel 4, please supply the name and address of the person to whom it should be sent. Reference
6.	I apply for an official search of the index map in respect of the land referred to in panel 2 above and shown _____ on the attached plan. *Any attached plan must contain sufficient details of the surrounding roads and other features to enable the land to be identified satisfactorily on the Ordnance Survey map. A plan may be unnecessary if the land can be identified by postal description.*
7.	Signature of applicant _____ Date _____

Explanatory notes

1. The purpose and scope of Official Searches of the Index Map are described in Practice Guide 10 'Official searches of the Index Map' obtainable from any Land Registry office. It can also be viewed online at www.landregistry.gov.uk.

2. Please send this application to the appropriate Land Registry office. This information is contained in Practice Guide 51 'Areas served by Land Registry offices'.

3. Please ensure that the appropriate fee payable under the current Land Registration Fee Order accompanies your application. If paying fees by cheque or postal order, these should be crossed and payable to "Land Registry". Where you have requested that the fee be paid by Credit Account, receipt of the certificate of result is confirmation that the appropriate fee has been debited.

© Crown copyright (ref: LR/HQ) 10/03

HOME IN SOLE NAME OF ONE PARTY TRANSFER TO OTHER 39

Application for official copies of register/plan or certificate in Form CI

Land Registry

OC1

Land Registry	Office

Use one form per title. If you need more room than is provided for in a panel, use continuation sheet CS and attach to this form.

1.	**Administrative area** if known
2.	**Title number** if known
3.	**Property**
	Postal number or description
	Name of road
	Name of locality
	Town
	Postcode
	Ordnance Survey map reference (if known)

4. **Payment of fee** *Place "X" in the appropriate box.*

   ☐ The Land Registry fee of £ _____ accompanies this application.

   ☐ Debit the Credit Account mentioned in panel 5 with the appropriate fee payable under the current Land Registration Fee Order.

   For official use only
   Impression of fees

5. **The application has been lodged by:**
   Land Registry Key No. (if appropriate)
   Name
   Address/DX No.

   Reference
   E-mail

Telephone No.	Fax No.

6. If the official copies are to be sent to anyone other than the applicant in panel 5, please supply the name and address of the person to whom they should be sent.

   Reference

MATRIMONIAL CONVEYANCING

7. Where the title number is **not** quoted in panel 2, place "X" in the appropriate box(es). As regards this property, my application relates to:

   ☐ freehold estate   ☐ caution against first registration   ☐ franchise   ☐ manor

   ☐ leasehold estate   ☐ rentcharge   ☐ profit a prendre in gross

8. In case there is an application for registration pending against the title, place "X" in the appropriate box:

   ☐ I require an official copy back-dated to the day prior to the receipt of that application   **or**

   ☐ I require an official copy on completion of that application

9. **I apply for:** *Place "X" in the appropriate box(es) and indicate how many copies are required.*

   ☐ ____ official copy(ies) of the **register** of the above mentioned property

   ☐ ____ official copy(ies) of the **title plan or caution plan** of the above mentioned property

   ☐ ____ a certificate in Form CI, in which case **either**:

   ☐ an estate plan has been approved and the plot number is _____

   or

   ☐ no estate plan has been approved and a certificate is to be issued in respect of the land shown _____ on the attached plan and copy

10. **Signature of applicant** _____   Date _____

© Crown copyright (ref: LR/HQ) 10/03

(b) Registered Land

The right of occupation of registered land is protected by registration of a Notice of Home Rights at HM Land Registry on form HR1 (No fee payable) (a copy of Form HR1 appears on the following page). (Land Registration Rules 2003, r.82(1) as amended by Land Registration (Amendment) (No 2) Rules 2005, r.12(2)).

3–04

It will be necessary to make an official search of the Index Map to ascertain the title number, unless this is already known, although an application for official copies may prove more useful as more information is disclosed. Notice of the application will not be served on the proprietor so as to avoid exacerbating the situation.

(c) Generally and cancellation

It is important to appreciate that the provisions for home rights in the Family Law Act 1996 (as amended by CPA 2004) only apply to a dwelling-house which has been the family home and that only one protection is allowed (s.32; Sch.4, para.2 as amended by CPA 2004, s.82; Sch.9, paras 15(1) and (2)). Thus if a husband and wife or civil partners live together in one house home rights cannot effectively be registered against a house owned solely by one party and occupied by him or her and a new partner.

3–05

Home rights properly registered before the presentation of a bankruptcy petition against one party are binding upon the trustee in bankruptcy (Insolvency Act 1986, s.336) although the power to make orders concerning the rights of occupation become exercisable by the court which has jurisdiction in relation to the bankruptcy (ss.336(2) and (3)).

Home rights come to an end on the death of either party (Family Law Act 1996, s.32; Sch.4(1)(a)) or on the termination of the marriage or civil partnership (s.32; Sch.4(l)(b)) (amended in both cases by CPA 2004, s.82; Sch.9, paras 15(1), (4) and (5)) unless the court has ordered otherwise. The production of a certified copy of the death certificate, decree absolute or other court order should ensure the cancellation of the Class F land charge. In the case of a Notice then HM Land Registry Form HR4 should be used accompanied by the appropriate document.

A copy of Form HR4 is printed immediately after Form HR1 on the following page.

In a disputed property case, because home rights effectively come to an end on the issue of the decree absolute or other court order the protective steps mentioned in the next section should be taken.

It should be appreciated that if one party to the marriage or civil partnership does not intend to occupy the family home that party is not entitled to register home rights against the owner (see *Barnett v Hassett* [1981] W.L.R. 1385 where the husband left the wife's house and did not wish to occupy it).

Any contract for the sale of a family home which provides for the purchaser to be given vacant possession on completion now implies a provision that the vendor will procure the cancellation of any notice in respect of home rights (Family Law Act 1996, s.32; Sch.4, para.3(1), (2)). Notwithstanding this provision, it is often of some reassurance to a purchaser if the party who has registered the Notice of Home Rights is joined as a party to the contract or to a separate consent to sale form; this confirms that that party knows that vacant possession is to be given and the appropriate notice is to be cancelled and can contain a specific release by that party of the home rights as from the date of sale. Negotiations between the parties solicitors will often have been on the basis that an application for the cancellation of the notice (Form HR4 (as referred to above) where the land is registered or Form K 13 where the land is unregistered—a copy of Form K13 is set out after Forms HR1 and HR4 on the following page) will be handed over on completion in return for one half of the net proceeds of sale (or whatever is agreed).

Form K13 must be signed by the party benefiting from the Class F Land Charge but form HR4 can be signed by the beneficiaries' solicitor. However in view of the negligence case of *Homes v Kennard* (1984) 128 S.J. 854 the writer would advise that the party concerned is always asked to sign the Form HR4 before it is submitted to HM Land Registry if time permits.

HOME IN SOLE NAME OF ONE PARTY TRANSFER TO OTHER 43

Application for   **Land Registry**
registration of a notice
of home rights   **HR1**

If you need more room than is provided for in a panel, use continuation sheet CS and attach to this form.

NOTE: Notice of this application will always be sent to the registered owner

1. **Administrative area and postcode** if known

2. **Title number(s)**

3. If you have already made this application by **outline application**, insert reference number:

4. **Property** *Insert full address of the property.*

5. **Address(es) for service of the applicant. The address(es) will be entered in the register and used for correspondence and the service of notice.** *You may give up to three addresses for service one of which must be a postal address but does not have to be within the UK. The other addresses can be any combination of a postal address, a box number at a UK document exchange or an electronic address.*

6. **Enter the full name of your husband, wife or civil partner**

7. **The applicant is:** *Please provide the full name of the person applying for the notice. Where a conveyancer lodges the application, the applicant is the client, not the conveyancer.*

8. **The application has been lodged by:**
Land Registry Key No. (if appropriate)
Name (if different from the applicant)
Address/DX No.

Reference
Email
Telephone No.   Fax No.

FOR OFFICIAL USE ONLY
Codes
Dealing
MHA
Status
Red

9. Have you registered a home rights charge (in respect of your marriage to or civil partnership with the person named in panel 6 above) in respect of any other dwelling-house? *Place "X" in the appropriate box.*

☐ No   ☐ Yes

If Yes:
Insert the address of the dwelling-house:

If the charge is registered under the Land Charges Act 1972, please insert the registration number and date of registration at Land Charges Department:

If the charge is registered under the Land Registration Act 2002, please insert title number:

NOTE: If your application is successful, the registration of the charge referred to above will be cancelled under section 32 of, and paragraph 2 of Schedule 4 to, the Family Law Act 1996.

10. Has an order been made under section 33(5) of the Family Law Act 1996? *Place "X" in the appropriate box.*

☐ No   ☐ Yes

If Yes, please place "X" in the appropriate box below and complete the relevant statement.

☐ I enclose an office copy of the order dated _____.

☐ I *(name of conveyancer acting)* _____ of _____
_____ certify that I am holding an office copy of the order dated _____ made under section 33(5) of the Family Law Act 1996 by _____ Court.

Signed: _____   Date: _____

11. Declaration
I declare that the information given above is true and that I am entitled by virtue of section 31(2) or 31(5) of the Family Law Act 1996 to a charge on the legal estate registered under the title number mentioned in panel 2.

12. Application
I apply under section 31(10)(a) or section 32 of, and paragraph 4(3)(b) of Schedule 4 to, the Family Law Act 1996 for registration, under section 32 of the Land Registration Act 2002, of notice of my home rights charge against the title mentioned in panel 2.

13. Signature of applicant or their conveyancer _____   Date _____

© Crown copyright (ref: LR/SC50) 7/05

HOME IN SOLE NAME OF ONE PARTY TRANSFER TO OTHER 45

Cancellation of a   **Land Registry**
home rights notice

HR4

For use with form AP1 only. If you need more room than is provided for in a panel, use continuation sheet CS and attach to this form.

1. **Administrative area and postcode** if known

2. **Title number**

3. **Property** *Insert full address of the property.*

4. **Application** *Place "X" in the appropriate box.*
   ☐ I
       of
   ☐ I/We   as solicitor(s) for
       apply to cancel the home rights entered against the above title.

   I/We enclose the following: *Place "X" in the appropriate box.*
       ☐ Original or certified copy death certificate or other evidence of the death of either spouse or either civil partner.
       ☐ Official or certified copy of the decree absolute or nullity of marriage.
       ☐ Official or certified copy of the order of dissolution or nullity of civil partnership.
       ☐ Official or certified copy of any order of court ending the home rights.
       ☐ A release in writing of the rights by any benefiting spouse or civil partner.
       ☐ The spouse or civil partner having the benefit of the rights has signed the release overleaf.
   ☐ I/We apply also to cancel the renewal of the said notice. Evidence that any order of court renewing the home rights has ceased to have effect is enclosed.

5. **Signature of applicant**
   or their conveyancer _____ Date _____

Notes to help you

When applying

- No fee is payable.

- Do not forget to enclose the evidence needed to support your application for cancellation.

- If your evidence for cancellation is a court order, a copy sealed by the court should be sent in with your application.

- Apply to the Land Registry office which deals with the property's area. To check this you can:

    (a) read Practice Guide *51 – Areas served by Land Registry offices*;

    (b) check on Land Registry's internet site at http://www.landregistry.gov.uk;

    (c) contact Land Registry Head Office as follows:

    The Information Centre
    Land Registry Head Office
    Lincoln's Inn Fields
    London WC2A 3PH
    Telephone 020 7917 8888   Fax 020 7955 0110

    PLEASE DO NOT SEND YOUR APPLICATION TO THIS ADDRESS

- We will write to let you know when your application has been completed.

Further help

- Public Guide *4 – Protecting home rights under the Family Law Act 1996* is available to help members of the public. It deals with applications to protect home rights. A copy is held by every Citizens Advice Bureau. It is also available in Welsh.

- Practice Guide *20 – Applications under the Family Law Act 1996* contains advice for legal practitioners about applications in respect of home rights.

- All three leaflets can be obtained free of charge from any Land Registry office. This information can also be accessed on Land Registry's internet site at the address shown above.

- If you have any questions about Land Registry procedures on home rights, please contact the Enquiries Officer at any Land Registry office. However, you should note that Land Registry staff are not allowed to give legal advice.

Release of home rights

I *(give full names)*

of *(address)*

release my home rights in the property shown overleaf

Signed   Date

Crown copyright (ref: LR/SC50) 7/05

HOME IN SOLE NAME OF ONE PARTY TRANSFER TO OTHER 47

Important: Please read the notes overleaf before completing the form	**Form K13**	**Land Charges Act 1972** (Family Law Act 1996) **Application for cancellation of a Land Charge of Class F**	**Fee Panel** If the fee is to be debited to your credit account put a cross (X) in this box. *(See Note 1 overleaf)*

Enter full name(s) and address(es) of applicants *(See Notes 2 and 3 overleaf)*	**Particulars of applicant** I, of hereby apply for cancellation in the register of the entry referred to below Signature Date

(See note 4 overleaf)	**Certificate of Solicitor(s)** We hereby certify that we are acting for the applicant and that we are satisfied that our client understands the nature of this application and the effect of the cancellation of the said entry on the register. Signature and address of the solicitors to the above applicant Signature Address

Delete (a) or (b) as appropriate	**Particulars of entry affected** Please cancel the undermentioned entry as to (a) the whole or (b) the following part

	Class **F**	Insert number and date of the registration	Official reference no.	Date of registration *(See Note 5 overleaf)*		
				Day	Month	Year
		Insert, if applicable, the number and date of any renewal of registration	Official reference no.	Date of registration *(See Note 5 overleaf)*		
				Day	Month	Year

Only one individual or body to be entered. *(See Note 6 overleaf)*	**Particulars of estate owner** Forename(s) **Surname** Address	**For official use only**

(See Note 7 overleaf)	**Key Number**		
Solicitor's name and address (including postcode) If no Solicitor is acting enter applicant's name and address (including postcode) *(See Notes 8 and 9 overleaf)*		1 *C	2	3
		4	5	6
	Solicitor's reference:			

MATRIMONIAL CONVEYANCING

Explanatory Notes

The following notes are supplied for assistance in making the application overleaf. Detailed information for the making of all kinds of application to the Land Charges Department is contained in a booklet entitled "Computerised Land Charges Department: a practical guide for solicitors" which is obtainable on application at the address shown below.

Fee payable	1. Fees must be paid by credit account or by cheque or postal order made payable to "HM Land Registry" (see guide referred to above).
Form completion	2. Please complete the form in **block letters** in writing or typewriting using black ink not liable to smear. No covering letter is required.
Applicant's name	3. Please give the name of the person on whose behalf the application is made. If the applicant is not the person on whose behalf the registration was made, the application must be accompanied by:-
	(a) a release in writing of the matrimonial home rights to which the charge relates, or
	(b) the evidence referred to in paragraph 4(1)9 Schedule 4 to the Family Law Act 1996 and, if the charge was registered or the registration of the charge was renewed pursuant to s.33(5) of the said Act, evidence proving to the satisfaction of the Chief Land Registrar that the order referred to in the application for registration or renewal has ceased to have effect.
Certificate of solicitor(s)	4. This certificate is only required where the application is signed by the person in whose favour the registration was made and solicitors are acting on his/her behalf.
Date of registration	5. Complete all boxes and refer to month by three letters:

Day		Month			Year			
0	4	S	E	P	1	9	8	1

Particulars of the estate owner	6. Please give the full name of the estate owner as entered on the register. Enter forenames and surnames on separate lines.
Key number	7. If you have been allocated a key number, please take care to enter this in the space provided overleaf, whether or not you are paying fees through your credit account.
Solicitor's reference	8. Any reference should be limited to 25 characters (including oblique strokes and punctuation).
Despatch of form	9. The completed form should be despatched to the address below, which is printed in a position to fit a standard window envelope.

The Superintendent
Land Charges Department
Registration Section
Plumer House, Tailyour Road,
Crownhill, PLYMOUTH PL6 5HY
DX 8249 PLYMOUTH (3)

Crown copyright (ref: LR/HQ) 11/01

HOME IN SOLE NAME OF ONE PARTY TRANSFER TO OTHER 49

Important: Please read the notes overleaf before completing the form.	**Form K3** **Land Charges Act 1972** **Application for registration of a Pending Action** Application is hereby made for the registration of a Pending Action in respect of the following particulars	**Fee panel** If the fee is to be debited to your credit account put a cross (X) in this box *(See Note 1 overleaf)*

Enter full name(s) and address(es) of chargee(s) *(See Notes 2 and 3 overleaf)*	**Particulars of chargee(s)** *Continue on form K10 (if necessary)*

	Particulars of action or proceeding Nature of action or proceeding Name of court and official reference number Title of action or proceeding Date commenced or filed

	PA	If application is made pursuant to a Priority Notice please state its official reference number

    (See Notes 4 and 5 overleaf)	**Particulars of land affected** County District Short description

Only one individual or body to be entered. *(See Note 6 overleaf)*	**Particulars of estate owner** Forename(s) **Surname** Title, trade or profession Address	**For official use only**

(See Note 7 overleaf)	**Key number**	

Solicitor's name and address (including postcode) If no Solicitor is acting enter applicant's name and address (including postcode) *(See Note 8 overleaf)*		1	2	3
		*C		
		4	5	6
	Solicitor's reference:			

I/We certify that the estate owner's title is not registered at the Land Registry.

Signature of solicitor or applicant   Date

MATRIMONIAL CONVEYANCING

Explanatory Notes

The following notes are supplied for assistance in making the application overleaf. Detailed information for the making of all kinds of applications to the Land Charges Department is contained in a booklet entitled "Computerised Land Charges Department: a practical guide for solicitors" which is obtainable on application at the address shown below.

Fee Payable	1.	Fees must be paid by credit account or by cheque or postal order made payable to "HM Land Registry" (see the "Guide" referred to above)
Form completion	2.	Please complete the form in block letters in writing or typewriting using black ink not liable to smear. No covering letter is required and no plan or other document should be lodged in support of the application. If the application is not made by a practising solicitor, it must be accompanied by a statutory declaration form K14.
Chargee's name(s)	3.	Please give the full name(s) and address(es) of the person(s) on and on whose behalf the application is being made.
County and District	4.	Enter as "County" the appropriate name as set out in Part 3 of the Appendix to Land Charges Practice Leaflet No.3. As stated therein, if the land referred to in the application lies within the Greater London Area, then "Greater London" should be stated as the county name.
Short description	5.	A short description, identifying the land as far as may be practicable, should be furnished.
Estate owner	6.	Please give the full name, address and description of the estate owner as defined in the Law of Property Act 1925 against whom registration is to be effected. A separate form is required for each full name. Enter forename(s) and surname on separate lines. The name of the company or other body should commence on the forename line and may continue on the surname line (the words "Forename(s)" and "Surname" should be deleted).
Key number	7.	If you have been allocated a key number, please take care to enter this in the space provided overleaf, whether or not you are paying fees through your credit account.
Solicitor's reference	8.	Any reference should be limited to 25 characters (including oblique strokes and punctuation).
Despatch of form	9.	When completed, this application form should be despatched to the address shown below which is printed in a position to fit within a standard envelope.

The Superintendent
Land Charges Department
Registration Section
Plumer House, Tailyour Road,
Crownhill, PLYMOUTH PL6 5HY
DX 8249 PLYMOUTH (3)

2 Protection of the transferee's position before lodging of transfer for registration

To avoid the transferor making a sale or charging the property (standing in that party's sole name) in the period between the decree absolute or equivalent order (when home rights cease—see above) and the lodging of the transfer at HM Land Registry, the following steps should be taken. **3–06**

(a) Unregistered Land

A pending action under the Land Charges Act 1972, s.5 (fee £1) should be registered by or on behalf of the wife (in Form K3) provided the divorce petition has contained a request for a transfer of real property under the Matrimonial Causes Act 1973, s.24; such a registration survives the decree absolute (see *Whittingham v Whittingham* [1978] 2 W.L.R. 936 and *Ferez-Adanzson v Perez-Rivas* [1987] 2 W.L.R. 500). **3–07**

The pending action land charge should effectively stop the transferor dealing with the property until completion of the transfer in the transferee's favour has taken place following the transferee's application for first registration as any purchaser or mortgagee will be put on notice by the entry at HM Land Charges Registry.

It is too late to register a pending action if a bankruptcy petition has been presented against the transferor; in *Re Flint* (1992) *The Times* July 16, it was held that a transfer of the family home by order of the court in matrimonial proceedings to the wife in the period between the presentation of a bankruptcy petition against the husband and the bankruptcy order was void.

As registration of all transfers of unregistered land contemplated by this book are now compulsory the transferee may gain further protection by applying for registration of a caution against first registration at HM Land Registry (LRA 2002, s.19). The transferee will thus receive notice if the transferor seeks to register the property with a possible view to disposing of it or charging it.

Application for the caution must be on Form CTI (Land Registration Rules 2003, r.82) which supports a statutory declaration to be declared by the applicant or his or her solicitor. An address for service in the UK must be given and the land must be clearly identified. A fee of £40 is payable (HM Land Registry Fees Order 2003 and a copy of Form CT1 is provided on the following page).

Caution against first registration

Land Registry

CT1

If you need more room than is provided for in a panel, use continuation sheet CS and attach to this form.

1. **Administrative area and postcode** if known

2. **Address or description of the property affected by the caution**

3. **Application and fee** *A fee calculator for all types of applications can be found on Land Registry's website at www.landregistry.gov.uk/fees*

   Caution against first registration   Fee paid £

   Fee payment method: *Place "X" in the appropriate box.*
   I wish to pay the appropriate fee payable under the current Land Registration Fee Order:

   ☐ by cheque or postal order, amount £ _____ made payable to "Land Registry".

   ☐ by Direct Debit under an authorised agreement with Land Registry.

   FOR OFFICIAL USE ONLY
   Record of fee paid

   Particulars of under/over payment

   Fees debited £

   Reference number

4. **The cautioner is:** *Please provide the full name of the person applying for the caution.*

   The application has been lodged by:
   Land Registry Key No. (if appropriate)
   Name (if different from the cautioner)
   Address/DX No.

   Reference
   E-mail
   Telephone No.   Fax No.

   FOR OFFICIAL USE ONLY
   Status codes

   RED

5. **The estate to which the caution relates is** *Place "X" in the appropriate box(es) and complete as necessary. In the case of a leasehold, rentcharge, franchise or profit a prendre in gross, please provide full details below of the particular leasehold, rentcharge, franchise or profit affected. Include the date, nature and parties of the instrument by which the estate was created, if known; the amount of the rentcharge; the nature of the franchise or profit; and length of the term, if leasehold.*

   ☐ the freehold

   ☐ a lease dated _____ for a term of _____ from _____ made between _____

   Is the lease discontinuous? ☐ Yes   ☐ No
   If Yes, please include full particulars of the discontinuous term, e.g. affected days, weeks, months etc.

   ☐ a rentcharge   ☐ a franchise   ☐ a profit a prendre in gross

6. **Extent of land to which the caution relates** *Place "X" in the appropriate box.*

   ☐ The property is clearly identified on the attached plan and shown _____ *Enter reference e.g. "edged red".*

   ☐ The description in panel 2 is sufficient to enable the property to be clearly identified on the Ordnance Survey map

7. **Address(es) for service of the cautioner. The address(es) will be entered in the cautions register and used for correspondence and the service of notice** *You may give up to three addresses for service **one** of which **must** be a postal address but does not have to be within the UK. The other addresses can be any combination of a postal address, a box number at a UK document exchange or an electronic address. Where the cautioner is a company, include the company's registered number (if any). For Scottish Companies use an SC prefix and for limited liability partnerships use an OC prefix before the registered number, if any.*

8. *Place "X" in the appropriate box and give the full name of the person making the declaration, or giving the certificate. You must make the declaration in panel 9 unless you are a conveyancer acting on behalf of the cautioner, in which case you can give a certificate in panel 10.*

   ☐ The declarant is (one of) the cautioner(s) or a person authorised by the cautioner to make the declaration in panel 9.
   The declarant's full name is

   ☐ The certificate in panel 10 has been completed by a conveyancer on behalf of the cautioner.
   The full name of the individual giving the certificate is

9. **The declarant solemnly and sincerely declares that the cautioner is interested in the estate referred to in panel 5 as**
   This panel must set out the nature of the cautioner's interest. Do not exhibit any documents.

   and I make this solemn declaration conscientiously believing the same to be true by virtue of the Statutory Declarations Act 1835.

   Signature of Declarant

   Declared at

   this   day of   before me,

   Name
   (BLOCK CAPITALS)

   Address

   Qualification
   This declaration must be made in the presence of a person empowered to administer oaths, such as a commissioner for oaths or a practising solicitor.

HOME IN SOLE NAME OF ONE PARTY TRANSFER TO OTHER 55

10. I certify that the cautioner is interested in the estate described in panel 5 as
This panel must set out the nature of the cautioner's interest. Do not exhibit any documents.

Signature _____

Name _____
(BLOCK CAPITALS)
Address _____

_____

_____

11. Signature of applicant
   or their conveyancer _____ Date _____

12. Consent to the lodging of this caution is given by

Name(s) *BLOCK CAPITALS*   Signature(s)

1. _____   1. _____

2. _____   2. _____

3. _____   3. _____

Caution applications do not require any consents. However, a person may consent to the lodging of a caution in accordance with rule 47 of the Land Registration Rules 2003. By so consenting that person may only apply to cancel the caution under section 18(1) of the Land Registration Act 2002 if one of the exceptions under rule 46 of the Land Registration Rules 2003 applies.

© Crown copyright (ref: LR/HQ/CD-ROM) 6/03

MATRIMONIAL CONVEYANCING

**Application to enter
a unilateral notice**

Land Registry

UN1

*To enter an agreed notice use Form AN1. To enter a notice to protect home rights use Form HR1.
If you need more room than is provided for in a panel, use continuation sheet CS and attach to this form.*

1.	Administrative area and postcode if known

2.	Title number(s)

3.	If you have already made this application by **outline application**, insert reference number:	

4.	Property

The interest to be protected by the unilateral notice affects *Place "X" in the appropriate box and complete as necessary.*

☐ the whole of the registered estate

☐ the part of the registered estate shown on the attached plan *State reference e.g. "edged red".*

☐ the registered charge dated _____ in favour of _____ referred to in the charges register

5.	Application and fee *A fee calculator for all types of applications can be found on Land Registry's website at www.landregistry.gov.uk/fees*	**FOR OFFICIAL USE ONLY** Record of fee paid

Unilateral notice   Fee paid £

Particulars of under/over payment

Fee payment method: *Place "X" in the appropriate box.*
I wish to pay the appropriate fee payable under the current Land Registration Fee Order:

☐ by cheque or postal order, amount £ _____ made payable to "Land Registry".

Fees debited £

☐ by Direct Debit under an authorised agreement with Land Registry.

Reference number

6.	**Documents lodged with this form (if any)** *If this application is accompanied by either Form AP1 or FR1 please only complete the corresponding panel on Form AP1 or DL. Number the documents in sequence; copies should also be numbered and listed as separate documents. If you supply the original document and a certified copy, we shall assume that you request the return of the original; if a certified copy is not supplied, we may retain the original document and it may be destroyed.*

7.	The applicant applies for the entry of a unilateral notice against the title(s) referred to in panel 2

8.	**The applicant is:** *Please provide the full name of the person applying for the notice. Where a conveyancer lodges the application, the applicant is the client, not the conveyancer.*

9.	The application has been lodged by: Land Registry Key No. (if appropriate) Name (if different from the applicant) Address/DX No. Reference Email Telephone No. Fax No.	**FOR OFFICIAL USE ONLY** Codes Dealing Status **RED**

HOME IN SOLE NAME OF ONE PARTY TRANSFER TO OTHER

10. Address(es) for service of the beneficiary. The address(es) will be entered in the register and used for correspondence and the service of notice. *List the full name and address of each person to be entered in the register as beneficiary of the notice. You may give up to three addresses for service **one** of which **must** be a postal address but does not have to be within the UK. The other addresses can be any combination of a postal address, a box number at a UK document exchange or an electronic address. For a company include company's registered number if any. For Scottish companies use an SC prefix and for limited liability partnerships use an OC prefix before the registered number, if any. For foreign companies give territory in which incorporated.*

11. *Complete this panel and **either** panel 12 **or** panel 13. Place "X" in the appropriate box.*

☐ The declarant is the beneficiary or a person authorised by the beneficiary to make the declaration in panel 12.
The declarant's full name is

☐ The certificate in panel 13 has been completed by a conveyancer on behalf of the beneficiary.
The conveyancer's full name is

Firm name (if any)

Address

12. **The declarant solemnly and sincerely declares that the beneficiary is interested in the property described in panel 4 as**
This panel must set out the nature of the beneficiary's interest.

The interest described above is not a public right or a customary right.

And I make this solemn declaration conscientiously believing the same to be true by virtue of the Statutory Declarations Act 1835.

Signature of declarant

Declared at

this   day of   before me,

Signature

Name
(BLOCK CAPITALS)

Address

Qualification
This declaration must be made in the presence of a person empowered to administer oaths, such as a commissioner for oaths or a practising solicitor.

13.	I certify that the beneficiary is interested in the property described in panel 4 as

This panel must set out the nature of the beneficiary's interest.

I certify that the interest described above is not a public right or a customary right.

Signature

Name
(BLOCK CAPITALS)

Address

14.	Signature of applicant or their conveyancer _____ Date _____

Crown copyright (ref: LR/SC50) 7/05

(b) Registered Land

3–08 A Unilateral Notice (formerly known as a caution against dealing) (LRA 2002, s.34) should be lodged at HM Land Registry in Form UN1.

Form UN1 incorporates a statutory declaration which must be made by either the applicant or his or her solicitor disclosing the nature of the applicant's interest (a copy of Form UN1 is provided following Form CT1 referred to above). A fee of £40 is payable (HM Land Registry Fees Order 2006) and an additional fee of £5.00 will be payable to the solicitor administering the statutory declaration.

(i) In the case where a court order has not yet been made, the nature of the applicant's interest may be shown as:

"the former *[wife] [husband]* of the registered proprietor having made application for a property adjustment order under section 24 of the Matrimonial Causes Act 1973 by proceedings in the [County Court between *[husband]* and [wife] bearing number]"

(ii) In the case where the court order in favour of the applicant has been made, but the transfer has not yet been executed and lodged at HM Land Registry and no earlier notice has been registered this might be:

"the registered proprietor *[husband] [wife]* has been ordered to transfer all his/her estate and interest in the property to *[wife] [husband]* by an order made in the [ ] County Court dated in proceedings between *[husband]* and *[wife]* bearing [ ]"

The effect of the registration of such a unilateral notice is that the Registrar will not, without the consent of the applicant, register any dealing by the registered proprietor until the period of notice specified in the notice to the applicant of the proposed dealing has expired.

Unless a unilateral notice is registered there is risk; before lodging the transfer the transferee's solicitor will make a Form OS3 search, but this search does not confer priority for the registration of any dealing (Land Registration (Official Searches) Rules 2003, rr.147–160). Some practitioners make a Form OC1 search (formerly a Form 94A search) which gives priority in favour of a purchaser, taking the view that the transferee is the equivalent of a purchaser. HM Land Registry have indicated that this priority might fail in the event of the lodging of a valid charge by the transferor's mortgagee, as strictly the transferee is not, in their view, a purchaser for valuable consideration.

3 Procedure

3–09 As from October 2003 land and charge certificates were abolished and therefore obtaining deeds to registered land is no longer a conveyancing issue.

In unregistered conveyancing it will still be necessary for the transferee's solicitor to obtain the title deeds in order to verify the title and make the mandatory application for first registration. It is unlikely that the transferor's solicitor will send out the original deeds until such time as the transfer is completed. The reason for this is that they cannot (unless they have taken an abstract) check on receiving the transfer for execution if proper indemnities are proferred in respect of any covenants and other matters to which the property is subject. It is considered more satisfactory to adhere to the conventional conveyancing procedure so that the transferor's solicitors will submit an epitome of title to the transferee's solicitors. Where the land is registered it may be that the transferor's solicitor will send official copies of the register to the transferee's solicitor but it is more likely that the latter will simply apply for them themselves or down load copies from Land Registry Direct. Amongst other things this will reveal at an early stage whether there are any undisclosed charges and consent issues.

In the case of a family home which does not have registered title, it would seem to be accepted practice to assume that the title was properly investigated at the time of the transferor's purchase, so that all the transferor's solicitors need to abstract to the transferee's solicitors is the conveyance to the transferor, any mortgage, any "sales-off" (or other transactions affecting the title), and details of the covenants affecting the property.

Following the receipt of the epitome of title or official copy entries, the transferee's solicitors will submit a draft transfer to the transferor's solicitors and engross the same after approval. Although the court order should specify a time-limit in which the transfer must be completed (so that compliance can be enforced—*see* Ch.8) such time-limit is rarely adhered to in practice. There can be no incentive for an embittered transferor to execute the transfer quickly. If a more than reasonable time has elapsed since the engrossed transfer was submitted for execution by the transferor, then the steps set out in Ch.8 are a guide as to the procedure to be followed before application is made to the court asking the court to execute the transfer on behalf of the reluctant transferor.

For the reason that there can so often be delay in obtaining the transferor's signature, it is recommended that only once the documentation has been agreed and executed should a "completion date" be arranged so that the transferee's solicitors can make the necessary searches against the transferor in HM Land Charges Registry or in favour of the transferee at HM Land Registry (as the case may be). In the latter case (unless the transferee is purchasing the property or the mortgagee is advancing monies when the ordinary search Form OS1 is appropriate) a search on Form OS3 should be made, although such a search does not confer priority for the registration of any dealing (Land Registration Rules 2003 (SI 2003/1417), r.10). The search fee in either case is £6 (HM Land Registry Fees Order 2006). If the property is being charged by way of mortgage by the transferee then priority can be obtained by the mortgagee's solicitors making the usual Form OS1 Search on behalf of the mortgagee, which gives a priority period of 30 days (Land Registration (Official Searches) Rules 1993 (SI 1993/3276), r.3).

4 Covenants for title

(a) Freehold

3–10 The position of covenants for title following the coming into force of the Law of Property (Miscellaneous Provisions) Act 1994 is dealt with in Ch.1 (*see* p.3) and for the reasons there mentioned the view is taken that the transferor should transfer with full title guarantee.

(b) Leasehold

3–11 Whilst the transferor should assign/transfer with full title guarantee, he or she may wish to be excused liability towards the assignee for a breach of the terms of the lease relating to repairs and the implied covenant should be amended accordingly (*see* p.6 and Precedent 2). The transferor will remain liable to the lessor for any future non-payment of rent or breach of covenant unless the lease is a "new tenancy" granted on or after January 1, 1996 (*see above* pp.5 and 6) and so in unregistered land the assignor should take the covenant from the assignee to observe and perform the covenants in the lease and for indemnity as set out in Precedent 3 (not required for registered land).

5 Where the property is subject to a mortgage

(a) First mortgage only

3–12 The court may order that:

> "The Respondent shall transfer with full title guarantee to the Petitioner absolutely within 28 days from the date of this Order the property at 1 Blackacre Drive, Blackacre, subject to the existing mortgage in favour of the Blackacre Building Society."

Alternatively, agreement to this effect may be reached between the parties and embodied in a "consent" order (as to the advantages of which, *see* Ch.1).

In such a case, the transferor will, if possible, wish to be released by the mortgagee from the future liability under the mortgage rather than rely upon an indemnity from the transferee, and although the mortgagee should be aware of the proceedings between the parties by virtue of the notification required to be made to it under r.2.59(4) of the Family Proceedings Rules 1991 (as amended) (*see* p.7), a formal application will doubtless have to be made by the transferor for a release. It must be remembered that a court cannot order a mortgagee to agree to a transfer subject to mortgage, nor can it order a mortgagee to release a party from the mortgage covenants.

If the transferee's level of income is sufficient and the property remains adequate security for the mortgage loan, the mortgagee will probably consent to the release of the transferor from liability under the mortgage so long as the transferee covenants to assume this and, depending upon the practice of the mortgagee, will specify what clauses it requires in the appropriate transfer. Some mortgagees insist on approving the draft transfer and regard must therefore be had to the practice of each mortgagee, in reality however most mortgagees now leave the drafting to the transferee's solicitor. The release of the transferor from his or her obligations under the mortgage (as in Precedent 3) will not release him or her from the covenants for title implied under the Law of Property Act 1925, s.76(1) by his or her having charged the property before July 1, 1995 as beneficial owner or by him or her since that date mortgaging the property with full title guarantee (*see above*, p.3) this lack of complete release is necessary for the mortgagee so that it still has the covenant for "further assurance" in the event that a defect in title becomes apparent and some mortgagees insist on a specific covenant to this effect (e.g. "The Society releases and discharges the Transferor from his other obligations under the mortgage other than as to title").

If the mortgagee will not consent to the transferor being released from the mortgage, then the transferor will have to be content with an indemnity from the transferee (*see* Precedent 4).

Strictly there is no need for the mortgagee to be a party to the transfer if it is not releasing the transferor from liability however as most mortgagees will have registered a restriction preventing dealings with the property without their specific consent, consent will need to be obtained. In practice most mortgagees require to join in the transfer. It is obviously in the transferor's interest that the mortgagee receives a covenant from the transferee to observe and perform the terms of the mortgage as this will put the mortgagee on further notice as to the primary responsibility notwithstanding that the transferor is not released. The exact terms of the covenant to be given should be checked with the mortgagee concerned.

Owing to the provisions of *Williams & Glyn's Bank Ltd v Boland* and *Williams & Glyn's Bank Ltd v Brown* [1981] A.C. 487 it would be prudent to obtain the consent to the transfer from any other occupier of the family home aged 18 years or more, coupled with confirmation from such occupier that he or she is agreeable to the rights of the mortgagee taking priority over his or her rights in the property or its proceeds of sale. Most banks and building societies have produced standard forms of consent (*see* Precedent 6).

It is suggested that the transfer be prepared and executed in duplicate so that the transferor has a record of the terms of the indemnity given to the transferee. Applications to enter a note of the transferor's covenant of indemnity to this effect should therefore be included in the transfer (*see* Precedent 4). The Land Registration Rules 2003, r.64 contain a discretion to the registrar to make a note on the register which may read as follows:

Note: The transfer to the proprietor contains a covenant by [him/her] with *[him/her]* to pay the monies secured by Charge No 1 and to indemnify[him/her] from all claims and demands in respect thereof.

It is not necessary for the bank or building society to be joined as a party to a registered land transfer where it is only receiving the benefit of a covenant to observe and perform the terms of the mortgage by the transferee (and not releasing the transferor) because it can enforce the covenant without being a party (*Chelsea and Walham Green Building Society v Armstrong* [1951] Ch. 853). It is suggested, however, that the bank or building society be joined so that it is specifically aware of the terms of the transfer.

As in unregistered conveyancing it is probably advisable that the transferor keeps a duplicate or certified copy of the transfer to the transferee so that he or she has a record of the terms of indemnity given to the transferee.

(b) Where in addition there is a second charge

3–13   If the former family home to be transferred to the transferee is subject to both a first and second charge it may be that whilst the first mortgagee is prepared to release the transferor, upon having a direct covenant by the transferee, the second mortgagee is not so agreeable. It is obviously to the transferor's advantage in such circumstances to seek to persuade the first mortgagee to offer the transferee a further advance of sufficient amount to repay the second charge. That failing, there can be a transfer between the transferor and transferee, to which the first mortgagee is a party, to release the transferor from liability under the first mortgage and take a covenant to observe and perform the same from the transferee who will also covenant with the transferor to indemnify him or her in respect of the second mortgage. The second mortgagee should also be a party to receive the additional covenant from the transferee. The Land Registration Rules 2003, r.64 will be applicable (*see* above).

6 Steps to be taken following completion of the transfer

(a) Stamp duty land tax

3–14   The precedents in this chapter (with the exception of Precedent 5 which is not following a court order) should not attract a charge to stamp duty land tax as a result of the Finance Act 2003, Sch.3 (*see* Ch.2 generally as to stamp duty land tax). In these cases SDLT 60 will need to be completed and signed by the transferee and submitted with the application to HM Land Registry.

All TR1 transfer forms contain a box at the beginning for stamp duty purposes. This is now redundant but has not yet been removed from the form. The author is advised by HM Land Registry that the TR1 will be amended next time it is reviewed but no date has been given.

(b) Cancellation at HM Land Registry or HM Land Charges Registry

No doubt as the family home was in the transferor's sole name the transferee will have registered home rights by way of a notice under the terms of the Family Law Act, 1996 as amended by the CPA 2004. Although such home rights come to an end by termination of the marriage or civil partnership following the decree absolute or equivalent, the notice has probably not been cancelled and this should be done at HM Land Registry (Form HR4 accompanied by a certified copy of the appropriate decree—no fee HM Land Registry Fees Order 2006 or by lodging Form K13 with a fee of £1.00 in the case of unregistered land where a Class F Land Charge has been registered).

3–15

Any pending action registered at HM Land Charges Registry should be cancelled (Form K11—fee £1, Land Charges Fees Rules 1990). A copy of Form K11 is printed on the following pages and a copy of Form HR4 appears on p.45.

Application to **cancel an entry in the Land Charges Register (other than class F)** [1][2]

HM Land Registry

Form K11
(Land Charges Act 1972)

(1) For Class F cancellation please use form K13.

(2) Please complete the appropriate sections of this form in typescript or BLOCK LETTERS using black ink which will not smear. No covering letter is required.

A separate form K11 must be used for each entry concerned

(3) Enter the full names of the applicants

(4) Please put a cross in the correct box. If the applicant is not that named in the original registration then evidence of title of the new applicant should be enclosed. Any documents lodged should be certified as true copies.

(5) Please put a cross in the correct box.

(6) If the entry is to be cancelled as to part only of the land please describe that part of the land.

(7) Please put a cross in the correct box

(8) If the entry is a Land Charge please enter the class and sub class here.

(9) An order of the Court directing vacation is necessary to cancel an entry relating to proceedings in bankruptcy or to a deed of arrangement.

(10) Please complete all boxes and refer to month by three letters e.g.
Day	Month	Year
0 3	O C T	2 0 0 1

(11) Please give full name(s) of the estate owner or debtor entered in the register. Enter forename(s) and surname on separate lines. You may use both lines for the name of a company or other body. (The words forename(s) and surname should then be deleted)

(12) Please enter your key number even if you are not paying fees through your credit account

(13) If no solicitor is acting enter full name and address (including postcode) of applicant

(14) Please limit to 25 characters including oblique strokes and punctuation.

Particulars of applicant(s) entitled to the benefit of the entry. [3]

Fee Panel
Please put a cross in this box if the fee is to be paid through your credit account.

(see Note 2 overleaf)

Certificate
I/We as solicitor(s) acting for the above mentioned applicant(s) hereby apply for cancellation in the register as shown below.
I/We certify that: [4]
☐ (a) The applicant(s) is/are the person(s) entitled to the benefit of the entry and is/are named as the chargee(s) in the original registration.
☐ (b) The applicant(s) is/are the successor(s) in title to the original chargee(s) and evidence of the applicant's title is enclosed.
☐ (c) The application is made pursuant to an order of the Court directing vacation of the entry and an office copy of the order is attached.
☐ (d) The restrictive covenants protected by the under mentioned entry are the covenants discharged by order of the Land Tribunal, an office copy of which is attached.

Signature of Solicitor/Applicants
(or attested seal of company)   Date

Particulars of entry

Please cancel the under mentioned entry as to either [5]   [6]
☐ the whole
or
☐ the following part

[7]   being part of the land affected by the original registration.

☐ Land Charges   [8] Class and sub class   Insert the number and date of the original registration below.
☐ Pending Action [9]
☐ Writ or Order [9]   Official reference no.   Date of registration [10]
☐ Deed of Arrangement [9] | Day | Month | Year |
☐ Annuity

Particulars of the estate owner [11]   For official use only

Forename(s)

Surname

Key Number [12]	Solicitor's name and address (including postcode) [13]	Name and address (including postcode) for despatch of acknowledgement (leave blank if it is to be sent to the solicitor/applicant's address)

Solicitors Reference [14]		1	2	3	4	5	6
For official use only	County	*C					

Please see also the Explanatory Notes overleaf

HOME IN SOLE NAME OF ONE PARTY TRANSFER TO OTHER 67

Explanatory Notes

1. If you need help to fill in this form please write to the address at the foot of this page and ask for the booklet 'Computerised Land Charges Department – a practical guide for solicitors'. A copy will be sent to you free of charge.

2. The fee payable for each application is set out in the current Land Charges Fee Order (which can be bought from The Stationary Office or from any law stationer). Fees may be paid either through your credit account, if you have one, or by cheque or postal order made payable to 'HM Land Registry'.

3. When you have completed this form please send it to the address shown below which is printed to fit within a standard window envelope.

The Superintendent
Land Charges Department
Cancellation Section
Plumer House, Tailyour Road,
Crownhill, PLYMOUTH PL6 5HY
DX 8249 PLYMOUTH (3)

Crown copyright (ref: LR/HQ) 5/01

(c) Court order

3–16 A certified copy of the court order (or examined abstract) will be required by HM Land Registry when the transfer is lodged for registration.

Where a new covenant is given by the transferee to the bank or building society a certified copy of the transfer containing the covenant should be lodged with the lender so it has a proper record there of the transferee's liability, the transfer incorporating the covenant itself being retained at the Land Registry.

(d) HM Land Registry fees

3–17 Where the transfer between the parties does not involve consideration (e.g. transfer following agreement between the parties or pursuant to a court order) then Scale 2 of HM Land Registry Fees Order 2006 will apply. However, where the land is unregistered and the transfer is subject to compulsory registration pursuant to the Land Registration Act 2002 the fee will be payable on Scale 1 even where it would otherwise qualify for a reduced fee under Scale 2—in both cases fees are based on the value of the land concerned after deducting the amount secured by any continuing charge.

It is simplest to mention the amount of the mortgage debt in the transfer as is done in Precedents 3, 4 and 5. The solicitor lodging the application may specify the value of the property transferred either by letter or on HM Land Registry Form AP1 (Application to change the register), or on form FRI (First Registration Application).

Where the transfer between the parties is one on sale, the fee is calculated in accordance with Scale 1, of the 2006 Fee Order on the amount of the consideration.

(e) Insurance

3–18 If the property is free from mortgage, the transferee should effect his or her own insurance cover following completion of the transfer.

If the property is subject to mortgage and the mortgagee concerned has effected cover, confirmation that the name of the insured has been changed to that of the transferee should be obtained from the mortgagee.

(f) Leasehold

3–19 The requirements of the lease as to registration of any assignment with the lessor should be observed. The transferor may wish to retain a copy of the assignment/transfer so as to have a record of the covenants received and limitation on those given.

If the lessor is owned by a company the shares in which are vested in the lessees then it will be necessary to have them transferred to the transferee. A stock transfer form should be prepared and sent to the transferor's solicitor with the transfer. The transferee's solicitor should receive, following completion, the transfer, a stock transfer form and the original share certificate.

MATRIMONIAL CONVEYANCING

PRECEDENTS

A—Transfer of entirety to other party. No mortgage. By court order

Transfer of whole of registered title(s)

Land Registry

TR1

PRECEDENT 1

If you need more room than is provided for in a panel, use continuation sheet CS and attach to this form.

1.	**Stamp Duty**
	Place "X" in the appropriate box or boxes and complete the appropriate certificate.
	☐ It is certified that this instrument falls within category [ ] in the Schedule to the Stamp Duty (Exempt Instruments) Regulations 1987
	☐ It is certified that the transaction effected does not form part of a larger transaction or of a series of transactions in respect of which the amount or value or the aggregate amount or value of the consideration exceeds the sum of £ [ ]
	☐ It is certified that this is an instrument on which stamp duty is not chargeable by virtue of the provisions of section 92 of the Finance Act 2001
2.	**Title Number(s) of the Property** *Leave blank if not yet registered.*
	[TITLE NUMBER] [OR LEAVE BLANK IF APPLYING FOR FIRST REGISTRATION]
3.	**Property**
	[ADDRESS]
4.	**Date**
5.	**Transferor** *Give full names and company's registered number if any.*
	[TRANSFEROR]
6.	**Transferee for entry on the register** *Give full name(s) and company's registered number, if any. For Scottish companies use an SC prefix and for limited liability partnerships use an OC prefix before the registered number, if any. For foreign companies give territory in which incorporated.*
	[TRANSFEREE]
	Unless otherwise arranged with Land Registry headquarters, a certified copy of the Transferee's constitution (in English or Welsh) will be required if it is a body corporate but is not a company registered in England and Wales or Scotland under the Companies Acts.
7.	**Transferee's intended address(es) for service (including postcode) for entry on the register** *You may give up to three addresses for service one of which must be a postal address but does not have to be within the UK. The other addresses can be any combination of a postal address, a box number at a UK document exchange or an electronic address.*
	[TRANSFEREE'S ADDRESS] (this will usually be the address of the property)
8.	**The Transferor transfers the Property to the Transferee**
9.	**Consideration** *Place "X" in the appropriate box. State clearly the currency unit if other than sterling. If none of the boxes applies, insert an appropriate memorandum in the additional provisions panel.*
	☐ The Transferor has received from the Transferee for the Property the sum of *In words and figures.*
	☐ *Insert other receipt as appropriate.* (See panel 12 below)
	☐ The transfer is not for money or anything which has a monetary value

HOME IN SOLE NAME OF ONE PARTY TRANSFER TO OTHER 71

10. The Transferor transfers with *Place "X" in the appropriate box and add any modifications.*

☐ full title guarantee ☐   ⊥   limited title guarantee

11. Declaration of trust *Where there is more than one Transferee, place "X" in the appropriate box.*

☐ The Transferees are to hold the Property on trust for themselves as joint tenants

☐ The Transferees are to hold the Property on trust for themselves as tenants in common in equal shares

☐ The Transferees are to hold the Property *Complete as necessary.*

12. Additional provisions *Insert here any required or permitted statements, certificates or applications and any agreed covenants, declarations, etc.*

12.1 The transfer is made pursuant to an order of the [ ] County Court dated [   ] in proceedings between the Transferor and the Transferee bearing number [   ]

Refer to continuation sheet (CS)

13. Execution *The Transferor must execute this transfer as a deed using the space below. If there is more than one Transferor, all must execute. Forms of execution are given in Schedule 9 to the Land Registration Rules 2003. If the transfer contains Transferee's covenants or declarations or contains an application by the Transferee (e.g. for a restriction), it must also be executed by the Transferee (all of them, if there is more than one).*

SIGNED as a DEED by (enter full name of individual) in the presence of: [TRANSFEROR]

Signature of Witness ……………………………………………..
Name (in BLOCK CAPITALS) ……………………………………….
Address ………………………………………………………………

SIGNED as a DEED by (enter full name
of individual) in the presence of: [TRANSFEREE]
                                  [Only necessary if covenant for indemnity given]

Signature of Witness ……………………………………………..
Name (in BLOCK CAPITALS) ……………………………………….
Address ………………………………………………………………

Continuation sheet for use with application and disposition forms	Land Registry **CS**
1. Continued from Form TR1	Title number(s) TITLE NUMBER

2. *Before each continuation, state panel to be continued, e.g. "Panel 12 continued".*

Panel 12 continued

12.2 The Transferee covenants with the Transferor that [he or she] will observe and perform the covenants and conditions referred to in the Charges Register so far as still subsisting and relating to the Property and will keep the Transferor and [his or her] personal representatives effectually indemnified against all losses resulting from their non-observance or breach.

Note to clause 12.2 – This clause is only necessary where the transferor entered into the original Restrictions affecting the property (if any) or in the conveyance to [him or her] covenanted to observe them. Otherwise [he or she] is not entitled to this indemnity.

Continuation sheet 1 of 1
Insert sheet number and total number of continuation sheets e.g. "sheet 1 of 3".
© Crown copyright (ref: LR/HQ/CD-ROM) 6/03

HOME IN SOLE NAME OF ONE PARTY TRANSFER TO OTHER 73

B—Assignment of leasehold property to other party. No mortgage. By court order

Transfer of whole   **Land Registry**
of registered title(s)
PRECEDENT 2   **TR1**

If you need more room than is provided for in a panel, use continuation sheet CS and attach to this form.

1. **Stamp Duty**

   Place "X" in the appropriate box or boxes and complete the appropriate certificate.

   ☐ It is certified that this instrument falls within category ☐ in the Schedule to the Stamp Duty (Exempt Instruments) Regulations 1987

   ☐ It is certified that the transaction effected does not form part of a larger transaction or of a series of transactions in respect of which the <u>amount or value or the aggregate amount or value</u> of the consideration exceeds the sum of £

   ☐ It is certified that this is an instrument on which stamp duty is not chargeable by virtue of the provisions of section 92 of the Finance Act 2001

2. **Title Number(s) of the Property** *Leave blank if not yet registered.*
   [TITLE NUMBER] [OR LEAVE BLANK IF APPLYING FOR FIRST REGISTRATION]

3. **Property**

   [ADDRESS]

4. **Date**

5. **Transferor** *Give full names and company's registered number if any.*

   [TRANSFEROR]

6. **Transferee for entry on the register** *Give full name(s) and company's registered number, if any. For Scottish companies use an SC prefix and for limited liability partnerships use an OC prefix before the registered number, if any. For foreign companies give territory in which incorporated.*

   [TRANSFEREE]

   Unless otherwise arranged with Land Registry headquarters, a certified copy of the Transferee's constitution (in English or Welsh) will be required if it is a body corporate but is not a company registered in England and Wales or Scotland under the Companies Acts.

7. **Transferee's intended address(es) for service (including postcode) for entry on the register** *You may give up to three addresses for service **one** of which **must** be a postal address but does not have to be within the UK. The other addresses can be any combination of a postal address, a box number at a UK document exchange or an electronic address.*

   [TRANSFEREE'S ADDRESS] (this will usually be the address of the property)

8. **The Transferor transfers the Property to the Transferee**

9. **Consideration** *Place "X" in the appropriate box. State clearly the currency unit if other than sterling. If none of the boxes applies, insert an appropriate memorandum in the additional provisions panel.*

   ☐ The Transferor has received from the Transferee for the Property the sum of *In words and figures.*

   ☐ *Insert other receipt as appropriate.* **(See panel 12 below)**

   ☐ The transfer is not for money or anything which has a monetary value

10.	The Transferor transfers with *Place "X" in the appropriate box and add any modifications.*
	☐ ☒ full title guarantee ☐ ☐ limited title guarantee

11. Declaration of trust *Where there is more than one Transferee, place "X" in the appropriate box.*
    - ☐ The Transferees are to hold the Property on trust for themselves as joint tenants
    - ☐ The Transferees are to hold the Property on trust for themselves as tenants in common in equal shares
    - ☐ The Transferees are to hold the Property *Complete as necessary.*

12. Additional provisions *Insert here any required or permitted statements, certificates or applications and any agreed covenants, declarations, etc.*

    12.1 The transfer is made pursuant to an order of the [ ] County Court dated [   ] in proceedings between the Transferor and the Transferee bearing number [   ]

    Refer to continuation sheet (CS)

13. Execution *The Transferor must execute this transfer as a deed using the space below. If there is more than one Transferor, all must execute. Forms of execution are given in Schedule 9 to the Land Registration Rules 2003. If the transfer contains Transferee's covenants or declarations or contains an application by the Transferee (e.g. for a restriction), it must also be executed by the Transferee (all of them, if there is more than one).*

    SIGNED as a DEED by (enter full name of individual) in the presence of: [TRANSFEROR]

    Signature of Witness ……………………………………………….
    Name (in BLOCK CAPITALS) …………………………………….
    Address …………………………………………………………….

    SIGNED as a DEED by (enter full name of individual) in the presence of: [TRANSFEREE]

    Signature of Witness ……………………………………………….
    Name (in BLOCK CAPITALS) …………………………………….
    Address …………………………………………………………….

| **Continuation sheet for use with application and disposition forms** | **Land Registry** | **CS** |

1. Continued from Form `TR1`   Title number(s) `TITLE NUMBER`

2. *Before each continuation, state panel to be continued, e.g. "Panel 12 continued".*

Panel 12 continued

12.2　The Transferee covenants with the Transferor that [he or she] will observe and perform the covenants and conditions referred to in the Charges Register so far as still subsisting and relating to the Property and will keep the Transferor and [his or her] personal representatives effectually indemnified against all losses resulting from their non-observance or breach.

Note to clause 12.2 – This clause is only necessary where the transferor entered into the original Restrictions affecting the property (if any) or in the conveyance to [him or her] covenanted to observe them. Otherwise [he or she] is not entitled to this indemnity.

12.3　The Covenant by the Transferor implied by section 4(1)(b) Law of Property (Miscellaneous Provisions) Act 1994 by reason of the property being transferred with Full Title Guarantee shall be limited so as not to extend to any breach of the terms of the registered lease on the part of the Transferor relating to the condition of the Property [Limitation of Transferors Liability in relation to repair: (see p.6)].

12.4　The Transferee covenants with the Transferor in the terms set out in Part IX, Schedule 2, Law of Property Act 1925.

Note to clause 12.4 – Only necessary on an application for first registration where the lease was granted before January 1, 1996 – "an old tenancy" (see p.62 at para.3–11).

Continuation sheet `1` of `1`
Insert sheet number and total number of continuation sheets e.g. "sheet 1 of 3".
© Crown copyright (ref: LR/HQ/CD-ROM) 6/03

C—Transfer of entirety to other party by order of the court. Property subject to mortgage. Transferee (with mortgagee's agreement) assuming liability. Transferor released

Transfer of whole of registered title(s)	Land Registry
PRECEDENT 3	**TR1**

If you need more room than is provided for in a panel, use continuation sheet CS and attach to this form.

1. **Stamp Duty**

    Place "X" in the appropriate box or boxes and complete the appropriate certificate.

    ☐ It is certified that this instrument falls within category ☐ in the Schedule to the Stamp Duty (Exempt Instruments) Regulations 1987

    ☐ It is certified that the transaction effected does not form part of a larger transaction or of a series of transactions in respect of which the amount or value or the aggregate amount or value of the consideration exceeds the sum of £

    ☐ It is certified that this is an instrument on which stamp duty is not chargeable by virtue of the provisions of section 92 of the Finance Act 2001

2. Title Number(s) of the Property *Leave blank if not yet registered.*

    [TITLE NUMBER] [OR LEAVE BLANK IF APPLYING FOR FIRST REGISTRATION]

3. Property

    [ADDRESS]

4. Date

5. Transferor *Give full names and company's registered number if any.*

    [TRANSFEROR]

6. Transferee **for entry on the register** *Give full name(s) and company's registered number, if any. For Scottish companies use an SC prefix and for limited liability partnerships use an OC prefix before the registered number, if any. For foreign companies give territory in which incorporated.*

    [TRANSFEREE]

    Unless otherwise arranged with Land Registry headquarters, a certified copy of the Transferee's constitution (in English or Welsh) will be required if it is a body corporate but is not a company registered in England and Wales or Scotland under the Companies Acts.

7. Transferee's intended **address(es) for service (including postcode) for entry on the register** *You may give up to three addresses for service **one** of which **must** be a postal address but does not have to be within the UK. The other addresses can be any combination of a postal address, a box number at a UK document exchange or an electronic address.*

    [TRANSFEREE'S ADDRESS] (this will usually be the address of the property)

8. **The Transferor transfers the Property to the Transferee**

9. Consideration *Place "X" in the appropriate box. State clearly the currency unit if other than sterling. If none of the boxes applies, insert an appropriate memorandum in the additional provisions panel.*

    ☐ The Transferor has received from the Transferee for the Property the sum of *In words and figures.*

    ☐ *Insert other receipt as appropriate.*   (See panel 12 below)

    ☐ The transfer is not for money or anything which has a monetary value

HOME IN SOLE NAME OF ONE PARTY TRANSFER TO OTHER 77

10. The Transferor transfers with *Place "X" in the appropriate box and add any modifications.*

　　☐ ☒　　full title guarantee ☐　　☐　　limited title guarantee

11. Declaration of trust *Where there is more than one Transferee, place "X" in the appropriate box.*

　　☐　The Transferees are to hold the Property on trust for themselves as joint tenants

　　☐　The Transferees are to hold the Property on trust for themselves as tenants in common in equal shares

　　☐　The Transferees are to hold the Property *Complete as necessary.*

12. Additional provisions *Insert here any required or permitted statements, certificates or applications and any agreed covenants, declarations, etc.*

　　12.1 The transfer is made pursuant to an order of the [ ] County Court dated [　　　] in proceedings between the Transferor and the Transferee bearing number [　]

　　Refer to continuation sheet (CS)

13. Execution *The Transferor must execute this transfer as a deed using the space below. If there is more than one Transferor, all must execute. Forms of execution are given in Schedule 9 to the Land Registration Rules 2003. If the transfer contains Transferee's covenants or declarations or contains an application by the Transferee (e.g. for a restriction), it must also be executed by the Transferee (all of them, if there is more than one).*

　　SIGNED as a DEED by (enter full name of individual) in the presence of:　　[TRANSFEROR]

　　Signature of Witness ……………………………………………
　　Name (in BLOCK CAPITALS) ……………………………………………
　　Address ……………………………………………

　　SIGNED as a DEED by (enter full name of individual) in the presence of:　　[TRANSFEREE]

　　Signature of Witness ……………………………………………
　　Name (in BLOCK CAPITALS) ……………………………………………
　　Address ……………………………………………

Continuation sheet for use with application and disposition forms

Land Registry

CS

1. Continued from Form TR1   Title number(s) TITLE NUMBER

2. *Before each continuation, state panel to be continued, e.g. "Panel 12 continued".*

Panel 12 continued

12.2　The Transferee covenants with the Transferor that [he or she] will observe and perform the covenants and conditions referred to in the Charges Register so far as still subsisting and relating to the Property and will keep the Transferor and [his or her] personal representatives effectually indemnified against all losses resulting from their non-observance or breach

Note to clause 12.2 – This clause is only necessary where the transferor entered into the original Restrictions affecting the property (if any) or in the conveyance to [him or her] covenanted to observe them. Otherwise [he or she] is not entitled to this indemnity.

12.3　The Covenant by the Transferor implied by section 4(1)(b) Law of Property (Miscellaneous Provisions) Act 1994 by reason of the property being transferred with Full Title Guarantee shall be limited so as not to extend to any breach of the terms of the registered lease on the part of the Transferor relating to the condition of the Property [Limitation of Transferor's Liability in relation to repair: (see p.6)].

12.4　The Property is transferred subject to the charge ("the registered charge") dated [ ] and registered on [ ] [under which there is now owing the sum of £   ].

12.5　The [Bank or Building Society] ("the lender") being the proprietor of the registered charge hereby releases and discharges the Transferor from all obligations under the registered charge.

12.6　The Transferee covenants with the lender to pay to the lender all principal money interest and costs and other monies due and to become due under or by virtue of the registered charge and will observe and be bound by the agreements, covenants and conditions contained or referred to in the registered charge.

Panel 13 continued

SIGNED on behalf of

[the lender]

　　　　　　　　　　　　　　　　　　　　　　　　　　　　　　　　　Authorised Signatory

HOME IN SOLE NAME OF ONE PARTY TRANSFER TO OTHER 79

D—Transfer of entirety to other party by order of the court. Mortgage. Transferor remaining liable. Transferee indemnifying

Transfer of whole of registered title(s)

PRECEDENT 4

Land Registry

TR1

If you need more room than is provided for in a panel, use continuation sheet CS and attach to this form.

1. Stamp Duty

Place "X" in the appropriate box or boxes and complete the appropriate certificate.

☐ It is certified that this instrument falls within category [ ] in the Schedule to the Stamp Duty (Exempt Instruments) Regulations 1987

☐ It is certified that the transaction effected does not form part of a larger transaction or of a series of transactions in respect of which the amount or value or the aggregate amount or value of the consideration exceeds the sum of £[ ]

☐ It is certified that this is an instrument on which stamp duty is not chargeable by virtue of the provisions of section 92 of the Finance Act 2001

2. Title Number(s) of the Property *Leave blank if not yet registered.*

[TITLE NUMBER] [OR LEAVE BLANK IF APPLYING FOR FIRST REGISTRATION]

3. Property

[ADDRESS]

4. Date

5. Transferor *Give full names and company's registered number if any.*

[TRANSFEROR]

6. Transferee for entry on the register *Give full name(s) and company's registered number, if any. For Scottish companies use an SC prefix and for limited liability partnerships use an OC prefix before the registered number, if any. For foreign companies give territory in which incorporated.*

[TRANSFEREE]

Unless otherwise arranged with Land Registry headquarters, a certified copy of the Transferee's constitution (in English or Welsh) will be required if it is a body corporate but is not a company registered in England and Wales or Scotland under the Companies Acts.

7. Transferee's intended address(es) for service (including postcode) for entry on the register *You may give up to three addresses for service **one** of which **must** be a postal address but does not have to be within the UK. The other addresses can be any combination of a postal address, a box number at a UK document exchange or an electronic address.*

[TRANSFEREE'S ADDRESS] (this will usually be the address of the property)

8. The Transferor transfers the Property to the Transferee

9. Consideration *Place "X" in the appropriate box. State clearly the currency unit if other than sterling. If none of the boxes applies, insert an appropriate memorandum in the additional provisions panel.*

☐ The Transferor has received from the Transferee for the Property the sum of *In words and figures.*

☐ *Insert other receipt as appropriate.* (See panel 12 below)

☐ The transfer is not for money or anything which has a monetary value

10. The Transferor transfers with *Place "X" in the appropriate box and add any modifications.*

    ☐ ☒ full title guarantee ☐   ☐ limited title guarantee

11. Declaration of trust *Where there is more than one Transferee, place "X" in the appropriate box.*

    ☐ The Transferees are to hold the Property on trust for themselves as joint tenants

    ☐ The Transferees are to hold the Property on trust for themselves as tenants in common in equal shares

    ☐ The Transferees are to hold the Property *Complete as necessary.*

12. Additional provisions *Insert here any required or permitted statements, certificates or applications and any agreed covenants, declarations, etc.*

    12.1 The transfer is made pursuant to an order of the [ ] County Court dated [   ] in proceedings between the Transferor and the Transferee bearing number [ ]

    Refer to continuation sheet (CS)

13. Execution *The Transferor must execute this transfer as a deed using the space below. If there is more than one Transferor, all must execute. Forms of execution are given in Schedule 9 to the Land Registration Rules 2003. If the transfer contains Transferee's covenants or declarations or contains an application by the Transferee (e.g. for a restriction), it must also be executed by the Transferee (all of them, if there is more than one).*

    SIGNED as a DEED by (enter full name of individual) in the presence of: [TRANSFEROR]

    Signature of Witness ………………………………………………..
    Name (in BLOCK CAPITALS) …………………………………………
    Address ………………………………………………………………..

    SIGNED as a DEED by (enter full name of individual) in the presence of: [TRANSFEREE]

    Signature of Witness ………………………………………………..
    Name (in BLOCK CAPITALS) …………………………………………
    Address ………………………………………………………………..

**Continuation sheet
for use with
application and
disposition forms**

Land Registry

CS

1. Continued from Form [TR1] Title number(s) [TITLE NUMBER]

2. *Before each continuation, state panel to be continued, e.g. "Panel 12 continued".*

   Panel 12 continued

   12.2 The Transferee covenants with the Transferor that [he or she] will observe and perform the covenants and conditions referred to in the Charges Register so far as still subsisting and relating to the Property and will keep the Transferor and [his or her] personal representatives effectually indemnified against all losses resulting from their non-observance or breach.

   Note to clause 12.2 – This clause is only necessary where the transferor entered into the original Restrictions affecting the property (if any) or in the conveyance to [him or her] covenanted to observe them. Otherwise he or she is not entitled to this indemnity.

   12.3 The Covenant by the Transferor implied by section 4(1)(b) Law of Property (Miscellaneous Provisions) Act 1994 by reason of the property being transferred with Full Title Guarantee shall be limited so as not to extend to any breach of the terms of the registered lease on the part of the Transferor relating to the condition of the Property [Limitation of Transferor's Liability in relation to repair: see p.6].

   12.4 The Property is transferred subject to the charge ("the registered charge") dated [ ] and registered on [ ] [under which there is now owing the sum of £   ].

   12.5 The Transferee covenants with the [Bank or Building Society] ("the lender") being the proprietor of the registered charge that the Transferee will pay to the lender all principal money interest and costs and other monies due and to become due under or by virtue of the registered charge and will observe and be bound by the agreements, covenants and conditions contained or referred to in the registered charge.

   12.6 The Transferee covenants with the Transferor that with effect from the date hereof [or other date if appropriate] the Transferee will pay and discharge all principal monies, interest, costs and other monies secured by or to become payable under the registered charge and will comply with the covenants contained in the registered charge and will at all times indemnify and keep indemnified the Transferor and the Transferor's estate and effects against all proceedings, costs, claims and demands whatsoever and the Transferor and Transferee apply to the Registrar pursuant to the Land Registration Rules 2003 to note this covenant on the register.

MATRIMONIAL CONVEYANCING

E—Transfer of entirety to other party. Sale. Property subject to first and second mortgages. Transferee assuming liability for the first and transferor released. Transferor remaining liable on second

Transfer of whole of registered title(s)	Land Registry
PRECEDENT 5	**TR1**

If you need more room than is provided for in a panel, use continuation sheet CS and attach to this form.

1. Stamp Duty

Place "X" in the appropriate box or boxes and complete the appropriate certificate.

☐ It is certified that this instrument falls within category [ ] in the Schedule to the Stamp Duty (Exempt Instruments) Regulations 1987

☒ It is certified that the transaction effected does not form part of a larger transaction or of a series of transactions in respect of which the amount or value or the aggregate amount or value of the consideration exceeds the sum of [   ] (as appropriate)

☐ It is certified that this is an instrument on which stamp duty is not chargeable by virtue of the provisions of section 92 of the Finance Act 2001

2. Title Number(s) of the Property *Leave blank if not yet registered.*
[TITLE NUMBER] [OR LEAVE BLANK IF APPLYING FOR FIRST REGISTRATION]

3. Property

[ADDRESS]

4. Date

5. Transferor *Give full names and company's registered number if any.*

[TRANSFEROR]

6. Transferee for entry on the register *Give full name(s) and company's registered number, if any. For Scottish companies use an SC prefix and for limited liability partnerships use an OC prefix before the registered number, if any. For foreign companies give territory in which incorporated.*

[TRANSFEREE]

Unless otherwise arranged with Land Registry headquarters, a certified copy of the Transferee's constitution (in English or Welsh) will be required if it is a body corporate but is not a company registered in England and Wales or Scotland under the Companies Acts.

7. Transferee's intended address(es) for service (including postcode) for entry on the register *You may give up to three addresses for service **one** of which **must** be a postal address but does not have to be within the UK. The other addresses can be any combination of a postal address, a box number at a UK document exchange or an electronic address.*

[TRANSFEREE'S ADDRESS] (this will usually be the address of the property)

8. The Transferor transfers the Property to the Transferee

9. Consideration *Place "X" in the appropriate box. State clearly the currency unit if other than sterling. If none of the boxes applies, insert an appropriate memorandum in the additional provisions panel.*

☐ The Transferor has received from the Transferee for the Property the sum of *In words and figures.*

☐ *Insert other receipt as appropriate.* (See panel 12 below)

☐ The transfer is not for money or anything which has a monetary value

HOME IN SOLE NAME OF ONE PARTY TRANSFER TO OTHER

10. The Transferor transfers with *Place "X" in the appropriate box and add any modifications.*

☐ ☒   full title guarantee ☐   ☐   limited title guarantee

11. Declaration of trust *Where there is more than one Transferee, place "X" in the appropriate box.*

☐ The Transferees are to hold the Property on trust for themselves as joint tenants
☐ The Transferees are to hold the Property on trust for themselves as tenants in common in equal shares
☐ The Transferees are to hold the Property *Complete as necessary.*

12. Additional provisions *Insert here any required or permitted statements, certificates or applications and any agreed covenants, declarations, etc.*

12.1 The transfer is made pursuant to an order of the [ ] County Court dated [   ] in proceedings between the Transferor and the Transferee bearing number [   ]

Refer to continuation sheet (CS)

13. Execution *The Transferor must execute this transfer as a deed using the space below. If there is more than one Transferor, all must execute. Forms of execution are given in Schedule 9 to the Land Registration Rules 2003. If the transfer contains Transferee's covenants or declarations or contains an application by the Transferee (e.g. for a restriction), it must also be executed by the Transferee (all of them, if there is more than one).*

SIGNED as a DEED by (enter full name of individual) in the presence of: [TRANSFEROR]

Signature of Witness ……………………………………………..
Name (in BLOCK CAPITALS) ……………………………………….
Address ……………………………………………………………..

SIGNED as a DEED by (enter full name of individual) in the presence of: [TRANSFEREE]

Signature of Witness ……………………………………………..
Name (in BLOCK CAPITALS) ……………………………………….
Address ……………………………………………………………..

Continuation sheet for use with application and disposition forms

Land Registry

CS

1. Continued from Form TR1   Title number(s) TITLE NUMBER

2. *Before each continuation, state panel to be continued, e.g. "Panel 12 continued".*

   Panel 12 continued

   12.2 The Covenant by the Transferor implied by section 4(1)(b) Law of Property (Miscellaneous Provisions) Act 1994 by reason of the property being transferred with Full Title Guarantee shall be limited so as not to extend to any breach of the terms of the registered lease on the part of the Transferor relating to the condition of the Property [Limitation of Transferor's Liability in relation to repair: see p.6].

   12.3 The Property is transferred subject to the charge ("the registered charge") dated [ ] and registered on [ ] [under which there is now owing the sum of £   ].

   12.4 The Property is transferred subject to the charge ("the second registered charge") dated [ ] and registered on [   ] [under which there is now owing the sum of £   ].

   12.5 The [Bank or Building Society] ("the lender") being the proprietor of the registered charge hereby releases and discharges the Transferor from all obligations under the registered charge.

   12.6 The Transferee covenants with the lender to pay to the lender all principal money interest and costs and other monies due and to become due under or by virtue of the registered charge and will observe and be bound by the agreements, covenants and conditions contained or referred to in the registered charge.

   12.7 The Transferee covenants with the Transferor that with effect from the date hereof [or other date if appropriate] the Transferee will pay and discharge all principal monies, interest, costs and other monies secured by or to become payable under the second registered charge and will comply with the covenants contained in the registered charge and will at all times indemnify and keep indemnified the Transferor and the Transferor's estate and effects against all proceedings, costs, claims and demands whatsoever and the Transferor and Transferee apply to the Registrar pursuant to the Land Registration Rules 2003 to note this covenant on the register.

   12.8 The Transferee covenants with the [Bank or Building Society] ("the second lender") being the registered proprietor of the second registered charge that the Transferee will pay to the second lender all principal money, interest, costs and other monies due and to become due under or by virtue of the second registered charge and will observe and be bound by the agreements, covenants and conditions contained or referred to in the second registered charge.

Continuation sheet 1 of 2
Insert sheet number and total number of continuation sheets e.g. "sheet 1 of 3".
© Crown copyright (ref: LR/HQ/CD-ROM) 6/03

1.	Continued from Form TR1	Title number(s) TITLE NUMBER

2. *Before each continuation, state panel to be continued, e.g. "Panel 12 continued".*

Panel 13 continued

SIGNED on behalf of

[the Lender]

                                      Authorised Signatory

F—Consent to transfer subject to mortgage by occupier

Precedent 6

The Property
The Lender
The Borrower
The Transferor
The Transferee
I, *[Occupier]*
being a person who is in or may go into occupation of the Property:

1 Consent to the transfer of the Property by the Transferor to the Transferee subject to the existing Mortgage in favour of the Lender

2 Agree that such present or future rights or interests that I may have or acquire in or over the Property shall be postponed and made subject to the rights and interests of the Lender under its Mortgage

3 Undertake that no claim to any such rights and interests shall be made by me against the Lender

4 Confirm that I have been advised that I can take independent legal advice on the effect of this document and confirm that the effect of this form of consent has been explained to me

Date
SIGNED by the Occupier
in the presence of:

Chapter 4

Home in Joint Names Transfer to Sole Name

This chapter deals with the situation where the family home is held in the joint names of the parties, either as beneficial joint tenants or as tenants in common. The home may be subject to a mortgage or free from charge. **4–01**

The court may order the transfer of the home to one party absolutely in the following manner:

> "It is ordered that the Respondent shall transfer to the Petitioner absolutely within 28 days from the date of this Order all his estate and interest with full title guarantee in the property 1 Blackacre Drive, Blackacre [subject to the existing Mortgage to the Blackacre Building Society, the Petitioner indemnifying the Respondent against all claims in respect thereof."

Alternatively agreement may be reached between the parties for some monetary payment so that the one party may keep the house in which case the consent order may be:

> "It is ordered that the Respondent shall within 28 days from the date of this Order pay to the Petitioner the sum of £   and
> It is ordered that on receipt of the said sum of £   the Petitioner do transfer all her estate and interest with full title guarantee in the property at 1 Blackacre Drive, Blackacre to the Respondent."

Chapter 6 deals with those cases where one party is ordered to convey or transfer his or her interest in the family home upon certain terms and conditions or upon certain trusts.

1 Severance

Dealing with the interest of one party in joint property would be incomplete without mention of the doctrine of severance. **4–02**

Just as solicitors acting for the transferee, where the family home stands in the transferor's sole name, will have given advice concerning the registration of Home Rights (*see* Ch.3); so, where the home stands in the joint names of the parties as beneficial joint tenants, will they have advised on severance of that joint tenancy in order to prevent the transferor acquiring the whole property by operation of law in the event of the transferee's death before the determination of the proceedings (Administration of Estates Act 1925, s.394) and see *Barton v Morris* [1985] 2 All E.R. 1032). The transferor's advisers will also have regard to the advantages of severance whilst proceedings are pending.

If severance of the joint tenancy takes place, it should be coupled with the making of a new will by the party severing the joint tenancy to deal with "the severed share". Although such will does not defeat the claim of the other party under the provisions of the Inheritance (Provision for Family and Dependants) Act 1975, if reasonable provision is not made for that party, it might be of "persuasive" use to the court in proceedings under that Act in deciding whether or not to award the surviving party a limited interest (e.g. until remarriage) or an absolute interest in the deceased's share of the family home (see Ch.11 for the effect on a will following dissolution of a marriage or civil partnership).

Despite an earlier move anyway from the concept it is now clear that severance, where no shares are agreed, operates to create a tenancy in common in equal shares (see Megarry and Wade, *Real Property* 5th edn., Stevens 1984, p.430, *R v Porter* [1990] 1 W.L.R. 1260 where the Court of Appeal held that in a joint venture, in the absence of any evidence, the Court was entitled to assume equal sharing and *Jones v Maynard* [1951] Ch. 572 followed in *Midland Bank Plc v Cooke [1995]* 4 All E.R. 562 where "equity favours equality between the co-tenants"). *Goodman v Gallant* [1986] 1 All E.R. 311 held that in the absence of any claim for rectification or recession of the original conveyance, evidence could not be subsequently given in support of an unequal division following severance.

This view has been reinforced despite *Springeue v Defoe* [1992] Fam. Law 459 (not a case between husband and wife but where equal shares were not inferred). Recent authorities include *Harwood v Harwood* [1991] 2 F.L.R. 274 and *Carlton v Goodman* [2002] 2 F.L.R. 259.

In the light of the case law practitioners should bear in mind that whilst severance is beneficial in that it stops one party acquiring the whole property in the event of the others death the actual claims are likely to be accrued to be equal with no assumption of implied resulting or constructive trusts. If a party has contributed more that 50 per cent it is vital that they are advised accordingly, otherwise there is likely to be a negligence claim against the solicitor acting. See further discussion on joint-ownership in Ch.5.

The procedure for severance differs depending upon whether title to the family home is registered or not.

(a) Unregistered land

4–03 The Law of Property Act 1925, s.36(2) (as amended by Trusts of Land and Appointment of Trustees Act 1996, Sch.2, para.(4) provides for severance of a joint tenancy either by:

(i) a notice in writing given by one joint tenant to the other; or

(ii) the doing of such other acts or things as would, in the case of personal estate, have been effectual to sever the tenancy in equity.

The mere issue of proceedings for a property adjustment order does not automatically sever a joint tenancy (*Harris v Goddard* [1983] 1 W.L.R. 1203) but the issue of proceedings under the Married Women's Property Act 1882, s.17 can cause severance to occur (*Re Draper's Conveyance* [1969] 1 Ch. 486) as does the bankruptcy of one of the parties (*Re Gorinan* (a bankrupt) [1990] 1 W.L.R. 616) or the fraudulent dealing with the property by one of the joint owners (see *First National Securities v Hegerty* [1984] 3 All E.R. 641 and *Ahmed v Kendrick* [1988] 2 F.L.R. 22 where a husband's fraudulent signature of his wife's name on a transfer was held to sever the joint tenancy). In the case of bankruptcy, the exact moment of severance is unclear (see *Encyclopedia of Forms and Precedents*, Vol. 16(2) [273], Butterworths)—only relevant in the event of an untimely death!

The parties may agree that the joint tenancy should be severed and if so they should properly evidence that fact. In *Nielson-Jones v Fedden* [1975] Ch. 222 it was held that it was not sufficient for the husband and wife to sign a memorandum to the effect that the husband was to have a free hand to sell the property and use the money to buy a new house for himself although in *Burgess v Rawnsley* [1975] Ch. 429 it was held that a beneficial joint tenancy was severed by the oral agreement of one joint tenant to sell her share in the property to the other even though that agreement was not specifically enforceable.

Service of a notice of severance (*see* Precedent 7) would appear to be effective to sever the joint tenancy if properly addressed to the other joint tenant and received at the property concerned.

It would appear not to matter that the party to whom the notice is addressed does not acknowledge receipt nor even if the party addressed never actually receives the notice itself (see *Re 88 Berkeley Road, London NW9; Rickwood v Turnsek* [1971] Ch. 648.

If the joint tenancy is severed by agreement then the notice of severance or declaration of trust which would have the same effect should specify in what proportions or shares the equitable interests of the former beneficial joint tenants are to be held. If however the shares of each party have never been determined, then at least proper service of the notice of severance ensures that severance has taken place with the advantage as mentioned earlier (*see* p.88).

Whilst the notice itself may be sufficient to sever the beneficial joint tenancy, to prevent a transfer by the survivor either through ignorance or fraud it would be prudent to endorse a memorandum on the last conveyance that severance has taken place. This should be sufficient to put a purchaser on notice so that he or she insists on paying the purchase monies to two trustees or a trust corporation so as to obtain a good receipt (Law of Property Act 1925, s.27). In the absence of such memorandum or the registration of a petition or receiving order in bankruptcy against any of the joint tenants in HM Land Charges Registry, a purchaser of the legal estate is entitled to treat the survivor as solely and beneficially interested if the transfer includes a statement that such survivor is solely and beneficially interested in the legal estate (Law of Property (Joint Tenants) Act 1964, s.1 as amended by Law of Property (Miscellaneous Provisions) Act 1994, s.21(1)).

(b) Registered land

4–04 The position in relation to registered land is that the Land Registration Act 2002 provides, as far as possible, that references to trusts shall be excluded from the register. A notice of severance or declaration of trust whilst being effective in equity, would have no effect on the register unless it was completed by an application to register a restriction so that the register shows that the survivor of the former two joint tenants is no longer able to give a valid receipt for capital monies (see Precedent 9). Such application (because the property is registered in joint names) preferably requires the signatures of both parties. Application will be in Form RX1 as required by the Land Registry Rules 2003, r.92. Severance results in the obligatory entry of a Form A restriction under Land Registration Act 2002, s.40 and the Land Registration Rules 2003, Sch.4); such Registration incurs no fee (Land Registration Fees Order 2006).

If, however, one of the joint proprietors refuses to join in the application to register a restriction, the party making the application should apply to HM Land Registry for a restriction to be entered on the basis of his or her application alone again using Form RX1. The registrar will require to be satisfied that severance has actually taken place. In the writer's experience it will be sufficient to lodge with the application:

(i) an explanation as to why the application has not been signed by both proprietors (e.g the parties are separated and one of them refuses to reply);

(ii) a copy of the notice of severance; and

(iii) a certificate of posting of the notice and confirmation of delivery.

It will be appreciated that the registration of a restriction does not specify the shares in which the net proceeds of sale of the property are to be held; so (if agreement) there should be a document (such as a declaration of trust) specifying those shares. However, registration of a restriction protects the share of any deceased former joint tenant whilst the future of the family home is being clarified.

2 Procedure

4–05 Where the property is unregistered neither party is solely entitled to hold the title deeds to the family home in joint names; but, if either party does hold the title deeds, then that party does, of course, hold them as trustee for both joint owners.

It would seem appropriate that the transferor's solicitors should be allowed custody of the title deeds and act, in effect, as the "vendor's solicitors". It is felt that the conventional conveyancing procedure should be adhered to for the reasons stated in Ch.3.

As the property was purchased jointly for the parties, it would seem unreasonable for the transferee's solicitors to insist on a full abstract of title. It should be assumed that the title was properly investigated at the time of the purchase by the parties. If the title to the family home is unregistered it is suggested, therefore, that the transferor's solicitors should submit to the transferee's solicitors merely a copy of the last conveyance, together with a copy of any mortgage affecting the property and memoranda of any "sales-off" or other documents affecting the legal title. In the case of registered land, sufficient particulars of the title or official copies of the registered title can be supplied to enable the transferee's solicitors to draw a transfer. Indeed the transferee's solicitors can apply themselves for official copies on Form OC1, by telephone or electronically from Land Registry Direct as stated in Ch.3.

Where the transferor is not legally represented or has disappeared, then obviously the transferee's solicitors should have complete conduct of the conveyancing and in these circumstances the transferee's solicitors may have already asked the court to give an order to this effect (*see* Ch.8). This should have the result that the title deeds (where still relevant) will be released by any mortgagee to the transferee's solicitors alone without the consent of the transferor.

Although the court order may specify a time-limit in which the transfer must be completed, this is rarely adhered to. If an unreasonable time has elapsed and the transferor refuses or fails to execute the conveyance or transfer, application can be made to the court (*see* Ch.8).

For the reason that there can so often be delay in obtaining the transferor's signature, it is recommended that only once the documentation has been agreed and executed is a "completion date" arranged so that the transferee's solicitors may (in the case of unregistered title) make a search against the transferor at HM Land Charges Registry. In the case of registered title, if the transferee is purchasing the transferor's interest in the property, a search in usual form (Form OS1) at HM Land Registry is appropriate; otherwise a search should be made on Form OS3, although as the transferee is a trustee of the legal estate with the transferor, this search can be of little value, particularly as it confers no priority (Land Registration (Official Searches) Rules 1993 (SI 1993/3276).

As often as not, however, a mortgagee will be involved and priority can be obtained by the mortgagee's solicitors making a Form OS1 search.

3 Form of transfer

As previously detailed all forms of transfer should be submitted to HM Land Registry on Form TR1, whilst it is still acceptable to submit an old form conveyance in respect of unregistered land the Land Registry prefer practitioners to utilise Form TR1 (or as appropriate) when submitting applications for first registration. All precedents in this book assume Form TR1 will be used. Nevertheless, this section requires a consideration of unregistered land and registered land separately.

4–06

(a) Unregistered Land

4–07 Where the parties are beneficial joint tenants there are two methods by which the family home can be vested in one party alone:

(i) the transferor can release his or her interest in the legal estate to the transferee (Law of Property Act 1925, s.36(2) as amended by the Trust of Land and Appointment of Trustees Act 1996, Sch.2, para.4)); or

(ii) the parties can convey the legal estate to the transferee alone (Law of Property Act 1925, s.72(4)).

The release operates to extinguish the legal estate of the releasor/transferor and vest the entirety in the transferee as other joint tenant. It is has previously been considered that a release would efficiently put an end to a joint tenancy but see below.

So far as a tenant in common is concerned however, he or she cannot release an undivided half share, as a tenant in common is solely seised of his or her respective interest. In this case, assuming that the trustees of the legal estate are tenants in common of the whole of the equity (as would usually be the case where husband and wife or civil partners are concerned) a transfer by the parties, as trustees of the legal estate, to the one party alone is the appropriate document. Whilst the transfer will vest the legal estate in the transferee, there should be an assignment to the transferee by the transferor of his or her equitable interest as well and this can be incorporated in the transfer document (*see* Precedent 17). It is not essential as the property is about to become registered in any event but deals with the equitable interest for completeness.

With the exception of inserting the assignment in the transfer as stated in the last paragraph it is recommended that all transfers are now dealt with on Form TR1 although HM Land Registry will accept a release (*see* para. (i) above) on an application for first registration as transferring the legal interest to the transferee.

(b) Registered land

4–08 The rule of keeping the equities off the title is strictly enforced in registered conveyancing.

Thus, since neither the registry nor persons dealing with the registered estate can have notice of any trust a release by one joint tenant to another is inappropriate (in contrast to unregistered conveyancing) to transfer the registered estate, and a transfer from the joint names to one name alone is the appropriate document. Strictly the transfer should contain no reference to the transferor's beneficial interest in the family home; this is a minor interest and will disappear with the alteration of the register.

Such a transfer will be appropriate whether the property was held by the parties as beneficial joint tenants or as tenants in common: in the latter case, as the transfer to the parties will not have contained a declaration to the effect that the survivor of them could give a good receipt for capital monies, a restriction will have automatically been entered on the register to the effect that no disposition by a sole proprietor of the land (not being a trust corporation) under which capital money arises is to be registered except under an order of the registrar (Land Registration Act 2002, s.40 and Land Registration Rules 2003, Sch.l2 Form A). When the property is transferred to a sole name, it is necessary, therefore, to apply to the registrar to remove this restriction and this can be achieved by sending with the application to HM Land Registry for registration a duly completed form RX4 (*see* Precedents 17 and 18). No fee is payable (Land Registration Fee Order 2006).

As the transfer deals only with the legal estate, it can be argued that there should properly be a release off the register by the transferor of his or her equitable interest in the family home to the transferee. In practice such a release is rarely prepared, the parties being satisfied with the evidence of the court order and the transfer itself. Any purchaser from the transferee is not concerned with this, as note he is merely interested to check that the transferee alone has power to transfer the property to him or her.

4 Covenants for title

(a) Freehold

Although this could be a matter of negotiation, there seems little reason why any conveyance or transfer should not be made with full title guarantee which then implies on the part of the transferor/covenantor the various covenants set out in the Law of Property (Miscellaneous Provisions) Act 1994 (*see* Ch.1, p.4). Indeed if mortgagees are involved, they appear to insist on a transfer with full title guarantee.   **4–09**

(b) Leasehold

The transferor may wish to be excused liability towards the assignee transferee for a breach of the terms of the lease relating to repairs and the implied covenant should be amended accordingly (*see* Precedent 13 and Ch.1, p.6).   **4–10**

The transferor will remain liable to the lessor for any future non-payment of rent or breach of covenant unless the lease is a "new tenancy" granted on or after January 1, 1996 (*see* note, p.6).

5 Where the property is subject to a mortgage

Although it may be agreed, or the court may order, that the family home be transferred to one party alone subject to the existing mortgage, the mortgagee may not be willing to release the transferor. In such case there will be a transfer to the transferee alone subject to the existing mortgage with the transferor taking an indemnity from the transferee.   **4–11**

It will be recalled (*see* Ch.3, p.63) that application under the Land Registration Rules 2003, r.64 should be made to note this indemnity on the Register. The advantages of having the transfer containing the indemnity executed in duplicate have already been noted (*see* Ch.3, p.63).

If however, the mortgagee is prepared to rely on the transferee's covenant, the transferor can be released from liability by the mortgagee, with the transferee alone remaining liable.

This may take place subsequent to the transfer to the transferee, so that a separate deed of release is required in favour of the transferor (*see* Precedent 19). No stamp duty land tax is payable on the deed (which should be prepared in duplicate so that the transferor has evidence of his or her release). If it is required to register this release at HM Land Registry (and that depends on the practice by the mortgagee) the original (plus copy) should be sent (together with a fee based on Scale 2) to HM Land Registry who would note on the Charges Register that the charge had been varied (Land Registration Fees Order 2006).

The transferee will have already covenanted with the mortgagee in the original mortgage to repay the mortgage debt, and there is no need therefore for the transferee to covenant further; surprisingly some mortgagees do, however, require this. Regard must therefore be had to the practice of each mortgagee in circumstances of this nature. For instance, some mortgagees require that any borrower giving up a share of the property give a Declaration of Solvency (*see* Precedent 87, Ch.10). Regard must also be had to *Williams & Glyn's Bank Ltd v Boland* [1981] A.C. 487 and the necessity for any consents to mortgage from those in occupation (*see* p.63 and Precedent 6).

It will be appreciated that if the transfer is one of sale between the parties as part of the settlement, it can be advantageous for the purposes of stamp duty land tax, inheritance tax and land registry fees to recite the amount of the mortgage debt and also to have a valuer's report. For stamp duty land tax purposes, the consideration is increased to the extent that the transferor's mortgage liability is released although this is not relevant if the transaction falls within Sch.3 to the Finance Act 2003 (*see further* Ch.2).

6 Steps to be taken following the completion of the transfer

(a) Stamp duty land tax

4–12   A form SDLT 1 is required only if there has been a transfer on sale (e.g. Precedent 11). This is also the case where the consideration is less than the nil rate of £125,000 as a return must be made and a certificate issued by HMRC prior to registration.

Generally no stamp duty land tax will be payable unless the conveyance is one on sale (or taking over of a mortgage liability) not resulting from a court order or agreement made in connection with the termination of a marriage or civil partnership but a self-certificate in form SDLT 60 must be completed and submitted to HM Land Registry with the transferees application for registration (*see* Ch.2).

(b) Court order

4–13 In all cases a certified copy of the court order, should be delivered with the application to HM Land Registry for registration of the transfer.

(c) HM Land Registry fees

4–14 Where the transfer is one on sale, the fees are based on the amount of the consideration in accordance with Scale 1 Land Registration Fees Order 2006.

Where the transfer between the parties does not involve consideration then Scale 2 of the Land Registration Fees Order 2006 applies: the fee is payable on the value of the share disposed of.

If the land is unregistered and the transfer is subject to compulsorily first registration pursuant to the Land Registration Act 2002 the fee will be payable on Scale 1 even where it would otherwise qualify for a reduced fee under Scale 2. In this case, as with a Scale 2 transfer, the fee is payable on the value of the land concerned.

The value of the land may be evidenced by a statement from the solicitors lodging the application, which should specify the value of the property transferred. In practice this is either a letter or a statement of value on HM Land Registry Form AP1 or FR1 as appropriate.

(d) Insurance

4–15 Insurance of the property should be placed in the name of the transferee alone, the transferor's name being deleted from the policy. Otherwise, in the event of a claim the insurance company may insist on receiving the signature of both parties before monies are paid out, and the transferor's whereabouts at that time may not be known. Mortgagees should be reminded accordingly.

(e) Leasehold

4–16 The requirements of the lease as to registration of any assignment with the lessor should be observed.

As stated in Ch.3, if the lessor is owned by a company the shares in which are vested in the lessees then it will be necessary to have these transferred from joint names into the sole name of the transferee. A stock transfer form should be prepared and sent to the transferor's solicitors with the transfer. The transferee's solicitors should receive, following completion, the transfer, the deeds, the stock transfer form and the original share certificate.

Any such stock transfer form will need to be sent to the local stamp office as it attracts a fixed duty of £5.00.

PRECEDENTS

A—Notice of severance by one party to the other severing joint tenancy

Precedent 7—Unregistered Land

I HEREBY GIVE YOU NOTICE severing our joint tenancy in equity of and in [*address of the family home preferably a description from the title deeds*] now held by yourself and myself as joint tenants both at law and in equity and henceforth the property shall be held by us as tenants in common in equity [in (equal) shares] AND I REQUEST you to acknowledge receipt of this Notice by signing and returning the Duplicate Notice enclosed herewith
Dated [*Signature of severing party*]
Duplicate
 I acknowledge receipt of this Notice of Severance of which the above is a duplicate.
Dated [*Signature of other joint owner*]

Precedent 8—Unregistered Land

Memorandum of Severance (endorsed on last conveyance)
By a Notice of Severance dated
Addressed by the within named [*severing party*] to the within named [*other joint owner*] the beneficial joint tenancy herein created was severed.

Precedent 9—Registered Land

 Application to enter a restriction use Form RX1 and ask for the following restriction to be entered:
Date we [*husband*] of and [*wife*] of apply to the Registrar to enter the following restriction against the title above referred to:

Restriction: No disposition by one proprietor of the land (being the survivor of joint proprietors and not being a trust corporation) under which capital money arises is to be registered except under an Order of the Registrar or of the Court.
SIGNED *etc* [*both parties*]

B—Transfer by one party as joint tenant to the other joint tenant. No mortgage. By order of court

Transfer of whole of registered title(s)

PRECEDENT 10

Land Registry

TR1

If you need more room than is provided for in a panel, use continuation sheet CS and attach to this form.

1.	**Stamp Duty**

Place "X" in the appropriate box or boxes and complete the appropriate certificate.

☐ It is certified that this instrument falls within category ☐ in the Schedule to the Stamp Duty (Exempt Instruments) Regulations 1987

☐ It is certified that the transaction effected does not form part of a larger transaction or of a series of transactions in respect of which the amount or value or the aggregate amount or value of the consideration exceeds the sum of £

☐ It is certified that this is an instrument on which stamp duty is not chargeable by virtue of the provisions of section 92 of the Finance Act 2001

2. **Title Number(s) of the Property** *Leave blank if not yet registered.*
[TITLE NUMBER] [OR LEAVE BLANK IF APPLYING FOR FIRST REGISTRATION]

3. **Property**
[ADDRESS]

4. **Date**

5. **Transferor** *Give full names and company's registered number if any.*
[BOTH PARTIES]

6. **Transferee for entry on the register** *Give full name(s) and company's registered number, if any. For Scottish companies use an SC prefix and for limited liability partnerships use an OC prefix before the registered number, if any. For foreign companies give territory in which incorporated.*

[TRANSFEREE]

Unless otherwise arranged with Land Registry headquarters, a certified copy of the Transferee's constitution (in English or Welsh) will be required if it is a body corporate but is not a company registered in England and Wales or Scotland under the Companies Acts.

7. **Transferee's intended address(es) for service (including postcode) for entry on the register** *You may give up to three addresses for service one of which must be a postal address but does not have to be within the UK. The other addresses can be any combination of a postal address, a box number at a UK document exchange or an electronic address.*

[TRANSFEREE'S ADDRESS] (this will usually be the address of the property)

8. **The Transferor transfers the Property to the Transferee**

9. **Consideration** *Place "X" in the appropriate box. State clearly the currency unit if other than sterling. If none of the boxes applies, insert an appropriate memorandum in the additional provisions panel.*

☐ The Transferor has received from the Transferee for the Property the sum of *In words and figures.*

☐ *Insert other receipt as appropriate.* (See panel 12 below)

☐ The transfer is not for money or anything which has a monetary value

10. The Transferor transfers with *Place "X" in the appropriate box and add any modifications.*

    ☐ ☒ full title guarantee ☐ ☐ limited title guarantee

11. Declaration of trust *Where there is more than one Transferee, place "X" in the appropriate box.*

    ☐ The Transferees are to hold the Property on trust for themselves as joint tenants

    ☐ The Transferees are to hold the Property on trust for themselves as tenants in common in equal shares

    ☐ The Transferees are to hold the Property *Complete as necessary.*

12. Additional provisions *Insert here any required or permitted statements, certificates or applications and any agreed covenants, declarations, etc.*

    12.1 The transfer is made pursuant to an order of the [ ] County Court dated [   ] in proceedings between [Transferor's name] and [Transferee's name] bearing number [   ]

    12.2 [Transferee's name] covenants with [Transferor's name] that [Transferee's name] will observe and perform the covenants and conditions referred to in the Charges Register so far as still subsisting and relating to the Property and will keep [Transferor's name] and [his or her] personal representatives effectually indemnified against all losses resulting from their non observance or breach.

    Note to clause 12.2 – This clause is only necessary when the parties entered into the original restrictions affecting the property (if any) or, in the conveyance to them, covenanted to observe them. Otherwise the Transferor is not entitled to them.

13. Execution *The Transferor must execute this transfer as a deed using the space below. If there is more than one Transferor, all must execute. Forms of execution are given in Schedule 9 to the Land Registration Rules 2003. If the transfer contains Transferee's covenants or declarations or contains an application by the Transferee (e.g. for a restriction), it must also be executed by the Transferee (all of them, if there is more than one).*

    SIGNED as a DEED by (enter full name of individual) in the presence of: [TRANSFEROR]

    Signature of Witness ……………………………………………………..
    Name (in BLOCK CAPITALS) …………………………………………
    Address ………………………………………………………………….

    SIGNED as a DEED by (enter full name of individual) in the presence of: [TRANSFEREE]

    Signature of Witness ……………………………………………………..
    Name (in BLOCK CAPITALS) …………………………………………
    Address ………………………………………………………………….

HOME IN JOINT NAMES TRANSFER TO SOLE NAME 99

C—Transfer by one joint tenant to the other joint tenant. Sale. No mortgage

Transfer of whole of registered title(s)

Land Registry

PRECEDENT 11

TR1

If you need more room than is provided for in a panel, use continuation sheet CS and attach to this form.

1. Stamp Duty

    Place "X" in the appropriate box or boxes and complete the appropriate certificate.

    ☐ It is certified that this instrument falls within category ☐ in the Schedule to the Stamp Duty (Exempt Instruments) Regulations 1987

    ☐ It is certified that the transaction effected does not form part of a larger transaction or of a series of transactions in respect of which the amount or value or the aggregate amount or value of the consideration exceeds the sum of ☐ (as appropriate)

    ☐ It is certified that this is an instrument on which stamp duty is not chargeable by virtue of the provisions of section 92 of the Finance Act 2001

2. Title Number(s) of the Property *Leave blank if not yet registered.*
[TITLE NUMBER] [OR LEAVE BLANK IF APPLYING FOR FIRST REGISTRATION]

3. Property

[ADDRESS]

4. Date

5. Transferor *Give full names and company's registered number if any.*
[BOTH PARTIES]

6. Transferee for entry on the register *Give full name(s) and company's registered number, if any. For Scottish companies use an SC prefix and for limited liability partnerships use an OC prefix before the registered number, if any. For foreign companies give territory in which incorporated.*

[TRANSFEREE]

Unless otherwise arranged with Land Registry headquarters, a certified copy of the Transferee's constitution (in English or Welsh) will be required if it is a body corporate but is not a company registered in England and Wales or Scotland under the Companies Acts.

7. Transferee's intended address(es) for service (including postcode) for entry on the register *You may give up to three addresses for service **one** of which **must** be a postal address but does not have to be within the UK. The other addresses can be any combination of a postal address, a box number at a UK document exchange or an electronic address.*

[TRANSFEREE'S ADDRESS] (this will usually be the address of the property)

8. The Transferor transfers the Property to the Transferee

9. Consideration *Place "X" in the appropriate box. State clearly the currency unit if other than sterling. If none of the boxes applies, insert an appropriate memorandum in the additional provisions panel.*

    ☐ The Transferor has received from the Transferee for the Property the sum of *In words and figures.*

    ☐ [AMOUNT OF CONSIDERATION IN WORDS AND NUMBERS]

    ☐ *Insert other receipt as appropriate.* (See panel 12 below)

    ☐ The transfer is not for money or anything which has a monetary value

10. The Transferor transfers with *Place "X" in the appropriate box and add any modifications.*

    ☐ ☒ full title guarantee ☐ ☐ limited title guarantee

11. Declaration of trust *Where there is more than one Transferee, place "X" in the appropriate box.*

    ☐ The Transferees are to hold the Property on trust for themselves as joint tenants

    ☐ The Transferees are to hold the Property on trust for themselves as tenants in common in equal shares

    ☐ The Transferees are to hold the Property *Complete as necessary.*

12. Additional provisions *Insert here any required or permitted statements, certificates or applications and any agreed covenants, declarations, etc.*

    12.1 [Transferee's name] covenants with [Transferor's name] that [Transferee's name] will observe and perform the covenants and conditions referred to in the Charges Register so far as still subsisting and relating to the Property and will keep [Transferor's name] and [his or her] personal representatives effectually indemnified against all losses resulting from their non observance or breach.

    Note to clause 12.1 – This clause is only necessary when the parties entered into the original restrictions affecting the property (if any) or, in the conveyance to them, covenanted to observe them. Otherwise the Transferor is not entitled to them.

13. Execution *The Transferor must execute this transfer as a deed using the space below. If there is more than one Transferor, all must execute. Forms of execution are given in Schedule 9 to the Land Registration Rules 2003. If the transfer contains Transferee's covenants or declarations or contains an application by the Transferee (e.g. for a restriction), it must also be executed by the Transferee (all of them, if there is more than one).*

    SIGNED as a DEED by (enter full name of individual) in the presence of: [TRANSFEROR]

    Signature of Witness ....
    Name (in BLOCK CAPITALS) ....
    Address ....

    SIGNED as a DEED by (enter full name of individual) in the presence of: [TRANSFEREE]

    Signature of Witness ....
    Name (in BLOCK CAPITALS) ....
    Address ....

HOME IN JOINT NAMES TRANSFER TO SOLE NAME   101

D—Transfer by one joint tenant to the other joint tenant by order of court. Mortgage. Transferor released

Transfer of whole of registered title(s)

Land Registry

TR1

PRECEDENT 12

If you need more room than is provided for in a panel, use continuation sheet CS and attach to this form.

1.	**Stamp Duty**

Place "X" in the appropriate box or boxes and complete the appropriate certificate.

☐ It is certified that this instrument falls within category ☐ in the Schedule to the Stamp Duty (Exempt Instruments) Regulations 1987

☐ It is certified that the transaction effected does not form part of a larger transaction or of a series of transactions in respect of which the <u>amount or value or the aggregate amount or value</u> of the consideration exceeds the sum of £ _____

☐ It is certified that this is an instrument on which stamp duty is not chargeable by virtue of the provisions of section 92 of the Finance Act 2001

2.	**Title Number(s) of the Property** *Leave blank if not yet registered.* [TITLE NUMBER] [OR LEAVE BLANK IF APPLYING FOR FIRST REGISTRATION]
3.	**Property** [ADDRESS]
4.	**Date**
5.	**Transferor** *Give full names and company's registered number if any.* [BOTH PARTIES]
6.	**Transferee for entry on the register** *Give full name(s) and company's registered number, if any. For Scottish companies use an SC prefix and for limited liability partnerships use an OC prefix before the registered number, if any. For foreign companies give territory in which incorporated.* [TRANSFEREE] *Unless otherwise arranged with Land Registry headquarters, a certified copy of the Transferee's constitution (in English or Welsh) will be required if it is a body corporate but is not a company registered in England and Wales or Scotland under the Companies Acts.*
7.	**Transferee's intended address(es) for service (including postcode) for entry on the register** *You may give up to three addresses for service **one** of which **must** be a postal address but does not have to be within the UK. The other addresses can be any combination of a postal address, a box number at a UK document exchange or an electronic address.* [TRANSFEREE'S ADDRESS] (this will usually be the address of the property)
8.	**The Transferor transfers the Property to the Transferee**
9.	**Consideration** *Place "X" in the appropriate box. State clearly the currency unit if other than sterling. If none of the boxes applies, insert an appropriate memorandum in the additional provisions panel.* ☐ The Transferor has received from the Transferee for the Property the sum of *In words and figures.* ☐ *Insert other receipt as appropriate.* (See panel 12 below) ☐ The transfer is not for money or anything which has a monetary value

10. The Transferor transfers with *Place "X" in the appropriate box and add any modifications.*

    ☐ ☒   full title guarantee ☐   ☐   limited title guarantee

11. Declaration of trust *Where there is more than one Transferee, place "X" in the appropriate box.*

    ☐ The Transferees are to hold the Property on trust for themselves as joint tenants

    ☐ The Transferees are to hold the Property on trust for themselves as tenants in common in equal shares

    ☐ The Transferees are to hold the Property *Complete as necessary.*

12. Additional provisions *Insert here any required or permitted statements, certificates or applications and any agreed covenants, declarations, etc.*

    12.1 The transfer is made pursuant to an order of the [ ] County Court dated [   ] in proceedings between [Transferor's name] and [Transferee's name] bearing number [   ]

    Refer to continuation sheet (CS)

13. Execution *The Transferor must execute this transfer as a deed using the space below. If there is more than one Transferor, all must execute. Forms of execution are given in Schedule 9 to the Land Registration Rules 2003. If the transfer contains Transferee's covenants or declarations or contains an application by the Transferee (e.g. for a restriction), it must also be executed by the Transferee (all of them, if there is more than one).*

    SIGNED as a DEED by (enter full name of individual) in the presence of: [TRANSFEROR]

    Signature of Witness ……………………………………………….
    Name (in BLOCK CAPITALS) ……………………………………
    Address ……………………………………………………………..

    SIGNED as a DEED by (enter full name of individual) in the presence of: [TRANSFEREE]

    Signature of Witness ……………………………………………….
    Name (in BLOCK CAPITALS) ……………………………………
    Address ……………………………………………………………..

Continuation sheet for use with application and disposition forms

Land Registry

CS

1. Continued from Form [TR1]   Title number(s) [TITLE NUMBER]

2. *Before each continuation, state panel to be continued, e.g. "Panel 12 continued".*

   Panel 12 continued

   12.2 [Transferee's name] covenants with [Transferor's name] that [Transferee's name] will observe and perform the covenants and conditions referred to in the Charges Register so far as still subsisting and relating to the Property and will keep [Transferor's name] and [his or her] personal representatives effectually indemnified against all losses resulting from their non observance or breach.

   Note to clause 12.2 – This clause is only necessary where the parties entered into the original restrictions affecting the property (if any) or, in the conveyance to them, covenanted to observe them. Otherwise the Transferor is not entitled to them.

   12.3 The Property is transferred subject to the charge (the registered charge) dated [   ] and registered on [ ] [under which there is now owing the sum of £   ].

   12.4 The [Bank or Building Society] (the lender) being the proprietor of the registered charge hereby releases and discharges [Transferor's name] from all obligations under the registered charge.

   Panel 13 continued

   SIGNED on behalf of

   [the Lender]

   Authorised Signatory

Continuation sheet [1] of [1]
Insert sheet number and total number of continuation sheets e.g. "sheet 1 of 3".
© Crown copyright (ref: LR/HQ/CD-ROM) 6/03

E—Leasehold—assignment by one joint tenant to the other joint tenant by order of the court. Mortgage. Transferor released

Transfer of whole of registered title(s)

PRECEDENT 13

Land Registry

TR1

If you need more room than is provided for in a panel, use continuation sheet CS and attach to this form.

1.	**Stamp Duty**
	Place "X" in the appropriate box or boxes and complete the appropriate certificate.
	☐ It is certified that this instrument falls within category ☐ in the Schedule to the Stamp Duty (Exempt Instruments) Regulations 1987
	☐ It is certified that the transaction effected does not form part of a larger transaction or of a series of transactions in respect of which the <u>amount or value or the aggregate amount or value</u> of the consideration exceeds the sum of £ ☐
	☐ It is certified that this is an instrument on which stamp duty is not chargeable by virtue of the provisions of section 92 of the Finance Act 2001
2.	**Title Number(s) of the Property** *Leave blank if not yet registered.* [TITLE NUMBER] [OR LEAVE BLANK IF APPLYING FOR FIRST REGISTRATION]
3.	**Property** [ADDRESS]
4.	**Date**
5.	**Transferor** *Give full names and company's registered number if any.* [BOTH PARTIES]
6.	**Transferee for entry on the register** *Give full name(s) and company's registered number, if any. For Scottish companies use an SC prefix and for limited liability partnerships use an OC prefix before the registered number, if any. For foreign companies give territory in which incorporated.* [TRANSFEREE] *Unless otherwise arranged with Land Registry headquarters, a certified copy of the Transferee's constitution (in English or Welsh) will be required if it is a body corporate but is not a company registered in England and Wales or Scotland under the Companies Acts.*
7.	**Transferee's intended address(es) for service (including postcode) for entry on the register** *You may give up to three addresses for service **one** of which **must** be a postal address but does not have to be within the UK. The other addresses can be any combination of a postal address, a box number at a UK document exchange or an electronic address.* [TRANSFEREE'S ADDRESS] (this will usually be the address of the property)
8.	**The Transferor transfers the Property to the Transferee**
9.	**Consideration** *Place "X" in the appropriate box. State clearly the currency unit if other than sterling. If none of the boxes applies, insert an appropriate memorandum in the additional provisions panel.* ☐ The Transferor has received from the Transferee for the Property the sum of *In words and figures.* ☐ *Insert other receipt as appropriate.* (See panel 12 below) ☐ The transfer is not for money or anything which has a monetary value

HOME IN JOINT NAMES TRANSFER TO SOLE NAME

10. The Transferor transfers with *Place "X" in the appropriate box and add any modifications.*

    ☐ ☒ full title guarantee ☐   ☐ limited title guarantee

11. Declaration of trust *Where there is more than one Transferee, place "X" in the appropriate box.*

    ☐ The Transferees are to hold the Property on trust for themselves as joint tenants

    ☐ The Transferees are to hold the Property on trust for themselves as tenants in common in equal shares

    ☐ The Transferees are to hold the Property *Complete as necessary.*

12. Additional provisions *Insert here any required or permitted statements, certificates or applications and any agreed covenants, declarations, etc.*

12.1 The transfer is made pursuant to an order of the [ ] County Court dated [   ] in proceedings between [Transferor's name] and [Transferee's name] bearing number [   ]

Refer to continuation sheet (CS)

13. Execution *The Transferor must execute this transfer as a deed using the space below. If there is more than one Transferor, all must execute. Forms of execution are given in Schedule 9 to the Land Registration Rules 2003. If the transfer contains Transferee's covenants or declarations or contains an application by the Transferee (e.g. for a restriction), it must also be executed by the Transferee (all of them, if there is more than one).*

SIGNED as a DEED by (enter full name of individual) in the presence of: |TRANSFEROR|

Signature of Witness ……………………………………………..
Name (in BLOCK CAPITALS) …………………………………….
Address ………………………………………………………..

SIGNED as a DEED by (enter full name of individual) in the presence of: |TRANSFEREE|

Signature of Witness ……………………………………………..
Name (in BLOCK CAPITALS) …………………………………….
Address ………………………………………………………..

Continuation sheet	**Land Registry**
for use with	
application and	**CS**
disposition forms	

| 1. Continued from Form | TR1 | Title number(s) | TITLE NUMBER |

2. *Before each continuation, state panel to be continued, e.g. "Panel 12 continued".*

Panel 12 continued

12.2   [Transferee's name] covenants with [Transferor's name] that [Transferee's name] will observe and perform the covenants and conditions referred to in the Charges Register so far as still subsisting and relating to the Property and will keep [Transferor's name] and [his or her] personal representatives effectually indemnified against all losses resulting from their non observance or breach.

       Note to clause 12.2 – This clause is only necessary where the parties entered into the original restrictions affecting the property (if any) or, in the conveyance to them, covenanted to observe them. Otherwise the Transferor is not entitled to them.

12.3   The covenant by the Transferor implied by section 4(1)(b) Law of Property (Miscellaneous Provisions) Act 1994 by reason of the Transferor transferring with Full Title Guarantee shall be limited so as not to extend to any breach of the terms of the registered lease on the part of the Transferor relating to the condition of the Property [Limitation of Transferor's Liability in relation to repair: see p.6].

12.4   The Property is transferred subject to the charge ("the registered charge") dated [ ] and registered on [ ] [under which there is now owing the sum of £   ].

12.5   The [Bank or Building Society] ("the lender") being the proprietor of the registered charge hereby releases and discharges [Transferor's name] from all obligations under the registered charge.

12.6   [Transferee's name] covenants with [Transferor's name] in the terms set out in Part IX, Sch.2, Law of Property Act 1925.

       Note to clause 12.6 – Only necessary on an application for first registration when the lease was granted before January 1, 1996 – "an old tenancy" (see p.57).

Panel 13 continued

SIGNED on behalf of

[the Lender]

                                               Authorised Signatory

HOME IN JOINT NAMES TRANSFER TO SOLE NAME   107

F—Transfer by one joint tenant to the other joint tenant. Sale. Mortgage. Transferor released

Transfer of whole of registered title(s)

Land Registry

TR1

PRECEDENT 14

If you need more room than is provided for in a panel, use continuation sheet CS and attach to this form.

1. **Stamp Duty**

    Place "X" in the appropriate box or boxes and complete the appropriate certificate.

    ☐ It is certified that this instrument falls within category ☐ in the Schedule to the Stamp Duty (Exempt Instruments) Regulations 1987

    ☐ It is certified that the transaction effected does not form part of a larger transaction or of a series of transactions in respect of which the amount or value or the aggregate amount or value of the consideration exceeds the sum of ☐☐☐☐☐ (as appropriate)

    ☐ It is certified that this is an instrument on which stamp duty is not chargeable by virtue of the provisions of section 92 of the Finance Act 2001

2. Title Number(s) of the Property *Leave blank if not yet registered.*
   [TITLE NUMBER] [OR LEAVE BLANK IF APPLYING FOR FIRST REGISTRATION]

3. Property

    [ADDRESS]

4. Date

5. Transferor *Give full names and company's registered number if any.*
   [BOTH PARTIES]

6. Transferee **for entry on the register** *Give full name(s) and company's registered number, if any. For Scottish companies use an SC prefix and for limited liability partnerships use an OC prefix before the registered number, if any. For foreign companies give territory in which incorporated.*

    [TRANSFEREE]

    Unless otherwise arranged with Land Registry headquarters, a certified copy of the Transferee's constitution (in English or Welsh) will be required if it is a body corporate but is not a company registered in England and Wales or Scotland under the Companies Acts.

7. Transferee's intended **address(es) for service (including postcode) for entry on the register** *You may give up to three addresses for service **one** of which **must** be a postal address but does not have to be within the UK. The other addresses can be any combination of a postal address, a box number at a UK document exchange or an electronic address.*

    [TRANSFEREE'S ADDRESS] (this will usually be the address of the property)

8. **The Transferor transfers the Property to the Transferee**

9. Consideration *Place "X" in the appropriate box. State clearly the currency unit if other than sterling. If none of the boxes applies, insert an appropriate memorandum in the additional provisions panel.*

    ☐ The Transferor has received from the Transferee for the Property the sum of *In words and figures.*
    ☐ [AMOUNT OF CONSIDERATION IN WORDS AND NUMBERS]

    ☐ *Insert other receipt as appropriate.* (See panel 12 below)

    ☐ The transfer is not for money or anything which has a monetary value

10.	The Transferor transfers with *Place "X" in the appropriate box and add any modifications.* ☐ ☒ full title guarantee ☐ ☐ limited title guarantee
11.	Declaration of trust *Where there is more than one Transferee, place "X" in the appropriate box.* ☐ The Transferees are to hold the Property on trust for themselves as joint tenants ☐ The Transferees are to hold the Property on trust for themselves as tenants in common in equal shares ☐ The Transferees are to hold the Property *Complete as necessary.*
12.	Additional provisions *Insert here any required or permitted statements, certificates or applications and any agreed covenants, declarations, etc.* 12.1 [Transferee's name] covenants with [Transferor's name] that [Transferee's name] will observe and perform the covenants and conditions referred to in the Charges Register so far as still subsisting and relating to the Property and will keep [Transferor's name] and [his or her] personal representatives effectually indemnified against all losses resulting from their non observance or breach. **Note to clause 12.1** – This clause is only necessary when the parties entered into the original restrictions affecting the property (if any) or, in the conveyance to them, covenanted to observe them. Otherwise the Transferor is not entitled to them. Refer to continuation sheet [CS]
13.	Execution *The Transferor must execute this transfer as a deed using the space below. If there is more than one Transferor, all must execute. Forms of execution are given in Schedule 9 to the Land Registration Rules 2003. If the transfer contains Transferee's covenants or declarations or contains an application by the Transferee (e.g. for a restriction), it must also be executed by the Transferee (all of them, if there is more than one).* SIGNED as a DEED by (enter full name of individual) in the presence of: [TRANSFEROR] Signature of Witness …………………………………………….. Name (in BLOCK CAPITALS) ……………………………………… Address ……………………………………………………………….. SIGNED as a DEED by (enter full name of individual) in the presence of: [TRANSFEREE] Signature of Witness …………………………………………….. Name (in BLOCK CAPITALS) ……………………………………… Address ………………………………………………………………..

Continuation sheet for use with application and disposition forms

Land Registry

CS

1. Continued from Form [TR1]   Title number(s) [TITLE NUMBER]

2. *Before each continuation, state panel to be continued, e.g. "Panel 12 continued".*

   Panel 12 continued

   12.2 The covenant by the Transferor implied by section 4(1)(b) Law of Property (Miscellaneous Provisions) Act 1994 by reason of the Transferor transferring with Full Title Guarantee shall be limited so as not to extend to any breach of the terms of the registered lease on the part of the Transferor relating to the condition of the Property [Limitation of Transferor's Liability in relation to repair: (see p.6)] (only required if leasehold).

   12.3 The Property is transferred subject to the charge ("the registered charge") dated [ ] and registered on [ ] [under which there is now owing the sum of £].

   12.5 The [Bank or Building Society] ("the lender") being the proprietor of the registered charge hereby releases and discharges [Transferor's name] from all obligations under the registered charge.

   Panel 13 continued

   SIGNED on behalf of

   [the Lender]

   Authorised Signatory

Continuation sheet [1] of [1]
Insert sheet number and total number of continuation sheets e.g. "sheet 1 of 3".
© Crown copyright (ref: LR/HQ/CD-ROM) 6/03

G—Leasehold assignment by one joint tenant to the other joint tenant. By agreement subject to mortgage. Transferor released

Transfer of whole of registered title(s)

PRECEDENT 15

Land Registry

TR1

If you need more room than is provided for in a panel, use continuation sheet CS and attach to this form.

1. **Stamp Duty**

   Place "X" in the appropriate box or boxes and complete the appropriate certificate.

   ☐ It is certified that this instrument falls within category ☐ in the Schedule to the Stamp Duty (Exempt Instruments) Regulations 1987

   ☐ It is certified that the transaction effected does not form part of a larger transaction or of a series of transactions in respect of which the amount or value or the aggregate amount or value of the consideration exceeds the sum of £

   ☐ It is certified that this is an instrument on which stamp duty is not chargeable by virtue of the provisions of section 92 of the Finance Act 2001

2. Title Number(s) of the Property *Leave blank if not yet registered.*
   [TITLE NUMBER] [OR LEAVE BLANK IF APPLYING FOR FIRST REGISTRATION]

3. Property
   [ADDRESS]

4. Date

5. Transferor *Give full names and company's registered number if any.*
   [BOTH PARTIES]

6. Transferee **for entry on the register** *Give full name(s) and company's registered number, if any. For Scottish companies use an SC prefix and for limited liability partnerships use an OC prefix before the registered number, if any. For foreign companies give territory in which incorporated.*
   [TRANSFEREE]

   Unless otherwise arranged with Land Registry headquarters, a certified copy of the Transferee's constitution (in English or Welsh) will be required if it is a body corporate but is not a company registered in England and Wales or Scotland under the Companies Acts.

7. Transferee's intended **address(es) for service (including postcode) for entry on the register** *You may give up to three addresses for service **one** of which **must** be a postal address but does not have to be within the UK. The other addresses can be any combination of a postal address, a box number at a UK document exchange or an electronic address.*
   [TRANSFEREE'S ADDRESS] (this will usually be the address of the property)

8. The Transferor transfers the Property to the Transferee

9. Consideration *Place "X" in the appropriate box. State clearly the currency unit if other than sterling. If none of the boxes applies, insert an appropriate memorandum in the additional provisions panel.*

   ☐ The Transferor has received from the Transferee for the Property the sum of *In words and figures.*

   ☐ *Insert other receipt as appropriate.* (See panel 12 below)

   ☐ The transfer is not for money or anything which has a monetary value

HOME IN JOINT NAMES TRANSFER TO SOLE NAME

10. The Transferor transfers with *Place "X" in the appropriate box and add any modifications.*

    ☐ ☒ full title guarantee ☐ ☐ limited title guarantee

11. Declaration of trust *Where there is more than one Transferee, place "X" in the appropriate box.*

    ☐ The Transferees are to hold the Property on trust for themselves as joint tenants
    ☐ The Transferees are to hold the Property on trust for themselves as tenants in common in equal shares
    ☐ The Transferees are to hold the Property *Complete as necessary.*

12. Additional provisions *Insert here any required or permitted statements, certificates or applications and any agreed covenants, declarations, etc.*

    12.1 This transfer is made pursuant to an agreement between the parties

    Refer to continuation sheet (CS)

13. Execution *The Transferor must execute this transfer as a deed using the space below. If there is more than one Transferor, all must execute. Forms of execution are given in Schedule 9 to the Land Registration Rules 2003. If the transfer contains Transferee's covenants or declarations or contains an application by the Transferee (e.g. for a restriction), it must also be executed by the Transferee (all of them, if there is more than one).*

    SIGNED as a DEED by (enter full name of individual) in the presence of: [TRANSFEROR]

    Signature of Witness …………………………………………………..
    Name (in BLOCK CAPITALS) ……………………………………….
    Address ……………………………………………………………..

    SIGNED as a DEED by (enter full name of individual) in the presence of: [TRANSFEREE]

    Signature of Witness …………………………………………………..
    Name (in BLOCK CAPITALS) ……………………………………….
    Address ……………………………………………………………..

Continuation sheet for use with application and disposition forms

Land Registry

CS

1. Continued from Form [TR1]   Title number(s) [TITLE NUMBER]

2. *Before each continuation, state panel to be continued, e.g. "Panel 12 continued".*

Panel 12 continued

12.2 [Transferee's name] covenants with [Transferor's name] that [Transferee's name] will observe and perform the covenants and conditions referred to in the Charges Register so far as still subsisting and relating to the Property and will keep [Transferor's name] and [his or her] personal representatives effectually indemnified against all losses resulting from their non observance or breach.

Note to clause 12.2 – This clause is only necessary when the parties entered into the original restrictions affecting the property (if any) or, in the conveyance to them, covenanted to observe them. Otherwise the Transferor is not entitled to them.

12.3 The covenant by the Transferor implied by section 4(1)(b) Law of Property (Miscellaneous Provisions) Act 1994 by reason of the Transferor transferring with Full Title Guarantee shall be limited so as not to extend to any breach of the terms of the registered lease on the part of the Transferor relating to the condition of the Property [Limitation of Transferor's Liability in relation to repair: (see p.6)].

12.4 The Property is transferred subject to the charge ("the registered charge") dated [ ] and registered on [ ] [under which there is now owing the sum of £   ].

12.5 The [Bank or Building Society] ("the lender") being the proprietor of the registered charge hereby releases and discharges [Transferor's name] from all obligations under the registered charge.

12.6 The Transferee covenants with the Transferor in the terms set out in Part IX, Sch.2, Law of Property Act 1925.

Note to clause 12.6 – Only necessary on an application for first registration when the lease was granted before January 1, 1996 – ("an old tenancy") (see p.62).

Panel 13 continued

SIGNED on behalf of

[the Lender]

Authorised Signatory

H—Transfer by one joint tenant to the other joint tenant by order of the court. Transferor not released but transferee indemnifying. Mortgagee not a party (*see* p.93 and 94)

Transfer of whole of registered title(s)

PRECEDENT 16

Land Registry

TR1

If you need more room than is provided for in a panel, use continuation sheet CS and attach to this form.

1. Stamp Duty

   Place "X" in the appropriate box or boxes and complete the appropriate certificate.

   ☐ It is certified that this instrument falls within category ☐ in the Schedule to the Stamp Duty (Exempt Instruments) Regulations 1987

   ☐ It is certified that the transaction effected does not form part of a larger transaction or of a series of transactions in respect of which the amount or value or the aggregate amount or value of the consideration exceeds the sum of £ _____

   ☐ It is certified that this is an instrument on which stamp duty is not chargeable by virtue of the provisions of section 92 of the Finance Act 2001

2. Title Number(s) of the Property *Leave blank if not yet registered.*
   [TITLE NUMBER] [OR LEAVE BLANK IF APPLYING FOR FIRST REGISTRATION]

3. Property

   [ADDRESS]

4. Date

5. Transferor *Give full names and company's registered number if any.*

   [BOTH PARTIES]

6. Transferee **for entry on the register** *Give full name(s) and company's registered number, if any. For Scottish companies use an SC prefix and for limited liability partnerships use an OC prefix before the registered number, if any. For foreign companies give territory in which incorporated.*

   [TRANSFEREE]

   Unless otherwise arranged with Land Registry headquarters, a certified copy of the Transferee's constitution (in English or Welsh) will be required if it is a body corporate but is not a company registered in England and Wales or Scotland under the Companies Acts.

7. Transferee's intended **address(es) for service (including postcode) for entry on the register** *You may give up to three addresses for service **one** of which **must** be a postal address but does not have to be within the UK. The other addresses can be any combination of a postal address, a box number at a UK document exchange or an electronic address.*

   [TRANSFEREE'S ADDRESS] (this will usually be the address of the property)

8. **The Transferor transfers the Property to the Transferee**

9. Consideration *Place "X" in the appropriate box. State clearly the currency unit if other than sterling. If none of the boxes applies, insert an appropriate memorandum in the additional provisions panel.*

   ☐ The Transferor has received from the Transferee for the Property the sum of *In words and figures.*

   ☐ *Insert other receipt as appropriate.* (See panel 12 below)

   ☐ The transfer is not for money or anything which has a monetary value

10. The Transferor transfers with *Place "X" in the appropriate box and add any modifications.*

    ☐ ☒ full title guarantee ☐ ☐ limited title guarantee

11. Declaration of trust *Where there is more than one Transferee, place "X" in the appropriate box.*

    ☐ The Transferees are to hold the Property on trust for themselves as joint tenants

    ☐ The Transferees are to hold the Property on trust for themselves as tenants in common in equal shares

    ☐ The Transferees are to hold the Property *Complete as necessary.*

12. Additional provisions *Insert here any required or permitted statements, certificates or applications and any agreed covenants, declarations, etc.*

    12.1 The transfer is made pursuant to an order of the [ ] County Court dated [   ] in proceedings between [Transferor's name] and [Transferee's name] bearing number [   ]

    Refer to continuation sheet (CS)

13. Execution *The Transferor must execute this transfer as a deed using the space below. If there is more than one Transferor, all must execute. Forms of execution are given in Schedule 9 to the Land Registration Rules 2003. If the transfer contains Transferee's covenants or declarations or contains an application by the Transferee (e.g. for a restriction), it must also be executed by the Transferee (all of them, if there is more than one).*

    SIGNED as a DEED by (enter full name of individual) in the presence of: [TRANSFEROR]

    Signature of Witness …………………………………………………..
    Name (in BLOCK CAPITALS) …………………………………………..
    Address ……………………………………………………………………..

    SIGNED as a DEED by (enter full name of individual) in the presence of: [TRANSFEREE]

    Signature of Witness …………………………………………………..
    Name (in BLOCK CAPITALS) …………………………………………..
    Address ……………………………………………………………………..

**Continuation sheet
for use with
application and
disposition forms**

Land Registry

CS

| 1. | Continued from Form | TR1 | Title number(s) | TITLE NUMBER |

2. *Before each continuation, state panel to be continued, e.g. "Panel 12 continued".*

Panel 12 continued

12.2 [Transferee's name] covenants with [Transferor's name] that [Transferee's name] will observe and perform the covenants and conditions referred to in the Charges Register so far as still subsisting and relating to the Property and will keep [Transferor's name] and [his or her] personal representatives effectually indemnified against all losses resulting from their non observance or breach.

Note to clause 12.2 – This clause is only necessary where the parties entered into the original restrictions affecting the property (if any) or, in the conveyance to them, covenanted to observe them. Otherwise the Transferor is not entitled to them.

12.3 The covenant by the Transferor implied by section 4(1)(b) Law of Property (Miscellaneous Provisions) Act 1994 by reason of the Transferor transferring with Full Title Guarantee shall be limited so as not to extend to any breach of the terms of the registered lease on the part of the Transferor relating to the condition of the Property [Limitation of Transferor's Liability in relation to repair: see p.6] (only required if leasehold).

12.4 With effect from the date hereof [or other date if appropriate] [Transferee's name] covenants with [Transferor's name] that [Transferee's name] will pay and discharge all principal monies, interest, costs and other monies secured by or to become payable under the Registered Charge and will comply with the covenants in the Registered Charge and will at all times indemnify and keep indemnified [Transferor's name] and his estate and effects against all proceedings, costs, claims and demands whatsoever and [Transferor's name] and [Transferee's name] apply to the Registrar pursuant to the Land Registration Rules 2003 to note this covenant on the register.

Continuation sheet 1 of 1
*Insert sheet number and total number of
continuation sheets e.g. "sheet 1 of 3".*
© Crown copyright (ref: LR/HQ/CD-ROM) 6/03

I—Transfer by one party to the other. Sale of transferor's share in the family home held by them as tenants in common in equal shares. No mortgage

Transfer of whole of registered title(s)

Land Registry

TR1

PRECEDENT 17

If you need more room than is provided for in a panel, use continuation sheet CS and attach to this form.

1. **Stamp Duty**

    Place "X" in the appropriate box or boxes and complete the appropriate certificate.

    ☐ It is certified that this instrument falls within category [ ] in the Schedule to the Stamp Duty (Exempt Instruments) Regulations 1987

    ☐ It is certified that the transaction effected does not form part of a larger transaction or of a series of transactions in respect of which the amount or value or the aggregate amount or value of the consideration exceeds the sum of [   ] (as appropriate)

    ☐ It is certified that this is an instrument on which stamp duty is not chargeable by virtue of the provisions of section 92 of the Finance Act 2001

2. **Title Number(s) of the Property** *Leave blank if not yet registered.*
    [TITLE NUMBER] [OR LEAVE BLANK IF APPLYING FOR FIRST REGISTRATION]

3. **Property**

    [ADDRESS]

4. **Date**

5. **Transferor** *Give full names and company's registered number if any.*
    [BOTH PARTIES]

6. **Transferee for entry on the register** *Give full name(s) and company's registered number, if any. For Scottish companies use an SC prefix and for limited liability partnerships use an OC prefix before the registered number, if any. For foreign companies give territory in which incorporated.*

    [TRANSFEREE]

    Unless otherwise arranged with Land Registry headquarters, a certified copy of the Transferee's constitution (in English or Welsh) will be required if it is a body corporate but is not a company registered in England and Wales or Scotland under the Companies Acts.

7. **Transferee's intended address(es) for service (including postcode) for entry on the register** *You may give up to three addresses for service one of which must be a postal address but does not have to be within the UK. The other addresses can be any combination of a postal address, a box number at a UK document exchange or an electronic address.*

    [TRANSFEREE'S ADDRESS] (this will usually be the address of the property)

8. **The Transferor transfers the Property to the Transferee**

9. **Consideration** *Place "X" in the appropriate box. State clearly the currency unit if other than sterling. If none of the boxes applies, insert an appropriate memorandum in the additional provisions panel.*

    ☐ The Transferor has received from the Transferee for the Property the sum of *In words and figures.*

    ☐ [AMOUNT OF CONSIDERATION IN WORDS AND NUMBERS]

    ☐ *Insert other receipt as appropriate.* (See panel 12 below)

    ☐ The transfer is not for money or anything which has a monetary value

HOME IN JOINT NAMES TRANSFER TO SOLE NAME

10. The Transferor transfers with *Place "X" in the appropriate box and add any modifications.*

☐ ☒ full title guarantee ☐ ☐ limited title guarantee

11. Declaration of trust *Where there is more than one Transferee, place "X" in the appropriate box.*

☐ The Transferees are to hold the Property on trust for themselves as joint tenants

☐ The Transferees are to hold the Property on trust for themselves as tenants in common in equal shares

☐ The Transferees are to hold the Property *Complete as necessary.*

12. Additional provisions *Insert here any required or permitted statements, certificates or applications and any agreed covenants, declarations, etc.*

12.1 [Transferee's name] covenants with [Transferor's name] that [Transferee's name] will observe and perform the covenants and conditions referred to in the Charges Register so far as still subsisting and relating to the Property and will keep [Transferor's name] and [his or her] personal representatives effectually indemnified against all losses resulting from their non observance or breach.

Note to clause 12.1 – This clause is only necessary when the parties entered into the original restrictions affecting the property (if any) or, in the conveyance to them, covenanted to observe them. Otherwise the transferor is not entitled to them.

Refer to continuation sheet [CS]

13. Execution *The Transferor must execute this transfer as a deed using the space below. If there is more than one Transferor, all must execute. Forms of execution are given in Schedule 9 to the Land Registration Rules 2003. If the transfer contains Transferee's covenants or declarations or contains an application by the Transferee (e.g. for a restriction), it must also be executed by the Transferee (all of them, if there is more than one).*

SIGNED as a DEED by (enter full name of individual) in the presence of: [TRANSFEROR]

Signature of Witness ……………………………………………..
Name (in BLOCK CAPITALS) ……………………………………
Address ……………………………………………………………..

SIGNED as a DEED by (enter full name of individual) in the presence of: [TRANSFEREE]

Signature of Witness ……………………………………………..
Name (in BLOCK CAPITALS) ……………………………………
Address ……………………………………………………………..

Continuation sheet for use with application and disposition forms	**Land Registry** **CS**
1. Continued from Form TR1	Title number(s) TITLE NUMBER

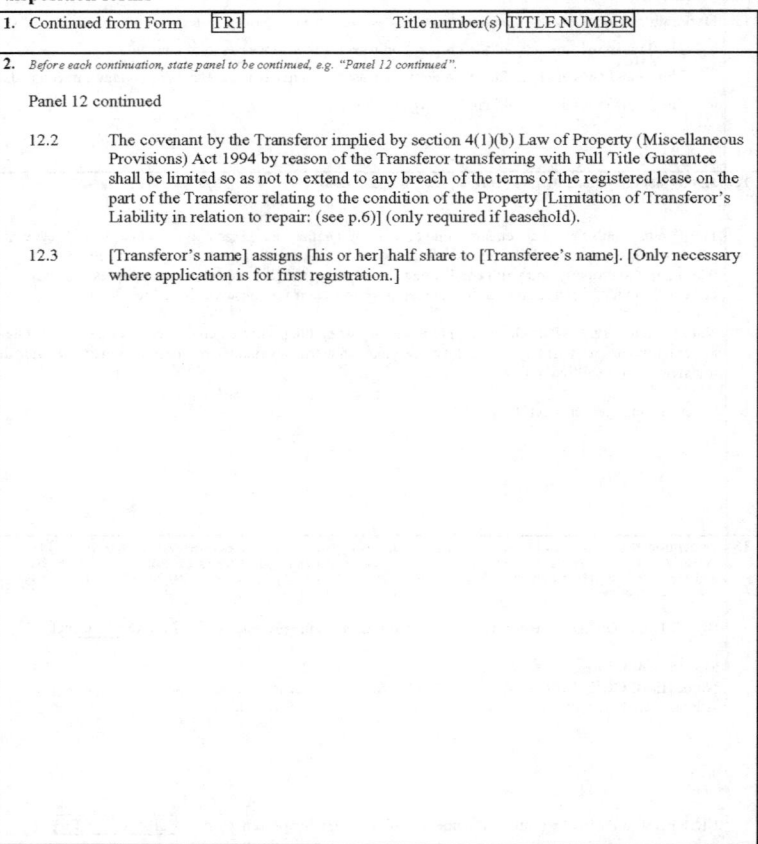

2. *Before each continuation, state panel to be continued, e.g. "Panel 12 continued".*

Panel 12 continued

12.2 The covenant by the Transferor implied by section 4(1)(b) Law of Property (Miscellaneous Provisions) Act 1994 by reason of the Transferor transferring with Full Title Guarantee shall be limited so as not to extend to any breach of the terms of the registered lease on the part of the Transferor relating to the condition of the Property [Limitation of Transferor's Liability in relation to repair: (see p.6)] (only required if leasehold).

12.3 [Transferor's name] assigns [his or her] half share to [Transferee's name]. [Only necessary where application is for first registration.]

Continuation sheet 1 of 1
Insert sheet number and total number of continuation sheets e.g. "sheet 1 of 3".
© Crown copyright (ref: LR/HQ/CD-ROM) 6/03

J—Transfer by one party to the other by order of court of transferor's share in family home held by them as tenants in common. No mortgage

Transfer of whole of registered title(s)

PRECEDENT 18

Land Registry

TR1

If you need more room than is provided for in a panel, use continuation sheet CS and attach to this form.

1.	**Stamp Duty**
	Place "X" in the appropriate box or boxes and complete the appropriate certificate.
	☐ It is certified that this instrument falls within category ☐ in the Schedule to the Stamp Duty (Exempt Instruments) Regulations 1987
	☐ It is certified that the transaction effected does not form part of a larger transaction or of a series of transactions in respect of which the <u>amount or value or the aggregate amount or value of the consideration exceeds the sum of</u> £
	☐ It is certified that this is an instrument on which stamp duty is not chargeable by virtue of the provisions of section 92 of the Finance Act 2001
2.	**Title Number(s) of the Property** *Leave blank if not yet registered.*
	[TITLE NUMBER] [OR LEAVE BLANK IF APPLYING FOR FIRST REGISTRATION]
3.	**Property**
	[ADDRESS]
4.	**Date**
5.	**Transferor** *Give full names and company's registered number if any.*
	[BOTH PARTIES]
6.	**Transferee for entry on the register** *Give full name(s) and company's registered number, if any. For Scottish companies use an SC prefix and for limited liability partnerships use an OC prefix before the registered number, if any. For foreign companies give territory in which incorporated.*
	[TRANSFEREE]
	Unless otherwise arranged with Land Registry headquarters, a certified copy of the Transferee's constitution (in English or Welsh) will be required if it is a body corporate but is not a company registered in England and Wales or Scotland under the Companies Acts.
7.	**Transferee's intended address(es) for service (including postcode) for entry on the register** *You may give up to three addresses for service **one** of which **must** be a postal address but does not have to be within the UK. The other addresses can be any combination of a postal address, a box number at a UK document exchange or an electronic address.*
	[TRANSFEREE'S ADDRESS] (this will usually be the address of the property)
8.	**The Transferor transfers the Property to the Transferee**
9.	**Consideration** *Place "X" in the appropriate box. State clearly the currency unit if other than sterling. If none of the boxes applies, insert an appropriate memorandum in the additional provisions panel.*
	☐ The Transferor has received from the Transferee for the Property the sum of *In words and figures.*
	☐ Insert other receipt as appropriate. (See panel 12 below)
	☐ The transfer is not for money or anything which has a monetary value

10.	The Transferor transfers with *Place "X" in the appropriate box and add any modifications.* ☐ ☒ full title guarantee ☐ ☐ limited title guarantee
11.	Declaration of trust *Where there is more than one Transferee, place "X" in the appropriate box.* ☐ The Transferees are to hold the Property on trust for themselves as joint tenants ☐ The Transferees are to hold the Property on trust for themselves as tenants in common in equal shares ☐ The Transferees are to hold the Property *Complete as necessary.*
12.	Additional provisions *Insert here any required or permitted statements, certificates or applications and any agreed covenants, declarations, etc.* 12.1 The transfer is made pursuant to an order of the [ ] County Court dated [ ] in proceedings between [Transferor's name] and [Transferee's name] bearing number [ ] Refer to continuation sheet (CS)
13.	Execution *The Transferor must execute this transfer as a deed using the space below. If there is more than one Transferor, all must execute. Forms of execution are given in Schedule 9 to the Land Registration Rules 2003. If the transfer contains Transferee's covenants or declarations or contains an application by the Transferee (e.g. for a restriction), it must also be executed by the Transferee (all of them, if there is more than one).* SIGNED as a DEED by (enter full name of individual) in the presence of: [TRANSFEROR] Signature of Witness …………………………………………….. Name (in BLOCK CAPITALS) ………………………………….. Address …………………………………………………………. SIGNED as a DEED by (enter full name of individual) in the presence of: [TRANSFEREE] Signature of Witness …………………………………………….. Name (in BLOCK CAPITALS) ………………………………….. Address ………………………………………………………….

Continuation sheet for use with application and disposition forms

Land Registry

CS

1. Continued from Form [TR1]   Title number(s) [TITLE NUMBER]

2. *Before each continuation, state panel to be continued, e.g. "Panel 12 continued".*

   Panel 12 continued

   12.2   [Transferee's name] covenants with [Transferor's name] that [Transferee's name] will observe and perform the covenants and conditions referred to in the Charges Register so far as still subsisting and relating to the Property and will keep [Transferor's name] and [his or her] personal representatives effectually indemnified against all losses resulting from their non observance or breach.

   Note to clause 12.2 – This clause is only necessary where the parties entered into the original restrictions affecting the property (if any) or, in the conveyance to them, covenanted to observe them. Otherwise the Transferor is not entitled to them.

   12.3   The covenant by the Transferor implied by section 4(1)(b) Law of Property (Miscellaneous Provisions) Act 1994 by reason of the Transferor transferring with Full Title Guarantee shall be limited so as not to extend to any breach of the terms of the registered lease on the part of the Transferor relating to the condition of the Property [Limitation of Transferor's Liability in relation to repair: (see p.6)] (only required if leasehold).

   12.4   [Transferor's name] assigns his half share to [Transferee's name]. [Only necessary where application is for first registration.]

Continuation sheet [1] of [1]
Insert sheet number and total number of continuation sheets e.g. "sheet 1 of 3".
© Crown copyright (ref: LR/HQ/CD-ROM) 6/03

Release of Transferor from mortgage by mortgagee at date subsequent to transfer to transferee subject to the mortgage
(*see* p.94)

Precedent 19

HM LAND REGISTRY

County and District

Or London Borough

Title Number:

Property:

Date

[Bank or Building Society] hereby releases and discharges [Transferor's name] from all obligations under the Legal Charge dated [   ] and registered on [   ]

Signed as a Deed
On behalf of
(Bank or Building Society)

Authorised Signatory

Chapter 5

Transfer of Ex-Partner's Interest to New Partner

This chapter deals principally with the situation where the parties hold the family home in their joint names (whether as beneficial joint tenants or as tenants in common) and, as a result of property adjustments, one party's interest in the home is conveyed or transferred to the other party's new spouse or partner. The expression "new partner" used in this chapter will include another person, whether the party concerned is married to that person or is their civil partner or not.

With the court having ordered the transferor's interest to be transferred to the transferee, or agreement to that effect having been reached, it may be that the transferee requests or desires that the house be transferred to the transferee and the transferee's new spouse or partner. Alternatively, the new partner may agree to purchase the transferor's interest in the property. In either event, particular regard will have to be had to the capital gains tax, inheritance tax and stamp duty land tax implications of such a transaction, and whilst these are dealt with more fully in Ch.2, the following points are mentioned as an aide-mémoire:

5–01

(i) If the new partner purchases the transferor's interest in the house, is this for full value and on the basis of an arm's length transaction? If not, there could be a potential liability for inheritance tax.

(ii) If the transferee becomes entitled to the whole house and requests that the family home be transferred to the transferee and the transferee's new partner (to whom the transferee is not married or enjoined by civil partnership), is the transferee making a gift for inheritance tax purposes to the "new partner"?

(iii) The HMRC capital gains tax concession mentioned in Ch.2 may not be available (on a strict interpretation of its wording) to the transferor where the transferor transfers his or her interest in the former principal private residence to someone other than his or her spouse or civil partner or ex-spouse or ex-civil partner.

(iv) A transfer to someone other than a party to the marriage or civil partnership will not attract the stamp duty land tax relief of Sch.3 of the Finance Act 2003, (*see* p.29) unless it is a voluntary disposition when Sch.3 will also apply. In view of the stamp duty land tax implications, the transferee should consider taking the transfer his or herself and subsequently transferring on to the transferee and the new partner.

The potential threat of the transfer to the transferee and new partner being put aside if the sale to the new partner could be considered to be at an undervalue must be borne in mind (*see* pp.17–19 and Insolvency Act 1986, s.339).

1 Procedure

(a) Is the transferee entitled to have the house transferred into joint names with the new partner?

5–02 If the court has ordered the transferor (or the transferor has agreed) to transfer his or her interest in the former family home to the transferee, there is no reason why he or she should agree, at the request of the transferee, to transfer it to the transferee and his or her new partner. If the transferor does not so agree, then the Precedents in Chs 3 and 4 are appropriate, and it is up to the transferee to make a further transfer or deed of gift once the property is vested in the transferee alone. Suitable precedent transfers on form TR1 can be found in the *Encyclopedia of Forms and Precedents*, Butterworths, Vol.17(2).

If the transferee and new partner are purchasing the transferor's share or interest in the property for full value, then usual sale and purchase considerations apply. If, however, it is agreed that the transferee should purchase the transferor's share and interest, and in reality the purchase monies are being provided by the new partner, then if the transferor refuses to convey his or her interest in the house to the transferee and the new partner, it is suggested that the transferee takes the transfer in the transferee's sole name as nominee and makes a subsequent transfer to the transferee and new partner jointly.

(b) Contract

5–03 Where the arrangement is agreed between the parties, the practitioner must consider whether or not it is desirable to have a binding contract. If the transferor is purchasing another house with the proceeds of sale of his or her interest in the family home, then, as he or she will have to commit to a contract in respect of this purchase, it is suggested that there should be a contract relating to the sale of the transferor's interest in the family home so that the transferor is fully safeguarded. This should ensure an adherence to a timetable which otherwise might be lacking in the case of an agreement between the parties not supported by a binding contract.

(c) Conduct of the conveyancing

5–04 It is appropriate for the transferor's solicitors to obtain the title deeds, where the land is unregistered, so that they may act as vendor's solicitors. It is envisaged that the transferee and the new partner will have a solicitor who acts for both of them.

Whilst the new partner is entitled to have the title investigated fully (at his or her own cost), in a case where the house is already in the joint names of the parties, it is thought that, in practice, the new partner will rely upon the title at the time of the transfer to the parties having been properly investigated. In the case of unregistered title the transferor's solicitors will, therefore, submit a copy of the last conveyance, mortgage (if any), any sales off or other transactions, together with copies of any covenants referred to in the last conveyance, to the new partner's solicitors who will themselves submit a draft transfer. In the case of registered title, official copies of the registered title should be supplied to enable the transferee's and new partner's solicitors to draw the relevant transfer. In order to save time these can be obtained by the transferee's solicitor by submitting form OC1 to HM Land Registry, electronically from Land Registry Direct or by telephone on 08709 088063.

Unless there is a contract governing the transaction, it is suggested that when the transfer has been executed by all parties a completion date should be arranged so that the necessary searches can be made by reference to that date and the matter completed. In the case of unregistered title, a search at HM Land Charges Registry against both the parties should be made, whilst a Form OS1 Search is appropriate in the case of registered land (except in the case of Precedent 23 when a Form OS3 Search is appropriate. It will be recalled that this does not confer priority (*see* Ch.3, pp.60–61)). These kind of searches can be applied for by post, electronically from Land Registry Direct or by telephone on 08709 088063.

2 Covenants for title

(a) Freehold

Although this could be a matter of negotiation, there seems little reason why any transfer by the transferor should not be made with full title guarantee which then implies on his or her part the various covenants set out in the Law of Property (Miscellaneous Provisions) Act 1994 (*see* Ch.1, p.4). In practical terms this might be a necessity if the transferee's mortgagee so insists. **5–05**

For similar reasons any transfer by the transferee should be made with full title guarantee.

(b) Leasehold

The transferor may wish to be excused liability towards the transferee and any new partner for a breach of the terms of the lease relating to repairs. The implied covenant should be amended accordingly (*see* Precedent 13 and Ch.1). **5–06**

For unregistered land, unless the lease is granted after January 1, 1996 (*see* Ch.1, p.6) the transferor should take a specific covenant from the transferee and new partner to observe and perform the covenants in the lease and for indemnity because he continues to be liable for any future non-payment of rent or breach of covenant.

3 Form of transfer

5–07 The approved Land Registry transfer (Form TR1) can be adapted to meet the situations covered in this chapter.

It will be recalled (*see* Ch.4, p.92–93) that the registrar is not affected with notice of any trust and that references to trusts are excluded from the register so far as possible (Land Registration Act 2002). Unless the registrar is instructed to the contrary, a transfer to the transferee and new partner will result in the registration of Form A restriction to the effect that no disposition by a sole proprietor of the land (not being a trust corporation) under which capital money arises is to be registered except under an order of the Registrar or of the court (i.e. the survivor of the transferee and new partner cannot give a good receipt for capital monies). If in effect, therefore, the transferee and new partner wish to hold the property as beneficial joint tenants, they must make the declaration contained in the standard form TR1.

If the transferee and new partner wish to hold as tenants in common, then it must be remembered that the register will not show their respective shares and they should make a separate declaration (which will be off the register) as to these, and this will be evidence at a later date should their shares be in dispute (for instance with the trustee in bankruptcy of either party). If the transfer refers to the shares of the tenants in common, it is thought that this is unobjectionable to the registrar, although no note of the shares will appear on the register (form TR1 provides for the shares to be entered if desired). The registrar does have a discretion to allow inspection of a filed transfer (Land Registration Rules 2003); but it is obviously better either to have a duplicate of the transfer or a separate declaration of trust so that exercise of the discretion does not have to be requested. This would in any event take time.

4 Where the property is subject to a mortgage

5–08 If the property is subject to a mortgage, then if the new partner's financial status is acceptable to the mortgagee it will doubtless be prepared to release the transferor's covenant in return for receiving a similar covenant from the new partner. The exact requirements of the mortgagee to be contained in the conveyance or transfer should be ascertained.

The necessity of obtaining consent to transfer subject to a mortgage from any other occupier of the family home aged 18 years or over should not be overlooked (*Williams & Glyn's Bank Ltd v Boland* [1981] A.C. 487). (*See* Precedent 6).

If the new partner's financial status is not acceptable to the mortgagee, so that the mortgagee is only prepared to agree to a transfer of the property to the transferee and new partner if the transferor remains liable under the original mortgage, then it would seem reasonable for the transferor to comply only with the terms of the court order or other agreement (to which of course the new partner is not a party) and not to transfer to the transferee and the new partner. If the transferor is to remain liable under the mortgage he or she should remain a trustee of the legal estate (which could stand in the names of the original parties and the new partner) so that he or she will know the state of the mortgage account and so that a further advance or a second charge cannot be created without his or her consent.

In a case where the transferor owns the house alone, subject to mortgage, and the transferee and new partner decide to buy him or her out, the most usual procedure would be for the transfer to the transferee and new partner to take place contemporaneously with the redemption of the existing mortgage and the taking of the new mortgage.

5 Advice to be given to parties taking as joint tenants or tenants in common

In the circumstances envisaged by this chapter the solicitor acting for the transferees will be dealing with joint ownership. It is absolutely vital that clear instructions are taken as to the type of joint ownership envisaged by the parties before box 11 of form TR1 is completed. 5–09

This subject has been touched upon in relation to the consequences of severance, thereby creating a tenancy in common, in para.1 of Ch.4. All transfers are required to be in either form TR1 or TR2 and three choices of joint ownership are given in box 11, namely:

(i) the transferees are to hold the property on trust for themselves as joint tenants; or

(ii) the transferees are to hold the property on trust for themselves as tenants in common in equal shares; or

(iii) the transferees are to hold the property (*complete as necessary*).

If the first option is used then the parties will purchase subject to the rule of survivorship. What many practitioners overlook especially when advising unmarried couples is that they also have the right to sever the joint tenancy at any time *inter vivos*. If this does happen, usually due to the relationship having broken down, there will be an assumption that they hold the property as tenants in common in equal shares. Clearly, if the couple have not contributed to the original purchase price equally this will create inequity between them. They will have only one option and that is to sue the purchasing solicitor. As previously stated in Ch.4 the case of *Goodman v Gallant* (1986) 1 F.L.R. 513 clearly upheld the view that where no declaration of the interests of the parties is made there is no room for the doctrine of implied, resulting or constructive trusts and it will be assumed that the parties are holding the property in equal shares. In that case on p.519 Slade LJ quotes Russell LJ in the case of *Wilson v Wilson* [1963] 1 W.L.R. 601 (at p.3180):

"If a freehold is conveyed to A and B on trust for themselves as joint tenants, each has the same beneficial interest in the nature of that property as the other. That is inherent in the nature of the beneficial interest created, as is the right of the whole on survivorship before severance. It is also inherent in the nature of the beneficial interest created that either may sever at any time *inter vivos,* and on severance the beneficial joint tenancy becomes a beneficial tenancy in common in undivided shares and right by survivorship no longer obtains. If there be two beneficial joint tenants, severance produces a beneficial tenancy in common in two equal shares."

This view is supported in the cases of *Harwood v Harwood* and *Carlton v Goodman* (*ref* to earlier in Ch.4) (albeit that these two cases are not directly concerned with severance). It may well be that the unmarried couple should consider holding the property as tenants in common from the outset as provided by the third option in para.11 of form TR 1 or TR2 and supplemented by a trust deed declaring the shares in which they hold the property. Wills could then be drawn to deal with their respective shares on death. Solicitors should also be aware that in drafting the trust document they should only act for one of the parties and that the other must be advised to obtain independent legal advice. If these procedures are followed then a future negligence claim can be avoided following the break down of the relationship between the parties. Obviously if the transferees are to marry or enter into a civil partnership following the dissolution of the previous marriage or civil partnership and transfer then much of the above can be ignored in view of the court's wide powers on the dissolution of such unions.

6 Steps to be taken following the completion of the transfer

(a) Stamp duty land tax

5–10 Where there has been a transfer on sale form SDLT 1 will be required. This is also the case where the consideration is less than the nil rate of £125,000 as a return must be made to HMRC and a certificate issued prior to registration at HM Land Registry.

None of the transfers which are the subject of this chapter fall within the provisions of Sch.3 to the Finance Act 2003 so far as it relates to divorces and termination of civil partnerships but it should be remembered a transfer for no consideration also falls within Sch.3. For those transfers on sale where the consideration (including any mortgage debt assumed) is more than £125,000, a form SDLT 1 will need to be submitted to HMRC with a cheque for the stamp duty land tax payable at the appropriate rate. A certificate will then be issued permitting registration at HM Land Registry to follow. In the case of transfers where the consideration is less than £125,000 a return in form SDLT 1 will also be required save that no cheque will be necessary. Precedents 23 and 24 are a hybrid between two reliefs both under Sch.3. It is suggested that an appropriately completed SDLT 1 should be submitted to HMRC as self-certificate SDLT 60 is not applicable. No duty should be payable. In contrast, Precedent 25 should whilst comprising a transfer to an ex-partner falls outside Sch.3 as there is also a sale to a third party. Form SDLT 1 should be submitted and duty paid at the appropriate rate on the sale element.

(b) Completion of the title

Where a new covenant is given by the new partner to the mortgagee, the mortgagee may require a certified copy of the transfer containing the covenant to be lodged with the official copies so that it has a proper record of the liability of the new partner, the transfer incorporating the covenant itself being at the Land Registry. **5–11**

(c) Cancellation of entries

In those cases where the house is in the sole name of the transferor, the transferee may have entered a notice of home rights (or a Class F land charge) at the Registry, and these should be cancelled. **5–12**

(d) HM Land Registry fees

The purchase by the new partner of the transferor's share in the former family home is a dealing for value within the Land Registration Fees Order 2006 and fees under Scale 1 on the amount of the consideration will be payable (Precedents 20, 21, 22 and 25). **5–13**

Where the transfer is pursuant to a court order and does not otherwise involve consideration (e.g. Precedents 23 and 24) Scale 2 applies. The fee is based on the value of the land less any charge to which the property remains subject. Where the transfer gives effect to the disposition of a share in registered land, the fee is based upon the value of that share.

As stated in previous chapters if the transfer constitutes an application for first registration then Scale 1 applies and a fee will be payable on the value of the land concerned.

The value of the land should be specified by the solicitor lodging the application to the Land Registry by letter or on Form AP1 or FR1.

(e) Insurance

The appropriate changes should be made to delete the transferor's name from the policy and add that of the new partner. **5–14**

PRECEDENTS

A—Transfer on sale by one joint tenant to stranger (new partner). Remaining joint tenant and stranger becoming joint tenants. No mortgage

Transfer of whole of registered title(s)

PRECEDENT 20

Land Registry

TR1

If you need more room than is provided for in a panel, use continuation sheet CS and attach to this form.

1.	**Stamp Duty**
	Place "X" in the appropriate box or boxes and complete the appropriate certificate.
	☐ It is certified that this instrument falls within category ☐ in the Schedule to the Stamp Duty (Exempt Instruments) Regulations 1987
	☐ It is certified that the transaction effected does not form part of a larger transaction or of a series of transactions in respect of which the amount or value or the aggregate amount or value of the consideration exceeds the sum of ☐ (as appropriate)
	☐ It is certified that this is an instrument on which stamp duty is not chargeable by virtue of the provisions of section 92 of the Finance Act 2001
2.	**Title Number(s) of the Property** *Leave blank if not yet registered.* [TITLE NUMBER] [OR LEAVE BLANK IF APPLYING FOR FIRST REGISTRATION]
3.	**Property** [ADDRESS]
4.	**Date**
5.	**Transferor** *Give full names and company's registered number if any.* [BOTH PARTIES]
6.	**Transferee for entry on the register** *Give full name(s) and company's registered number, if any. For Scottish companies use an SC prefix and for limited liability partnerships use an OC prefix before the registered number, if any. For foreign companies give territory in which incorporated.* [TRANSFEREE AND NEW PARTNER] *Unless otherwise arranged with Land Registry headquarters, a certified copy of the Transferee's constitution (in English or Welsh) will be required if it is a body corporate but is not a company registered in England and Wales or Scotland under the Companies Acts.*
7.	**Transferee's intended address(es) for service (including postcode) for entry on the register** *You may give up to three addresses for service one of which must be a postal address but does not have to be within the UK. The other addresses can be any combination of a postal address, a box number at a UK document exchange or an electronic address.* [TRANSFEREE'S AND NEW PARTNER'S ADDRESS] (this will usually be the address of the property)
8.	The Transferor transfers the Property to the Transferee
9.	**Consideration** *Place "X" in the appropriate box. State clearly the currency unit if other than sterling. If none of the boxes applies, insert an appropriate memorandum in the additional provisions panel.*
	☐ The Transferor has received from the Transferee for the Property the sum of *In words and figures.* [AMOUNT OF CONSIDERATION IN WORDS AND NUMBERS]
	☐ *Insert other receipt as appropriate.* (See panel 12 below)
	☐ The transfer is not for money or anything which has a monetary value

TRANSFER OF EX-PARTNER'S INTEREST TO NEW PARTNER 131

10. The Transferor transfers with *Place "X" in the appropriate box and add any modifications.*

    ☐ ☒ full title guarantee ☐ ☐ limited title guarantee

11. Declaration of trust *Where there is more than one Transferee, place "X" in the appropriate box.*

    ☐ The Transferees are to hold the Property on trust for themselves as joint tenants

    ☐ The Transferees are to hold the Property on trust for themselves as tenants in common in equal shares

    ☐ The Transferees are to hold the Property *Complete as necessary.*

    NB: This will need to be discussed and instructions taken as to the client's wishes.

12. Additional provisions *Insert here any required or permitted statements, certificates or applications and any agreed covenants, declarations, etc.*

    12.1 [Transferee's name] covenants with [Transferor's name] that [Transferee's name] will observe and perform the covenants and conditions referred to in the Charges Register so far as still subsisting and relating to the Property and will keep [Transferor's name] and [his or her] personal representatives effectually indemnified against all losses resulting from their non observance or breach.

    Note to clause 12.1 – This clause is only necessary when the parties entered into the original restrictions affecting the property (if any) or, in the conveyance to them, covenanted to observe them. Otherwise the Transferor is not entitled to them.

    Refer to continuation sheet [CS]

13. Execution *The Transferor must execute this transfer as a deed using the space below. If there is more than one Transferor, all must execute. Forms of execution are given in Schedule 9 to the Land Registration Rules 2003. If the transfer contains Transferee's covenants or declarations or contains an application by the Transferee (e.g. for a restriction), it must also be executed by the Transferee (all of them, if there is more than one).*

    SIGNED as a DEED by (enter full name of individual) in the presence of: [TRANSFEROR]

    Signature of Witness ……………………………………………………..
    Name (in BLOCK CAPITALS) …………………………………………..
    Address …………………………………………………………………...

    SIGNED as a DEED by (enter full name of individual) in the presence of: [TRANSFEREE]

    Signature of Witness ……………………………………………………..
    Name (in BLOCK CAPITALS) …………………………………………..
    Address …………………………………………………………………...

Continuation sheet for use with application and disposition forms

Land Registry

CS

1. Continued from Form [TR1]   Title number(s) [TITLE NUMBER]

2. *Before each continuation, state panel to be continued, e.g. "Panel 12 continued".*

   Panel 12 continued

   12.2 The covenant by the Transferor implied by section 4(1)(b) Law of Property (Miscellaneous Provisions) Act 1994 by reason of the Transferor transferring with Full Title Guarantee shall be limited so as not to extend to any breach of the terms of the registered lease on the part of the Transferor relating to the condition of the Property [Limitation of Transferor's Liability in relation to repair: see p.6] (only required if leasehold).

   Panel 13 continued

   SIGNED as a DEED by (enter full name of individual) in the presence of: [NEW PARTNER]

Continuation sheet [1] of [1]

B—Transfer on sale by one party of share in family home (held by self and other party as tenants in common in equal shares) to new partner. Transferees holding as tenants in common. No mortgage

Transfer of whole of registered title(s)	**Land Registry**
PRECEDENT 21	**TR1**

If you need more room than is provided for in a panel, use continuation sheet CS and attach to this form.

1. Stamp Duty

Place "X" in the appropriate box or boxes and complete the appropriate certificate.

☐ It is certified that this instrument falls within category ☐ in the Schedule to the Stamp Duty (Exempt Instruments) Regulations 1987

☐ It is certified that the transaction effected does not form part of a larger transaction or of a series of transactions in respect of which the amount or value or the aggregate amount or value of the consideration exceeds the sum of ☐ (as appropriate)

☐ It is certified that this is an instrument on which stamp duty is not chargeable by virtue of the provisions of section 92 of the Finance Act 2001

2. Title Number(s) of the Property *Leave blank if not yet registered.*
[TITLE NUMBER] [OR LEAVE BLANK IF APPLYING FOR FIRST REGISTRATION]

3. Property

[ADDRESS]

4. Date

5. Transferor *Give full names and company's registered number if any.*
[BOTH PARTIES]

6. Transferee for entry on the register *Give full name(s) and company's registered number, if any. For Scottish companies use an SC prefix and for limited liability partnerships use an OC prefix before the registered number, if any. For foreign companies give territory in which incorporated.*

[TRANSFEREE and NEW PARTNER]

Unless otherwise arranged with Land Registry headquarters, a certified copy of the Transferee's constitution (in English or Welsh) will be required if it is a body corporate but is not a company registered in England and Wales or Scotland under the Companies Acts.

7. Transferee's intended address(es) for service (including postcode) for entry on the register *You may give up to three addresses for service **one** of which **must** be a postal address but does not have to be within the UK. The other addresses can be any combination of a postal address, a box number at a UK document exchange or an electronic address.*

[TRANSFEREE'S and NEW PARTNER'S ADDRESS] (this will usually be the address of the property)

8. The Transferor transfers the Property to the Transferee

9. Consideration *Place "X" in the appropriate box. State clearly the currency unit if other than sterling. If none of the boxes applies, insert an appropriate memorandum in the additional provisions panel.*

☐ The Transferor has received from the Transferee for the Property the sum of *In words and figures.*
☐ [AMOUNT OF CONSIDERATION IN WORDS AND NUMBERS]

☐ Insert other receipt as appropriate.   (See panel 12 below)

☐ The transfer is not for money or anything which has a monetary value

10.	The Transferor transfers with *Place "X" in the appropriate box and add any modifications.* ☐ ☒ full title guarantee ☐ ☐ limited title guarantee
11.	Declaration of trust *Where there is more than one Transferee, place "X" in the appropriate box.* ☐ The Transferees are to hold the Property on trust for themselves as joint tenants ☐ The Transferees are to hold the Property on trust for themselves as tenants in common in equal shares ☐ The Transferees are to hold the Property *Complete as necessary.* NB: This will need to be discussed and instructions taken as to the client's wishes.
12.	Additional provisions *Insert here any required or permitted statements, certificates or applications and any agreed covenants, declarations, etc.* 12.1 The Transferee covenants with [Transferor's name] to observe and perform the covenants and conditions referred to in the Charges Register so far as still subsisting and relating to the Property and will keep [Transferor's name] and [his or her] personal representatives effectually indemnified against all losses resulting from their non observance or breach. **Note to clause 12.1** – This clause is only necessary when the parties entered into the original restrictions affecting the property (if any) or, in the conveyance to them, covenanted to observe them. Otherwise the transferor is not entitled to them. Refer to continuation sheet [CS]
13.	Execution *The Transferor must execute this transfer as a deed using the space below. If there is more than one Transferor, all must execute. Forms of execution are given in Schedule 9 to the Land Registration Rules 2003. If the transfer contains Transferee's covenants or declarations or contains an application by the Transferee (e.g. for a restriction), it must also be executed by the Transferee (all of them, if there is more than one).* SIGNED as a DEED by (enter full name of individual) in the presence of: [TRANSFEROR] Signature of Witness …………………………………………………….. Name (in BLOCK CAPITALS) ………………………………………. Address …………………………………………………………………….. SIGNED as a DEED by (enter full name of individual) in the presence of: [TRANSFEREE] Signature of Witness …………………………………………………….. Name (in BLOCK CAPITALS) ………………………………………. Address ……………………………………………………………………..

Continuation sheet for use with application and disposition forms

Land Registry

CS

| 1. Continued from Form | TR1 | Title number(s) | TITLE NUMBER |

2. *Before each continuation, state panel to be continued, e.g. "Panel 12 continued".*

Panel 12 continued

12.2   The covenant by the Transferor implied by section 4(1)(b) Law of Property (Miscellaneous Provisions) Act 1994 by reason of the Transferor transferring with Full Title Guarantee shall be limited so as not to extend to any breach of the terms of the registered lease on the part of the Transferor relating to the condition of the Property [Limitation of Transferor's Liability in relation to repair: (see p.6)] (only required if leasehold).

12.3   [Transferor's name] assigns to [New Partner's name] the one half share of [Transferor's name] in equity. [Only where land is registered.]

Panel 13 continued

SIGNED as a DEED by (enter full name of individual) in the presence of: [NEW PARTNER]

Continuation sheet 1 of 1
Insert sheet number and total number of continuation sheets e.g. "sheet 1 of 3".
© Crown copyright (ref: LR/HQ/CD-ROM) 6/03

C—Transfer on sale by one party of share in family home. Original parties joint tenants. Transferee and new partner taking as tenants in common. Mortgage. Transferee and new partner responsible. Transferor released

Transfer of whole of registered title(s)

PRECEDENT 22

Land Registry

TR1

If you need more room than is provided for in a panel, use continuation sheet CS and attach to this form.

1. Stamp Duty

Place "X" in the appropriate box or boxes and complete the appropriate certificate.

☐ It is certified that this instrument falls within category [ ] in the Schedule to the Stamp Duty (Exempt Instruments) Regulations 1987

☐ It is certified that the transaction effected does not form part of a larger transaction or of a series of transactions in respect of which the amount or value or the aggregate amount or value of the consideration exceeds the sum of [ ] (as appropriate)

☐ It is certified that this is an instrument on which stamp duty is not chargeable by virtue of the provisions of section 92 of the Finance Act 2001

2. Title Number(s) of the Property *Leave blank if not yet registered.*
[TITLE NUMBER] [OR LEAVE BLANK IF APPLYING FOR FIRST REGISTRATION]

3. Property

[ADDRESS]

4. Date

5. Transferor *Give full names and company's registered number if any.*
[BOTH PARTIES]

6. Transferee for entry on the register *Give full name(s) and company's registered number, if any. For Scottish companies use an SC prefix and for limited liability partnerships use an OC prefix before the registered number, if any. For foreign companies give territory in which incorporated.*

[TRANSFEREE and NEW PARTNER]

Unless otherwise arranged with Land Registry headquarters, a certified copy of the Transferee's constitution (in English or Welsh) will be required if it is a body corporate but is not a company registered in England and Wales or Scotland under the Companies Acts.

7. Transferee's intended address(es) for service (including postcode) for entry on the register *You may give up to three addresses for service **one** of which **must** be a postal address but does not have to be within the UK. The other addresses can be any combination of a postal address, a box number at a UK document exchange or an electronic address.*

[TRANSFEREE'S and NEW PARTNER'S ADDRESS] (this will usually be the address of the property)

8. The Transferor transfers the Property to the Transferee

9. Consideration *Place "X" in the appropriate box. State clearly the currency unit if other than sterling. If none of the boxes applies, insert an appropriate memorandum in the additional provisions panel.*

☐ The Transferor has received from the Transferee for the Property the sum of *In words and figures.*
[AMOUNT OF CONSIDERATION IN WORDS AND NUMBERS]

☐ *Insert other receipt as appropriate.* (See panel 12 below)

☐ The transfer is not for money or anything which has a monetary value

TRANSFER OF EX-PARTNER'S INTEREST TO NEW PARTNER 137

10. The Transferor transfers with *Place "X" in the appropriate box and add any modifications.*
    ☐ ☒ full title guarantee ☐   ☐ limited title guarantee

11. Declaration of trust *Where there is more than one Transferee, place "X" in the appropriate box.*
    ☐ The Transferees are to hold the Property on trust for themselves as joint tenants
    ☐ The Transferees are to hold the Property on trust for themselves as tenants in common in equal shares
    ☐ The Transferees are to hold the Property *Complete as necessary.*
    NB: This will need to be discussed and instructions taken as to the client's wishes. See "Advice to be given to parties taking as joint tenants or tenants in common" in paragraph 5 of this chapter.

12. Additional provisions *Insert here any required or permitted statements, certificates or applications and any agreed covenants, declarations, etc.*

    12.1 The Transferee covenants with [Transferor's name] to observe and perform the covenants and conditions referred to in the Charges Register so far as still subsisting and relating to the Property and will keep [Transferor's name] and [his or her] personal representatives effectually indemnified against all losses resulting from their non observance or breach.

    Note to clause 12.1 – This clause is only necessary when the parties entered into the original restrictions affecting the property (if any) or, in the conveyance to them, covenanted to observe them. Otherwise the transferor is not entitled to them.

    Refer to continuation sheet [CS]

13. Execution *The Transferor must execute this transfer as a deed using the space below. If there is more than one Transferor, all must execute. Forms of execution are given in Schedule 9 to the Land Registration Rules 2003. If the transfer contains Transferee's covenants or declarations or contains an application by the Transferee (e.g. for a restriction), it must also be executed by the Transferee (all of them, if there is more than one).*

    SIGNED as a DEED by (enter full name of individual) in the presence of: |TRANSFEROR|

    Signature of Witness ……………………………………………………..
    Name (in BLOCK CAPITALS) …………………………………………..
    Address ……………………………………………………………………

    SIGNED as a DEED by (enter full name of individual) in the presence of: |TRANSFEREE|

    Signature of Witness ……………………………………………………..
    Name (in BLOCK CAPITALS) …………………………………………..
    Address ……………………………………………………………………

Continuation sheet for use with application and disposition forms

Land Registry

CS

1. Continued from Form TR1   Title number(s) TITLE NUMBER

2. *Before each continuation, state panel to be continued, e.g. "Panel 12 continued".*

Panel 12 continued

12.2 The covenant by the Transferor implied by section 4(1)(b) Law of Property (Miscellaneous Provisions) Act 1994 by reason of the Transferor transferring with Full Title Guarantee shall be limited so as not to extend to any breach of the terms of the registered lease on the part of the Transferor relating to the condition of the Property [Limitation of Transferor's Liability in relation to repair: see p.6] (only required if leasehold).

12.3 The Property is transferred subject to the charge ("the Registered Charge") dated [] and Registered on [   ] [under which there is now owing the sum of £   ].

12.4 The [Bank or Building Society] ("the lender") being the proprietor of the registered charge relieves and discharges [Transferor's name] from all obligations under the registered charge.

12.5 [New Partner's name] hereby covenants with the lender that he/she will pay to the lender all principal money, interest, costs and other monies due or to become due under the registered charge and will observe and be bound by the agreements, covenants and conditions contained or referred to in the registered charge.

Panel 13 continued

SIGNED as a DEED by (enter full name of individual) in the presence of: [NEW PARTNER]

Signed on behalf of

[the Lender]

Continuation sheet 1 of 1
Insert sheet number and total number of continuation sheets e.g. "sheet 1 of 3".
© Crown copyright (ref: LR/HQ/CD-ROM) 6/03

TRANSFER OF EX-PARTNER'S INTEREST TO NEW PARTNER 139

D—One party to receive whole property (in sole name of other party) by court order, but requests transfer to self and new partner as joint tenants. No mortgage

Transfer of whole of registered title(s)

Land Registry

PRECEDENT 23

TR1

If you need more room than is provided for in a panel, use continuation sheet CS and attach to this form.

1. **Stamp Duty**

   Place "X" in the appropriate box or boxes and complete the appropriate certificate.

   ☐ It is certified that this instrument falls within category ☐ in the Schedule to the Stamp Duty (Exempt Instruments) Regulations 1987

   ☐ It is certified that the transaction effected does not form part of a larger transaction or of a series of transactions in respect of which the amount or value or the aggregate amount or value of the consideration exceeds the sum of ☐ (as appropriate)

   ☐ It is certified that this is an instrument on which stamp duty is not chargeable by virtue of the provisions of section 92 of the Finance Act 2001

2. **Title Number(s) of the Property** *Leave blank if not yet registered.*
   [TITLE NUMBER] [OR LEAVE BLANK IF APPLYING FOR FIRST REGISTRATION]

3. **Property**
   [ADDRESS]

4. **Date**

5. **Transferor** *Give full names and company's registered number if any.*
   [BOTH PARTIES]

6. **Transferee for entry on the register** *Give full name(s) and company's registered number, if any. For Scottish companies use an SC prefix and for limited liability partnerships use an OC prefix before the registered number, if any. For foreign companies give territory in which incorporated.*

   [TRANSFEREE and NEW PARTNER]

   Unless otherwise arranged with Land Registry headquarters, a certified copy of the Transferee's constitution (in English or Welsh) will be required if it is a body corporate but is not a company registered in England and Wales or Scotland under the Companies Acts.

7. **Transferee's intended address(es) for service (including postcode) for entry on the register** *You may give up to three addresses for service one of which must be a postal address but does not have to be within the UK. The other addresses can be any combination of a postal address, a box number at a UK document exchange or an electronic address.*

   [TRANSFEREE'S and NEW PARTNER'S ADDRESS] (this will usually be the address of the property)

8. **The Transferor transfers the Property to the Transferee**

9. **Consideration** *Place "X" in the appropriate box. State clearly the currency unit if other than sterling. If none of the boxes applies, insert an appropriate memorandum in the additional provisions panel.*

   ☐ The Transferor has received from the Transferee for the Property the sum of *In words and figures.*
   ☐ [AMOUNT OF CONSIDERATION IN WORDS AND NUMBERS]

   ☐ *Insert other receipt as appropriate.* (See panel 12 below)

   ☒ The transfer is not for money or anything which has a monetary value

10.	The Transferor transfers with *Place "X" in the appropriate box and add any modifications.*
	☐ ☒ full title guarantee ☐ ☐ limited title guarantee

11.	Declaration of trust *Where there is more than one Transferee, place "X" in the appropriate box.*
	☐ The Transferees are to hold the Property on trust for themselves as joint tenants
	☐ The Transferees are to hold the Property on trust for themselves as tenants in common in equal shares
	☐ The Transferees are to hold the Property *Complete as necessary.*
	NB: This will need to be discussed and instructions taken as to the client's wishes.

12. Additional provisions *Insert here any required or permitted statements, certificates or applications and any agreed covenants, declarations, etc.*

12.1 The transfer is made pursuant to an order of the [County Court] dated [ ] in proceedings between the Transferor and [Transferee's name] bearing number [ ] and pursuant to a direction by [Transferee's name] to the Transferor.

Refer to continuation sheet [CS]

13. Execution *The Transferor must execute this transfer as a deed using the space below. If there is more than one Transferor, all must execute. Forms of execution are given in Schedule 9 to the Land Registration Rules 2003. If the transfer contains Transferee's covenants or declarations or contains an application by the Transferee (e.g. for a restriction), it must also be executed by the Transferee (all of them, if there is more than one).*

SIGNED as a DEED by (enter full name of individual) in the presence of: [TRANSFEROR]

Signature of Witness ………………………………………………………..
Name (in BLOCK CAPITALS) ……………………………………………..
Address …………………………………………………………………………..

SIGNED as a DEED by (enter full name of individual) in the presence of: [TRANSFEREE]

Signature of Witness ………………………………………………………..
Name (in BLOCK CAPITALS) ……………………………………………..
Address …………………………………………………………………………..

TRANSFER OF EX-PARTNER'S INTEREST TO NEW PARTNER

Continuation sheet for use with application and disposition forms	**Land Registry**	**CS**

1. Continued from Form **TR1**   Title number(s) **TITLE NUMBER**

2. *Before each continuation, state panel to be continued, e.g. "Panel 12 continued".*

   Panel 12 continued

   12.2   The Transferor by [himself or herself] and by the direction of [Transferee's name] transfers and [Transferee's name] transfers and confirms the property to the Transferee.

   12.3   The Transferee covenants with [Transferor's name] to observe and perform the covenants and conditions referred to in the Charges Register so far as still subsisting and relating to the Property and will keep [Transferor's name] and [his or her] personal representatives effectually indemnified against all losses resulting from their non observance or breach.

   Note to Clause 12.3—This clause is only necessary when the parties entered into the original restrictions affecting the property (if any) or, in the conveyance to them, covenanted to observe them. Otherwise the transferor is not entitled to them.

   12.4   The covenant by the Transferor implied by section 4(1)(b) Law of Property (Miscellaneous Provisions) Act 1994 by reason of the Transferor transferring with Full Title Guarantee shall be limited so as not to extend to any breach of the terms of the registered lease on the part of the Transferor relating to the condition of the Property [Limitation of Transferor's Liability in relation to repair: see p.6] (only required if leasehold).

   Panel 13 continued

   SIGNED as a DEED by (enter full name of individual) in the presence of: **[NEW PARTNER]**

Continuation sheet **1** of **1**
Insert sheet number and total number of continuation sheets e.g. "sheet 1 of 3".
© Crown copyright (ref: LR/HQ/CD-ROM) 6/03

E—House in joint names of the parties. One party entitled to sole interest by court order. Transfer to that party and new partner. Mortgage. Transferor released

Transfer of whole of registered title(s)

Land Registry

TR1

PRECEDENT 24

If you need more room than is provided for in a panel, use continuation sheet CS and attach to this form.

1. **Stamp Duty**

   Place "X" in the appropriate box or boxes and complete the appropriate certificate.

   ☐ It is certified that this instrument falls within category [ ] in the Schedule to the Stamp Duty (Exempt Instruments) Regulations 1987

   ☐ It is certified that the transaction effected does not form part of a larger transaction or of a series of transactions in respect of which the amount or value or the aggregate amount or value of the consideration exceeds the sum of [ ] (as appropriate)

   ☐ [ADJUDICATION]

   ☐ It is certified that this is an instrument on which stamp duty is not chargeable by virtue of the provisions of section 92 of the Finance Act 2001

2. **Title Number(s) of the Property** *Leave blank if not yet registered.*
   [TITLE NUMBER] [OR LEAVE BLANK IF APPLYING FOR FIRST REGISTRATION]

3. **Property**
   [ADDRESS]

4. **Date**

5. **Transferor** *Give full names and company's registered number if any.*
   [BOTH PARTIES]

6. **Transferee for entry on the register** *Give full name(s) and company's registered number, if any. For Scottish companies use an SC prefix and for limited liability partnerships use an OC prefix before the registered number, if any. For foreign companies give territory in which incorporated.*

   [TRANSFEREE and NEW PARTNER]

   Unless otherwise arranged with Land Registry headquarters, a certified copy of the Transferee's constitution (in English or Welsh) will be required if it is a body corporate but is not a company registered in England and Wales or Scotland under the Companies Acts.

7. **Transferee's intended address(es) for service (including postcode) for entry on the register** *You may give up to three addresses for service one of which must be a postal address but does not have to be within the UK. The other addresses can be any combination of a postal address, a box number at a UK document exchange or an electronic address.*

   [TRANSFEREE'S and NEW PARTNER'S ADDRESS] (this will usually be the address of the property)

8. **The Transferor transfers the Property to the Transferee**

9. **Consideration** *Place "X" in the appropriate box. State clearly the currency unit if other than sterling. If none of the boxes applies, insert an appropriate memorandum in the additional provisions panel.*

   ☐ The Transferor has received from the Transferee for the Property the sum of *In words and figures.*

   ☐ [AMOUNT OF CONSIDERATION IN WORDS AND NUMBERS]

   ☐ *Insert other receipt as appropriate.* (See panel 12 below)

   ☒ The transfer is not for money or anything which has a monetary value

TRANSFER OF EX-PARTNER'S INTEREST TO NEW PARTNER 143

10. The Transferor transfers with *Place "X" in the appropriate box and add any modifications.*

   ☐ ☒   full title guarantee ☐   ☐   limited title guarantee

11. Declaration of trust *Where there is more than one Transferee, place "X" in the appropriate box.*

   ☐ The Transferees are to hold the Property on trust for themselves as joint tenants

   ☐ The Transferees are to hold the Property on trust for themselves as tenants in common in equal shares

   ☐ The Transferees are to hold the Property *Complete as necessary.*

      NB: This will need to be discussed and instructions taken as to the client's wishes. See "Advice to be given to parties taking as joint tenants or tenants in common" in paragraph 5 of this chapter.

12. Additional provisions *Insert here any required or permitted statements, certificates or applications and any agreed covenants, declarations, etc.*

12.1 The transfer is made pursuant to an order of the [County Court] dated [ ] in proceedings between the transferor and [Transferee's name] bearing number [ ] and pursuant to a direction by [Transferee's name] to the Transferor.

Refer to continuation sheet [CS]

13. Execution *The Transferor must execute this transfer as a deed using the space below. If there is more than one Transferor, all must execute. Forms of execution are given in Schedule 9 to the Land Registration Rules 2003. If the transfer contains Transferee's covenants or declarations or contains an application by the Transferee (e.g. for a restriction), it must also be executed by the Transferee (all of them, if there is more than one).*

SIGNED as a DEED by (enter full name of individual) in the presence of: [TRANSFEROR]

Signature of Witness ……………………………………………..
Name (in BLOCK CAPITALS) …………………………………….
Address …………………………………………………………….

SIGNED as a DEED by (enter full name of individual) in the presence of: [TRANSFEREE]

Signature of Witness ……………………………………………..
Name (in BLOCK CAPITALS) …………………………………….
Address …………………………………………………………….

Continuation sheet for use with application and disposition forms

Land Registry

CS

1. Continued from Form TR1   Title number(s) TITLE NUMBER

2. *Before each continuation, state panel to be continued, e.g. "Panel 12 continued".*

   Panel 12 continued

   12.2 [Transferor's name] and [Transferee's name] with [Transferor's name] directing as to all his interest in the property transfers the property to the Transferee.

   12.3 The Property is transferred subject to the charge ("the Registered Charge") dated [] and Registered on [   ] [under which there is now owing the sum of £   ].

   12.4 The [Bank or Building Society] ("the lender") being the proprietor of the registered charge relieves and discharges [Transferor's name] from all obligations under the registered charge.

   12.5 [New Partner's name] hereby covenants with the lender that he/she will pay to the lender all principal money, interest, costs and other monies due or to become due under the registered charge and will observe and be bound by the agreements, covenants and conditions contained or referred to in the registered charge.

   12.6 The Transferee covenants with [Transferor's name] to observe and perform the covenants and conditions referred to in the Charges Register so far as still subsisting and relating to the Property and will keep [Transferor's name] and his personal representatives effectually indemnified against all losses resulting from their non observance or breach.

   Note to Clause 12.6–This clause is only necessary when the parties entered into the original restrictions affecting the property (if any) or, in the conveyance to them, covenanted to observe them. Otherwise the transferor is not entitled to them.

   12.7 The covenant by the Transferor implied by section 4(1)(b) Law of Property (Miscellaneous Provisions) Act 1994 by reason of the Transferor transferring with Full Title Guarantee shall be limited so as not to extend to any breach of the terms of the registered lease on the part of the Transferor relating to the condition of the Property [Limitation of Transferor's Liability in relation to repair: (see p.6)] (only required if leasehold).

   Panel 13 continued

   SIGNED as a DEED by (enter full name of individual) in the presence of: [NEW PARTNER]

   Signed on behalf of
   [the Lender]

   Authorised Signatory

TRANSFER OF EX-PARTNER'S INTEREST TO NEW PARTNER   145

F—House in sole name of one party. Transferee entitled to 50 per cent by court order. Sale of other 50 per cent to new partner. Transferee and new partner to hold as joint tenants

Transfer of whole of registered title(s)

Land Registry

TR1

PRECEDENT 25

If you need more room than is provided for in a panel, use continuation sheet CS and attach to this form.

1. **Stamp Duty**

   Place "X" in the appropriate box or boxes and complete the appropriate certificate.

   ☐ It is certified that this instrument falls within category ☐ in the Schedule to the Stamp Duty (Exempt Instruments) Regulations 1987

   ☐ It is certified that the transaction effected does not form part of a larger transaction or of a series of transactions in respect of which the amount or value or the aggregate amount or value of the consideration exceeds the sum of _____ (as appropriate)

   ☐ [ADJUDICATION]

   ☐ It is certified that this is an instrument on which stamp duty is not chargeable by virtue of the provisions of section 92 of the Finance Act 2001

2. Title Number(s) of the Property *Leave blank if not yet registered.*
   [TITLE NUMBER] [OR LEAVE BLANK IF APPLYING FOR FIRST REGISTRATION]

3. Property

   [ADDRESS]

4. Date

5. Transferor *Give full names and company's registered number if any.*
   [TRANSFEROR]

6. Transferee **for entry on the register** *Give full name(s) and company's registered number, if any. For Scottish companies use an SC prefix and for limited liability partnerships use an OC prefix before the registered number, if any. For foreign companies give territory in which incorporated.*

   [TRANSFEREE and NEW PARTNER]

   Unless otherwise arranged with Land Registry headquarters, a certified copy of the Transferee's constitution (in English or Welsh) will be required if it is a body corporate but is not a company registered in England and Wales or Scotland under the Companies Acts.

7. Transferee's intended **address(es) for service (including postcode) for entry on the register** *You may give up to three addresses for service **one** of which **must** be a postal address but does not have to be within the UK. The other addresses can be any combination of a postal address, a box number at a UK document exchange or an electronic address.*

   [TRANSFEREE'S and NEW PARTNER'S ADDRESS] (this will usually be the address of the property)

8. **The Transferor transfers the Property to the Transferee**

9. Consideration *Place "X" in the appropriate box. State clearly the currency unit if other than sterling. If none of the boxes applies, insert an appropriate memorandum in the additional provisions panel.*

   ☐ The Transferor has received from the Transferee for the Property the sum of *In words and figures.*

   ☐ [AMOUNT OF CONSIDERATION IN WORDS AND NUMBERS]

   ☐ *Insert other receipt as appropriate.* (See panel 12 below)

   ☐ The transfer is not for money or anything which has a monetary value

10. The Transferor transfers with *Place "X" in the appropriate box and add any modifications.*

　　☐ ☒ 　full title guarantee ☐ 　☐ 　limited title guarantee

11. Declaration of trust *Where there is more than one Transferee, place "X" in the appropriate box.*

　　☐ The Transferees are to hold the Property on trust for themselves as joint tenants

　　☐ The Transferees are to hold the Property on trust for themselves as tenants in common in equal shares

　　☐ The Transferees are to hold the Property *Complete as necessary.*

　　NB: This will need to be discussed and instructions taken as to the client's wishes. See "Advice to be given to parties taking as joint tenants or tenants in common" in paragraph 5 of this chapter.

12. Additional provisions *Insert here any required or permitted statements, certificates or applications and any agreed covenants, declarations, etc.*

　　12.1 This transfer is made pursuant to an order of the [County Court] dated [ ] in proceedings between the Transferor and [Transferee's name] bearing number [ ] and in consideration of the consideration)(see panel 9 above) paid by [New Partner's name] to the tranferor.

　　Refer to continuation sheet [CS]

13. Execution *The Transferor must execute this transfer as a deed using the space below. If there is more than one Transferor, all must execute. Forms of execution are given in Schedule 9 to the Land Registration Rules 2003. If the transfer contains Transferee's covenants or declarations or contains an application by the Transferee (e.g. for a restriction), it must also be executed by the Transferee (all of them, if there is more than one).*

　　SIGNED as a DEED by (enter full name of individual) in the presence of: 　　[TRANSFEROR]

　　Signature of Witness ……………………………………………..
　　Name (in BLOCK CAPITALS) …………………………………….
　　Address ……………………………………………………………..

　　SIGNED as a DEED by (enter full name of individual) in the presence of: 　　[TRANSFEREE]

　　Signature of Witness ……………………………………………..
　　Name (in BLOCK CAPITALS) …………………………………….
　　Address ……………………………………………………………..

TRANSFER OF EX-PARTNER'S INTEREST TO NEW PARTNER 147

Continuation sheet for use with application and disposition forms

Land Registry

CS

1. Continued from Form TR1   Title number(s) TITLE NUMBER

2. *Before each continuation, state panel to be continued, e.g. "Panel 12 continued".*

Panel 12 continued

12.2 The Transferor by [himself or herself] and by the direction of [Transferee's name] and by the direction of [New Partner's name] transfer the property to the Transferee.

12.3 The Transferee covenants with [Transferor's name] to observe and perform the covenants and conditions referred to in the Charges Register so far as still subsisting and relating to the Property and will keep [Transferor's name] and his personal representatives effectually indemnified against all losses resulting from their non-observance or breach.

Note to Clause 12.3 This clause is only necessary when the parties entered into the original restrictions affecting the property (if any) or, in the conveyance to them, covenanted to observe them. Otherwise the transferor is not entitled to them.

12.4 The covenant by the Transferor implied by section 4(1)(b) Law of Property (Miscellaneous Provisions) Act 1994 by reason of the Transferor transferring with Full Title Guarantee shall be limited so as not to extend to any breach of the terms of the registered lease on part of the Transferor relating to the condition of the Property [Limitation of Transferor's Liability in relation to repair: (see p.6)] (only required if leasehold).

Panel 13 continued

SIGNED as a DEED by (enter full name of individual) in the presence of: NEW PARTNER

Note to Clause 12.3 This clause is only necessary when the parties entered into the original restrictions affecting the property (if any) or, in the conveyance to them, covenanted to observe them. Otherwise the transferor is not entitled to them.

Chapter 6

Home to be Held on Certain Terms and Conditions

Whether the family home is held in the joint names of the parties or in one of their sole names, it is not unusual for the court to order that the house be retained but upon certain terms and conditions. Such an order may be made so as to ensure that there is a home for the children of the relationship. It may recognise that once the youngest child has left home the parent providing day-to-day care may again be able to take up gainful employment but until that time will need to be provided with a home rent free. It may also recognise that the other parent should be entitled to a financial stake in the family home, such stake being made available at the end of the period specified in the court order or at a time previously agreed between the parties.

6–01

A typical court order (in this case the family home being in one party's sole name) might be as follows:

"It is ordered that the Respondent do transfer with full title guarantee the property known as 1 Blackacre Drive, Blackacre, to himself and the Petitioner (or to other trustees) to hold the same as to 60 per cent for himself and as to 40 per cent for the Petitioner. The Petitioner shall have the occupation of the property for herself and the children of the family to the exclusion of the Respondent upon the conditions set out in the form of the draft declaration of trust annexed. The property is not to be sold until:

 (i) (a) (name) (date of birth) [the youngest child] attains the age of eighteen years or

 (b) (name) shall cease full time education whichever is the later or

 (ii) the death of the Petitioner or

 (iii) the Petitioner shall remarry

whichever shall first occur."

The above type of order is commonly known as a *Mesher* order (after *Mesher v Mesher and Hall* [1980] 1 All E.R. 126), and whilst it has been criticised largely on the grounds that the parent looking after the children faces a sale of the house several years hence (e.g. when the youngest child ceases full-time education) and the prospect then of receiving only a proportion of the sale proceeds with which to purchase alternative accommodation (*see Mortimer v Mortimer-Griffiths* [1986] 2 F.L.R. 315) the court is still of the view that such an order might provide the best solution (*see Clutton v Clutton* [1991] 1 All E.R. 340).

This type of order frequently contains a provision that a sale is triggered in the event of:

> (a) "the cohabitation of the petitioner for a period in excess of six months". Practitioners criticise this on the grounds that it is a mean clause, it invites the one parent to take a keener interest in the personal affairs of the parent providing day-to-day care for the children than is desirable, the burden of proof is difficult, and it loses sight of the fact that the purpose of the order in the first place was to provide a home for the children until the youngest ceased full-time education. In short, its insertion can cause difficulties.
>
> (b) "the wife ceasing to reside at the property".

As an event triggering a sale, this provision can also cause difficulty. The period of non-residence should be sufficiently reasonable to cover hospitalisation, looking after an elderly relative and so on. Despite such difficulties such a provision can be a vital capital gains tax saving requirement for the non-resident party (see heading "tax considerations" below).

In general, because of these and other difficulties, practitioners acting for the parent staying on in the home would favour an order not requiring sale until either death or remarriage (*see Martin v Martin* [1977] 3 All E.R. 762) whilst those acting for the non-resident parent might prefer a deferred charge entitling him or her to a percentage of the proceeds of sale (*see* Ch.7).

It is important that the events which trigger a sale should be understood. (*See Omielan v Omielan* [1996] 2 F.L.R. 306 where the court held it had no power in the absence of fraud, misrepresentation or non-disclosure to defer sale until another event which had not been mentioned in the original order.)

1 Comment on the Mesher order

6–02 Whilst this type of order is fairly common, it must be appreciated that it has defects as compared with an outright transfer of the family home. Certain facts need to be considered:

> (i) *Repairs*—The court cannot expressly order a party to pay for or contribute towards the cost of repairs to the house the subject of the court order because its powers are limited to ordering periodical payments and lump sums. The preamble to the court order might indicate that it is made (for example) on the basis that the party in occupation will keep the property in good repair; this is certainly "persuasive" in the event of a row. Or, in the case of a consent

order, the party in occupation might undertake to pay for repairs. It is in the interests of both parties that agreement be reached as to the responsibility for maintenance and repairs. In the absence of any agreement, or undertaking, then probably out of necessity the party in occupation will have to pay for repairs, and explore the possibility when the trust comes to an end of applying to the court (under "liberty to apply") for a variation of the division of the sale proceeds so that he or she is reimbursed.

In *Harvey v Harvey* [1987] 1 F.L.R. 67 the house was held by both parties as trustees with provision for postponement of sale. The husband refused to co-operate in obtaining a second mortgage and improvement grant to deal with necessary repairs, and the court ordered the appointment of a Receiver of the other party's interest limited to those purposes.

(ii) *Changing* house—Most court orders relate to a specific property and do not make provision for the party in occupation to move house and occupy another property upon similar terms and conditions. In the absence of any provision concerning this in the court order, the agreement/declaration of trust made by the parties should seek to cover this.

(iii) *Ending of the court order period*—In practice, problems can appear when one of the specified events happens (e.g. the youngest child attaining 18 years), for many court orders have provided who should pay outgoings and mortgage payments during the "trust period" but made no provision thereafter during the period whilst the house is being sold. Again, this is something that should be covered in any agreement or declaration of trust.

Practitioners will also be aware of the difficulty in getting the occupying party out so that the other party can obtain his or her share of the proceeds of sale (*see Crosthwaite v Crosthwaite* [1989] 2 F.L.R. 86).

(iv) *Charging* Clause—Specific provision should be made for this in the court order as the trustees (particularly if there are infants) cannot give themselves power to charge in the declaration of trust without authority.

(v) Does *there need to be a transfer?*—Where agreement has been reached between the parties that the former family home be held upon terms similar to those set out in the court order it has been known (in a natural desire to save costs) for the agreement to remain based on correspondence between parties or their solicitors, no other documentation being prepared. This is not satisfactory.

If the former family home was in one party's sole name, then in the event of his or her death the other party has to prove his or her interest in it, and the correspondence will have to be unearthed to prove to HMRC that, although the house is in the sole name of one party, his or her estate would not be beneficially entitled to the whole of the proceeds of sale. Further, a sale of the house in such circumstances cannot be arranged until a grant of representation to the deceased party's estate is obtained. The registration of home rights is not sufficient protection as the death of the estate owner brings this protection to an end (Family Law Act 1996, s.32; Sch.4(1)(a)) (as amended by CPA 2004).

If it is the non-owning party who dies, his or her personal representatives may not be aware of the interest in the house or may have difficulty in producing proof of the same, much to the detriment of the estate.

Similar difficulties can occur if the former family home was in the names of both parties as beneficial joint tenants, for on the death of either it would appear to a purchaser that the survivor had the right to sell (Law or Property (Joint Tenants) Act 1964, s.1(1)) unless he or she is put on notice by a restriction at HM Land Registry.

In the event of the insolvency of either party, one would wish to be able to prove beyond doubt to a trustee in bankruptcy the interests of the parties in the property.

Where a court order is made, it is not sufficient for a copy of that to be placed with the title deeds with nothing further being done, for the court order can be misplaced or removed. In each case, therefore, the agreement between the parties or the court order should be properly carried into effect by way of a conveyance, severance, transfer or declaration of trust, the form of which is the subject of this chapter. As we have seen, the declaration of trust can deal with matters outside the court order, as long as both parties agree.

2 Procedure

6–03 Unless monetary payment is to pass from one party to the other (for instance, as in a case where the house is in the sole name of one party and both parties agree that it is to be transferred to them both jointly and held upon certain trusts provided the non-owning party pays the other a sum of money—*see* Ch.7), when the transferor may require such money for his own purchase of another property, a contract between the parties would appear to be unnecessary. A court order enables either party to go back to the court if unreasonable delay in carrying out the terms of the order is experienced, and if there is to be a transfer of the family home following an agreement between the parties (not incorporated into a court order) it is always open to either party to make application to the court at any time.

If the house was unregistered and formerly in the sole name of one party it would be quite appropriate for the other party's solicitors to insist on a full abstract of title commencing with a good root of title (although in practice it seems to be accepted that the title was properly investigated at the time of the owning party's purchase); but in the case of a house already in joint names it is thought that this could be dispensed with, the solicitors assuming that a proper investigation of title to the property was made at the time when the house was purchased by the parties.

The court may have ordered one party's solicitor to conduct the conveyancing; but if not so, it would seem appropriate for particulars of title or official copies to be supplied to the other party's solicitors. As previously stated official copies can in any event be obtained by the transferee's solicitors by use of form OS1, by telephone or from Land Registry Direct. It would then be for those solicitors to draft the relevant transfer and declaration of trust (as appropriate) and submit these to the other party's solicitors for approval.

Once the documentation is agreed it is suggested that a "completion date" should be arranged so that the relevant searches can be made (*see* Ch.3, p.61) and any payment of monies requisitioned in time for the "completion date".

3 Covenants for title

Where the precedents in this chapter envisage the house standing in the sole name of one party and a transfer to both parties to hold as trustees or to outside trustees, then there seems to be no reason why the transfer should not be with full title guarantee; the transferor would be required to do so if he or she was selling the property and the reason for the transfer is akin to consideration.

6–04

If the house is already in joint names and is to be held upon certain trusts then:

(a) there is no transfer; all that may be required is an appointment of new trustees coupled with a declaration of trust; no covenants for title are necessary; or

(b) the property may be transferred to new trustees, who could reasonably insist on receiving a full title guarantee, coupled with a declaration of trust.

If the property is leasehold and the subject of an "old tenancy" practitioners may need to incorporate a specific covenant by the assignee to observe and perform the covenants under the lease and for indemnity (*see* Ch.1, p.6).

4 Tax considerations

Chapter 2 has outlined the relevant tax provisions to be considered when a sole party is disposing of his or her share or interest in the family home. In the cases that followed (i.e. the disposal of the whole of the family home to one party (Ch.3); a transfer of one joint owner's interest in the family home to other (Ch.4); and the transfer of an ex-partner's interest in the family home to the other party's new partner (Ch.5), once the transferor had disposed of his or her interest no further tax considerations applied so far as the transferor was concerned (unless there was an element of gift involved in the transfer not at arm's length and the transferor died within seven years, thus bringing in a charge to inheritance tax).

6–05

In the situations covered in this chapter, however, the liable party is retaining an interest in the family home until the happening of a certain event. One must, therefore, bear in mind the tax which may become chargeable on the happening of such event. The creation of different interests in the family home (e.g. the right of one party to have occupation until the youngest child attains 18 years or until his or her death) would appear to create a settlement both for capital gains tax and inheritance tax purposes (*Booth v Ellard* [1980] 1 W.L.R. 1443).

(a) Creation of the settlement

6–06 It is unlikely that the creation of the settlement will incur any liability to inheritance tax as being a transfer for value (Inheritance Tax Act 1984, s.3). First, if the decree absolute of divorce or other order has not been pronounced the parties are still married or enjoined by civil partnership (*Fender v St John-Mildmay* [1938] A.C. 1); and we have seen that transfers between spouses or civil partners (provided they are both domiciled in the UK) are exempt from a charge to inheritance tax (*see* Ch.2, p.26) even if they are living apart.

Secondly, the Inheritance Tax Act 1984, s.11 provides that a disposition is not a transfer for value for inheritance tax if made by one party for the maintenance of the other. This section gives relief in respect of a disposition made on the occasion of the dissolution of the marriage or civil partnership or if it varies a disposition made on that occasion. There is no definition of "maintenance" in the Act.

Thirdly, if the marriage or civil partnership is dissolved the disposition may be one where no gratuitous benefit is intended (see Inheritance Tax Act 1984, s.10) as it is to settle the claim of the former partner (*see* Ch.2, pp.24–25).

It is thought that, if the capital gains tax concession mentioned in Ch.2 would apply should one party transfer the whole of his or her interest in the family home to the other absolutely, it will also apply in these circumstances. No capital gains tax would, therefore, be incurred on the creation of the settlement.

(b) Termination of the settlement

6–07 When the interest of the party in occupation of the house ceases during his or her lifetime (e.g. when the youngest child becomes 18 years of age) there should be no charge to inheritance tax on that part of the settled property that reverts back to the other party (Inheritance Tax Act 1984, s.53(3)) nor on that part which is retained by the party in occupation (s.53(2)). If however, the non-occupying party dies before the other party (i.e. whilst his or her right of occupation subsists) the reversionary interest in the proceeds of sale is not excluded property and there will be a charge to inheritance tax (Inheritance Tax Act 1984, s.48(1)).

As far as capital gains tax is concerned, it is considered that the gain referrable to the occupying party's share in the house will be free from a charge to capital gains tax if the house throughout the term of the settlement has been that party's only or main residence (Taxation of

Chargeable Gains Act 1992, s.222). The non-occupying party would appear to be liable to capital gains tax on any increase in value of his or her share of the former family home between the date of the transfer into settlement and the date of the deferred sale. (This party will not have occupied the property as his or her only or main residence nor is there a disposal between spouses or civil partners—*see* Ch.2.) However, the position is open to doubt where the non-occupying party has not elected that some other house should be treated for capital gains tax purposes as his or her main residence for the period. If HMRC accept that the court order or agreement between the parties created a settlement on the ground that the interests of the beneficiaries are not of the same quality as the occupying party has a right of occupation (see *Booth v Ellard* [1980] 1 W.L.R. 1443). Taxation of Chargeable Gains Act, 1992, s.225 provides that the gain accruing to a trustee on the disposal of settled property shall in effect be free from capital gains tax where during the period of ownership the house has been the only or main residence of the person entitled to occupy it under the terms of the settlement. This should give relief to the non-occupying party for capital gains tax for the period from when the settlement is established (i.e. the court order or when the agreement between the parties was finalised) until its termination. Such genuine scenarios would seem not to be caught by the new s.226(a) (TCGA 1992 introduced by the Finance Act 2004) anti-avoidance provisions. All practitioners should however note that if the capital gains tax liability is to be avoided by the non-occupying party it is vital that the occupying party continues to live in the property. In order to protect the non-occupying party therefore all declarations of trust should contain a provision that the trust comes to an end and the property is to be sold if the occupying party fails to live in the property for periods totalling six months in any one year.

If the non-occupying party dies whilst the other's occupation subsists then no charge to capital gains tax will arise at that stage, because of the death exemption (TCGA 1992, s.73) and his or her estate will acquire a new base value for capital gains tax purposes.

5 Form of the transfer

(a) Unregistered land

If the house is in the sole name of one party it should be transferred, for reasons mentioned earlier, to trustees who can be the former partners, or one of them and an outsider, or not less than two outsiders (often one being nominated by each of the parties). A transfer to trustees may not give rise to compulsory first registration although this is somewhat unclear unless there was already a trust in existence and the transfer is merely to give effect to an appointment of new trustees. It is suggested that in all situations where a transfer of title is involved that an application for first registration is made in any event.

If the house is already in the joint names of the parties, then such tenancy, if held as beneficial joint tenants, should be severed and a

6–08

memorandum of severance should be endorsed on the conveyance to the parties (*see* Precedent 29). It is important to put a purchaser on notice that he or she will only get a good receipt if he or she pays any purchase money to two trustees or to a trust corporation (Law of Property Act 1925, s.27 (as amended)). This severance does not give rise to any application for first registration.

Following the spirit of the property legislation of 1925 and 2002, the trusts relating to the house should be kept off the title. If the house is placed in the names of outsider trustees, then a separate declaration of trust should be made by them to evidence the terms upon which they hold the property. This is probably not necessary if the house is to be held by the parties as trustees upon the terms of a court order (which will be sufficient evidence in itself), but it is strongly advised if the house is to be held by the parties as trustees upon the terms of an agreement reached between them. Any potential problems will hopefully be settled whilst the terms of the declaration of trust are being agreed. As both the parties have an interest in the property, each should be provided with a copy of any declaration of trust.

The Trustee Act 1925, s.36 allows a surviving trustee to appoint a new trustee to replace (for instance) a trustee who has died. To protect both the parties (and their respective estates) any declaration of trust might provide that any trustee appointed to replace either of them should be appointed by the deceased party's personal representatives. It would be prudent, to avoid argument, to have this expressly mentioned in any court order.

(b) *Registered land*

6–09 Any reference to a trust will be excluded from the register (Land Registration Act 2002). A panel is provided in form TR1 for the parties to confirm that they hold as tenants in common and it is suggested that the declaration of trust is referred to by reference to the parties and its date. Details will not appear on the register.

The legal title should be protected by the machinery provided by the Land Registration Act, whilst the trusts should be contained in a separate declaration of trust made by the registered proprietors.

Where land is transferred to two or more proprietors, then (in the absence of a request for its exclusion) the registrar will automatically register a Form A restriction to the effect that no disposition by a sole proprietor of land (not being a trust corporation) under which capital money arises will be registered except under an order of the registrar (Land Registration Act 2002, s.44; Land Registration Rules 2003 (SI 2003/1417), r.94).

It is probably better to go further than this, for one party may die and the other (by virtue of Trustee Act 1925, s.36) could appoint a new trustee malleable to his or her wishes and to the detriment of the deceased party's estate. It is, therefore, suggested that application be made to the registrar on form RX1 to enter a restriction under which no disposition is to be registered after the death of one of the proprietors without the consent of the personal representatives of the deceased proprietor. It would avoid argument if this is specifically mentioned in any court order. This additional restriction related to any disposition and not just to those where capital monies arise (Land Registration Rules 2003 (SI 2003/1417), r.92). As far as Precedent 26 is concerned the following restriction should be requested:

> "Except under an order of the Registrar no disposition by the proprietors of the land is to be registered after the death of any of the proprietors without the consent of the personal representatives of the deceased proprietor."

In relation to Precedents 27 and 33 the following restriction should be requested:

> "Except under an order of the Registrar no disposition by the proprietors of the land should be registered after the death of [X] without the consent of the Transferor or [his or her] personal representatives and after the death of [Y] without the consent of [the other party's name] or [his or her] personal representatives."

Obviously there must be evidence outside the registry of the trusts affecting the former family home and the declaration of trust set out at Precedent 28 is appropriate. Each trustee should have a copy.

6 Trusts of Land and Appointment of Trustees Act 1996

The Trustee Act 1925, s.36 dealing with the appointment of a new trustee has already been mentioned (*see* p.151 above). The above Act (which came into force on January 1, 1997) recognises the difficulties caused by a mentally disordered trustee (s.20) or a trustee who is "difficult" or indifferent. 6–10

Unless the provisions of the above Act are excluded (s.21(5)) s.19 allows the beneficiaries to direct the retirement of a trustee and direct the appointment of someone else in the absence of a person nominated for the purposes of appointing new trustees by the instrument creating the trust.

The precedents in this chapter envisage that there will be someone nominated to appoint a new trustee (*i.e.* usually each of the parties) and so the provisions of the Act in relation to the appointment of trustees will not be relevant.

In the absence of such nomination, the parties (as beneficiaries between them absolutely entitled, s.19(1)(b)) will be able to direct the retirement of a trustee and direct the appointment of a new one. This will not be the case if a beneficiary is not of full age (s.19(l)(b)) such as would be the case if the house (or its proceeds of sale) were partially held for a child who has not yet attained majority.

The Act abolishes the doctrine of conversion (s.3); all land held on trust is a trust of land with the trustees of land having all the powers of an absolute owner (s.6) and power to postpone a sale of land (s.4).

7 Contents of the declaration of trust

6-11 The declaration of trust referred to in the previous section should contain not only the trusts upon which the former family home is held but in addition clauses relating to:

> (i) *Repairs*—Outside trustees will particularly wish to ensure that they are under no obligation to see to the maintenance and repair of the property, and under no liability in respect of lack of maintenance and repair (*see* p.150–151).
>
> (ii) *Changing house*—See pp.148–149.
>
> (iii) *Charging clause*—If any of the trustees are professional people (such as a solicitor) or such a trustee is likely to be appointed in the future, the trust document should contain the usual charging clause (*see* p.151). If the trust is of the former family home alone, there will be no available cash out of which fees can be paid. During the life of the trust, it is unlikely that a professional trustee will actually have to do anything. The charging clause will enable him or her to collect fees at the end of the trust. The alternative, if it is contemplated that fees will be incurred during the life of the trust, is to take a separate deed of covenant from the parties, or either of them, whereby they or one of them agree to discharge the fees concerned.
>
> (iv) *Infants*—If a child (or children) of the parties is to be a beneficiary at the end of the trust and is likely to be an infant at that time, the trustees should perhaps be given power to pay the child's share of the proceeds to the parent or guardian. The Trustee Act 1925, ss.31–32, should be extended if monies are to be retained until such child or children come of age, so that the trustees have flexibility in their use of both income and capital of a child's share of the trust fund, as should the power of investment so that it is not limited by the Trustee Investments Act 1961.
>
> (v)*Insurance*—The Trustee Act 1925, s.19(1) limits a trustee's power to insure to insurance against fire to three-quarters of the value of the property; as the trustees will probably not have any cash, the occupying party should be made responsible for insurance (*see* p.159–160).

8 Where the property is subject to a mortgage

6-12 In spite of the trusts imposed on the former family home or its proceeds of sale, the non-occupying party may remain liable in respect of any mortgage secured thereon, the intent being in effect that this should be deducted from or charged on his or her equitable share. Thus, if the house has to be transferred to the parties as trustees, the building society will probably require the occupying party to covenant with the society in respect of the mortgage and that party will require an indemnity from the other in respect thereof.

If the house is already in the joint names of the parties subject to a mortgage and the non-occupying party alone is to assume liability, then again the other party will require an indemnity. It is not likely that the mortgagee will release the occupying party as one of the owners of the legal estate from liability under the mortgage. Such indemnity can be contained in the declaration of trust to be made between the parties.

The necessity of obtaining consents to transfers subject to a mortgage from occupiers of the family home aged 18 years and over must not be overlooked in view of the effect of *Williams & Glyn's Bank Ltd v Boland* [1981] A.C. 487 (*see* Precedent 6).

9 Steps to be taken following the completion of the transfer and declaration of trust

(a) Stamp duty land tax

If the parties themselves are to be the trustees of the settlement then any transfer between them will fall within Sch.3 to the Finance Act 2003 as being a transfer pursuant to a divorce or termination of a civil partnership and self-certificate SDLT 60 can be completed and sent to HM Land Registry. Where third party trustees are involved there will be a transfer for no consideration and this is also within Sch.3 and the same rule will apply and SDLT 60 will suffice. 6–13

(b) Cancellation at HM Land Charges Registry or Land Registry

Any Class F Land Charge should be cancelled (Form K13—fee £1) as should any notice of home rights at HM Land Registry (Form HR4, copy of decree absolute, no fee). Similarly it will be appropriate to cancel any pending action land charge (Form K1 1—fee £1). 6–14

(c) Completion of abstract

Where there has been a court order, a copy marked as examined against the original or a certified copy should be placed with the deeds or official copies although this would appear to be unnecessary where the property already stands in the joint names of the parties and a separate declaration of trust is made. The copy of the court order should be kept with the declaration of trust. 6–15

Similarly, a certified copy of the order should be lodged at HM Land Registry with the application for transfer or for first registration.

(d) HM Land Registry fees

The transfers in this chapter fall within the Land Registration Fees Order 2006. Fees are payable, on the basis of Scale 2, on the value of the land less charges secured if there is a transfer of the whole. Where a transfer not for 6–16 value gives effect to the disposition of a share in registered land, the fee payable is based on the value of that share. The value of the land may be evidenced by a statement from the solicitors lodging the application (either by letter or on the Land Registry Form AP1).

Where application is made for registration of a restriction only, no fee is payable (*see* Precedent 30).

(e) Insurance

6–17 If the family home is in the sole name of one party then it is best to change the insurance arrangements once agreement is reached or the court order made; the non-occupying party may neglect or refuse to pay the premium, or worse, cancel the policy to obtain a refund. If the family home is transferred into the names of trustees, then it is best that the policy be in the name of the occupier of the property with the interest of the trustees being noted on the policy. This enables the occupier to submit a prompt claim to the insurers in the event of, for instance, a fire at the property.

(f) Leasehold

6–18 If the property concerned is leasehold, the requirements of the lease as to giving notice of any assignment should be observed.

As stated in Ch.3, it may be necessary to have any shares in a lessor or management company transferred into the names of the trustees.

… HOME TO BE HELD ON CERTAIN TERMS AND CONDITIONS

PRECEDENTS

A—Transfer of family home (in sole name of one party) to both parties to hold on terms of court order

Transfer of whole of registered title(s)	Land Registry
PRECEDENT 26	**TR1**

If you need more room than is provided for in a panel, use continuation sheet CS and attach to this form.

1. **Stamp Duty**

   Place "X" in the appropriate box or boxes and complete the appropriate certificate.

   ☐ It is certified that this instrument falls within category ☐ in the Schedule to the Stamp Duty (Exempt Instruments) Regulations 1987

   ☐ It is certified that the transaction effected does not form part of a larger transaction or of a series of transactions in respect of which the amount or value or the aggregate amount or value of the consideration exceeds the sum of _____

   ☐ It is certified that this is an instrument on which stamp duty is not chargeable by virtue of the provisions of section 92 of the Finance Act 2001

2. **Title Number(s) of the Property** *Leave blank if not yet registered.*
   [TITLE NUMBER] [OR LEAVE BLANK IF APPLYING FOR FIRST REGISTRATION]

3. **Property**

   [ADDRESS]

4. **Date**

5. **Transferor** *Give full names and company's registered number if any.*
   [TRANSFEROR]

6. **Transferee for entry on the register** *Give full name(s) and company's registered number, if any. For Scottish companies use an SC prefix and for limited liability partnerships use an OC prefix before the registered number, if any. For foreign companies give territory in which incorporated.*

   [TRANSFEROR and TRANSFEREE]

   Unless otherwise arranged with Land Registry headquarters, a certified copy of the Transferee's constitution (in English or Welsh) will be required if it is a body corporate but is not a company registered in England and Wales or Scotland under the Companies Acts.

7. **Transferee's intended address(es) for service (including postcode) for entry on the register** *You may give up to three addresses for service **one** of which **must** be a postal address but does not have to be within the UK. The other addresses can be any combination of a postal address, a box number at a UK document exchange or an electronic address.*

   [TO BE AGREED BY THE PARTIES]

8. **The Transferor transfers the Property to the Transferee**

9. **Consideration** *Place "X" in the appropriate box. State clearly the currency unit if other than sterling. If none of the boxes applies, insert an appropriate memorandum in the additional provisions panel.*

   ☐ The Transferor has received from the Transferee for the Property the sum of *In words and figures.*

   ☒ *Insert other receipt as appropriate.* (See panel 12 below)

   ☐ The transfer is not for money or anything which has a monetary value

10. The Transferor transfers with *Place "X" in the appropriate box and add any modifications.*

☐ ☒ full title guarantee ☐   ☐ limited title guarantee

11. Declaration of trust *Where there is more than one Transferee, place "X" in the appropriate box.*

☐ The Transferees are to hold the Property on trust for themselves as joint tenants

☐ The Transferees are to hold the Property on trust for themselves as tenants in common in equal shares

☐ The Transferees are to hold the Property *Complete as necessary.*
UPON TRUST AS TENANTS IN COMMON PURSUANT TO THE TERMS OF A DECLARATION OF TRUST DATED [   ] AND MADE BETWEEN TRANSFEROR (1) AND TRANSFEREE (2)
NB: An application to add an additional restriction must be made on form RX1 as stated on p.156-157 Para.6-09.

12. Additional provisions *Insert here any required or permitted statements, certificates or applications and any agreed covenants, declarations, etc.*

   12.1   The transfer is made pursuant to an order of the [   ] County Court dated [   ] in proceedings between [Transferor's name] and [Transferee's name] bearing number [   ].

   12.2   Transferees apply to the Registrar to enter the following restriction (in additional to the usual obligatory restriction).

   Refer to continuation sheet [CS]

13. Execution *The Transferor must execute this transfer as a deed using the space below. If there is more than one Transferor, all must execute. Forms of execution are given in Schedule 9 to the Land Registration Rules 2003. If the transfer contains Transferee's covenants or declarations or contains an application by the Transferee (e.g. for a restriction), it must also be executed by the Transferee (all of them, if there is more than one).*

   SIGNED as a DEED by (enter full name of individual) in the presence of: [TRANSFEROR]

   Signature of Witness ....
   Name (in BLOCK CAPITALS) ....
   Address ....

   SIGNED as a DEED by (enter full name of individual) in the presence of: [TRANSFEREE]

   Signature of Witness ....
   Name (in BLOCK CAPITALS) ....
   Address ....

Continuation sheet for use with application and disposition forms

Land Registry

CS

1. Continued from Form TR1   Title number(s) TITLE NUMBER

2. *Before each continuation, state panel to be continued, e.g. "Panel 12 continued".*

   Panel 12 continued

   12.2   The Transferee covenants with the Transferor to observe and perform the covenants and conditions referred to in the Charges Register so far as still subsisting and relating to the property and will keep the Transferor and his personal representatives effectually indemnified against all losses resulting from their non observance or breach.

   Note to Clause 12.2–This clause is only necessary when the parties entered into the original restrictions affecting the property (if any) or, in the conveyance to them, covenanted to observe them. Otherwise the transferor is not entitled to them.

B—Transfer of family home (in sole name of one party) to independent trustees to hold on terms agreed between the parties

Transfer of whole of registered title(s)

PRECEDENT 27

Land Registry

TR1

If you need more room than is provided for in a panel, use continuation sheet CS and attach to this form.

1.	**Stamp Duty** *Place "X" in the appropriate box or boxes and complete the appropriate certificate.* ☐ It is certified that this instrument falls within category ☐ in the Schedule to the Stamp Duty (Exempt Instruments) Regulations 1987 ☐ It is certified that the transaction effected does not form part of a larger transaction or of a series of transactions in respect of which the amount or value or the aggregate amount or value of the consideration exceeds the sum of ☐ ☐ It is certified that this is an instrument on which stamp duty is not chargeable by virtue of the provisions of section 92 of the Finance Act 2001
2.	**Title Number(s) of the Property** *Leave blank if not yet registered.* [TITLE NUMBER] [OR LEAVE BLANK IF APPLYING FOR FIRST REGISTRATION]
3.	**Property** [ADDRESS]
4.	**Date**
5.	**Transferor** *Give full names and company's registered number if any.* [TRANSFEROR]
6.	**Transferee for entry on the register** *Give full name(s) and company's registered number, if any. For Scottish companies use an SC prefix and for limited liability partnerships use an OC prefix before the registered number, if any. For foreign companies give territory in which incorporated.* [INDEPENDENT TRUSTEES [X] AND [Y]] *Unless otherwise arranged with Land Registry headquarters, a certified copy of the Transferee's constitution (in English or Welsh) will be required if it is a body corporate but is not a company registered in England and Wales or Scotland under the Companies Acts.*
7.	**Transferee's intended address(es) for service (including postcode) for entry on the register** *You may give up to three addresses for service one of which must be a postal address but does not have to be within the UK. The other addresses can be any combination of a postal address, a box number at a UK document exchange or an electronic address.* [ADDRESS OF INDEPENDENT TRUSTEES]
8.	**The Transferor transfers the Property to the Transferee**
9.	**Consideration** *Place "X" in the appropriate box. State clearly the currency unit if other than sterling. If none of the boxes applies, insert an appropriate memorandum in the additional provisions panel.* ☐ The Transferor has received from the Transferee for the Property the sum of *In words and figures.* ☒ *Insert other receipt as appropriate.* (See panel 12 below) ☐ The transfer is not for money or anything which has a monetary value

10.	The Transferor transfers with *Place "X" in the appropriate box and add any modifications.* ☐ ☒ full title guarantee ☐ ☐ limited title guarantee

11.	Declaration of trust *Where there is more than one Transferee, place "X" in the appropriate box.* ☐ The Transferees are to hold the Property on trust for themselves as joint tenants ☐ The Transferees are to hold the Property on trust for themselves as tenants in common in equal shares ☐ The Transferees are to hold the Property *Complete as necessary.* UPON TRUST AS TENANTS IN COMMON PURSUANT TO THE TERMS OF A DECLARATION OF TRUST DATED [ ] AND MADE BETWEEN [X] AND [Y] etc … NB: An application to add an additional restriction must be made on form RX1 as stated on p. 156–157 Para.6–09.

12.	Additional provisions *Insert here any required or permitted statements, certificates or applications and any agreed covenants, declarations, etc.*	
	12.1	The Transferee covenants with the Transferor to observe and perform the covenants and conditions referred to in the Charges Register so far as still subsisting and relating to the property and to keep the Transferor and [his or her] personal representatives effectually indemnified against all losses resulting from their non-observance or breach.
		Note to Clause 12.1–This clause is only necessary when the parties entered into the original restrictions affecting the property (if any) or, in the conveyance to them, covenanted to observe them. Otherwise the transferor is not entitled to them.
	Refer to continuation sheet (CS)	

13.	Execution *The Transferor must execute this transfer as a deed using the space below. If there is more than one Transferor, all must execute. Forms of execution are given in Schedule 9 to the Land Registration Rules 2003. If the transfer contains Transferee's covenants or declarations or contains an application by the Transferee (e.g. for a restriction), it must also be executed by the Transferee (all of them, if there is more than one).*
	SIGNED as a DEED by (enter full name of individual) in the presence of: [TRANSFEROR]
	Signature of Witness ……………………………………………………. Name (in BLOCK CAPITALS) ………………………………………… Address ………………………………………………………………..
	SIGNED as a DEED by (enter full name of individual) in the presence of: [X]
	Signature of Witness ……………………………………………………. Name (in BLOCK CAPITALS) ………………………………………… Address ………………………………………………………………..

Continuation sheet for use with application and disposition forms

Land Registry

CS

1. Continued from Form [TR1]   Title number(s) [TITLE NUMBER]

2. *Before each continuation, state panel to be continued, e.g. "Panel 13 continued".*

   12.

   Panel 13 continued

   SIGNED as a DEED by (enter full name of individual) in the presence of: [Y]

Continuation sheet [1] of [1]
Insert sheet number and total number of continuation sheets e.g. "sheet 1 of 3".
© Crown copyright (ref: LR/HQ/CD-ROM) 6/03

Precedent 28—Declaration of Trust

THIS DECLARATION OF TRUST is made the   day of 200[ ] by [X] of   and [Y] of   (1) ("the Trustees" which expression shall include all other trustee or trustees of this trust) and [occupying party's name] of (2) ("W")

WHEREAS:

(A) By a transfer bearing the same date as but executed before this Declaration and made between (a) [name of sole owning party] and (2) the Trustees ("The Transfer") the freehold property known as 1 Blackacre Drive, Blackacre [registered at HM Land Registry with Title [Absolute] under Title No] was transferred to the Trustees (omit words in square brackets if this is part of an application for first registration).

(B) The Trustees make this Declaration to set out the trusts and the powers and provisions subject to which the property is held

NOW IT IS HEREBY DECLARED as follows:

1 The following expressions shall have the following meanings:

1.1 "The property" shall mean ALL THAT the property more particularly described in the Transfer and any house bungalow flat or maisonette purchased by the Trustees in accordance with the provisions of this declaration in substitution for the property

1.2 "The specified events" shall mean:

1.2.1.1 the eighteenth birthday of [A—youngest child] who was born on [date] or

1.2.1.2 the date upon which [A] shall cease full-time education whichever is the later or

1.3 the death of W or

1.4 the re-marriage of W [or entering into a registered civil partnership as appropriate]

1.5 W ceasing to occupy the property for any period in the aggregate in excess of six months in any one year whichever shall first occur

2 The Trustees shall hold the property as trustees of land.

3 The Trustees shall permit W to reside in and continue to reside in the home without payment made by [him or her] to the Trustees until one of the specified events shall happen or until such time as [he or she] shall have signified to the Trustees in writing [his or her] wish no longer to reside in the house.

4 As often as W shall request in writing the Trustees may at their discretion sell the property currently held by them upon the trusts set out in this declaration and with the net proceeds of sale purchase any other available property designated by W (but if such property be leasehold only if the unexpired residue of the term granted by the lease exceeds 60 years at the date of designation) the total cost of which (including all legal estate agents and survey fees and stamp duty land tax and HM Land Registry fees) does not exceed those proceeds (unless any excess is provided by W in which case such proportion of the future sale proceeds as such excess shall bear to the

cost of purchase shall belong to W absolutely on any such future sale) and the Trustees shall hold the property upon the trusts set out in this declaration but if on such substitution there should remain any surplus money in the hands of the Trustees they shall hold such surplus money upon the trusts of Clause 6 below.

5 W covenants with the Trustees that for as long as [he or she] shall continue to reside in the property [he or she] will pay the rent (if any) and other outgoings and keep the property in good repair and insured comprehensively to its full value in an insurance office approved by the Trustees and in the joint names of [himself or herself] and the Trustees (or in his or her sole name with the Trustees interest noted) and [he or she] shall within seven days of any demand being made produce to the Trustees or one of them such policy of insurance and the last receipt for payment of the premium and [he or she] will comply with all the terms and conditions affecting the property as if [he or she] was the absolute owner of it and was bound therein and W further covenants to indemnify the Trustees and each of them and their respective estates and effects against any loss damage liability charge or expense caused by or arising out of the failure by [him or her] to observe any of those terms and conditions.

6 Upon the happening of any one of the specified events the Trustees shall sell the dwelling and shall hold the net proceeds of sale (which for the avoidance of doubt shall mean the sum remaining after payment of all proper legal and estate agents' charges and disbursements in connection with the sale):

6.1 as to [ ] per cent for [name of non-occupying spouse] or [his or her] personal representatives (as the case may be)

6.2 as to [ ] per cent for W or [his or her] personal representatives (as the case may be)

and until such sale shall take place W if remaining in occupation shall remain liable to pay the outgoings referred to in clause 5 above and keep the dwelling in good repair and insured as required by this declaration.

7 The Trustees and each of them shall be entitled to be indemnified out of the property against all costs expenses damages claims and demands incurred or sustained by them by reason of their holding the property upon the trusts of this declaration and in furtherance of such indemnity the Trustees shall be deemed to have all the powers (including the power of sale) given to a mortgagee under the Law of Property Act 1925 and shall be entitled to exercise it to indemnify themselves or either of them under the provisions of this clause.

8.1 If after written demand made by the Trustees W shall have failed within a period of six weeks from the date of such demand to pay the rent or to put the property in good repair or to insure it as required by this declaration the Trustees may at their entire discretion pay the rent or carry out such repairs as are necessary to put the property into good repair or take out a policy of insurance (as the case may be) and the Trustees and each of them shall be entitled to an indemnity in respect of any costs or charges incurred by them in so doing and in furtherance of such indemnity the Trustees shall be deemed to have the same powers as those set out in the above clause PROVIDED ALWAYS that the Trustees shall not be liable to see to any such insurance or repair and shall be under no liability in that respect.

8.2 The Trustees may borrow money using the property as security if required on such terms as to interest and repayment and otherwise as they may think fit for the purpose of carrying out such repairs as required by this declaration.

9 The power of appointing a trustee in substitution for [X] shall be vested in [*name of non-occupying party*] during [his or her] lifetime and after [his or her] death in [his or her] personal representatives and the power of appointing a trustee in substitution for [Y] shall be vested in W during [his or her] lifetime and after [his or her] death in [his or her] personal representatives.

[10 *Charging clause if professional trustees:*

Any trustee of this declaration engaged in a profession or business shall be entitled to be paid all usual professional or other charges for business transacted and acts done by [him or her] or by a partner of [his or her] in connection with the trusts of this declaration (whether or not in the course of his profession or business) including acts which a trustee not being in a profession or business could have done personally].

IN WITNESS whereof this Declaration has been executed as a deed on the date appearing above.
SIGNED *etc*

C—Family home (parties joint tenants) to be held on terms of court order. Occupying party to repair and insure

Precedent 29—Unregistered Land

Memorandum [to be endorsed on last conveyance]

Memorandum Following an Order in the   County Court date and in proceedings between [*occupying party's name*] and [*non-occupying party's name*] bearing number the joint tenancy in equity created by this Conveyance was severed

Precedent 30—Registered Land

Application to enter a restriction—use Form RX1 and ask for the following restriction to be entered:

Restriction Except under an Order of the Registrar no disposition is to be registered after the death of either of the proprietors without the consent of the personal representatives of the deceased proprietor
SIGNED *etc*

Precedent 31—Declaration of Trust (unregistered and registered land)

THIS DECLARATION OF TRUST is made the   day of   200   By [*first party's name*] of("SP1") and   [*second party's name*] of   ("SP2")

WHEREAS:

—unregistered land

(A) By a Transfer ("the Transfer") dated   and made between (1) [*Transferor's name*] and (2) SP1 and SP2 the Property briefly described in the Schedule below was transferred to SP1 and SP2 in fee simple as beneficial joint tenants

(B) Following an Order in the   County Court dated in proceedings between SP1 and SP2 bearing number   the joint tenancy created by the Transfer was severed as the parties admit and it was ordered that the Property be held upon the terms set out in this declaration

—registered land

(A) SP1 and SP2 are registered as the proprietors at HM Land Registry of the property described in the Schedule below

(B) Following an Order in the   County Court dated and in proceedings between SP1 and SP2 bearing number   it was ordered that the Property be held upon the terms set out in this declaration and the parties have made application to HM Land Registry to enter a Restriction to the effect that except under an order of the Registrar no disposition is to be registered after the death of either of them without the consent of the deceased's personal representatives

NOW IT IS HEREBY DECLARED as follows:

1 IN pursuance of the Court Order as from [*date of Court Order*] SP1 and SP2 shall HOLD the Property as trustees of land upon the terms of the Court Order and in accordance with that order as to [ ] per cent of the net proceeds of sale for SP1 and as to [ ] per cent of the net proceeds of sale for SP2.

2 SP2 covenants with SP1 that [he or she] will pay all outgoings in respect of the Property and that [he or she] will keep the Property in good repair and insured comprehensively to its full value in an insurance office approved by the SP1 and in the joint names of SP1 and SP2 and [he or she] shall within seven days of any demand being made produce to SP1 such policy of insurance and the last receipt for premium in respect thereof

IN WITNESS *etc*

THE SCHEDULE
[*brief description of property from title documents*]

D—Family home (parties joint tenants) subject to mortgage, to be held on terms of court order. Non-occupying party responsible for mortgage (interest only)

Precedent 32—Declaration of Trust—memorandum of severance (**Precedent 29**) or restriction (**Precedent 30**) having been completed

THIS DECLARATION OF TRUST is made the   day of   200[] By [*First party's name*] of   (1) ("SP1") and [*Second party's name*] of   (2) ("SP2")

HOME TO BE HELD ON CERTAIN TERMS AND CONDITIONS

WHEREAS:

(A) [*Recital of conveyance/transfer to the parties as appropriate—Precedent 30, recital (A)*]

(B) By a Mortgage ("the Mortgage") dated   and made between (1) SP1 and SP2 and (2) [Bank or Building Society] ("the lender") the Property was charged to the lender to secure the sum of £

(C) The sum of £   is now owing to the Lender on the security of the Mortgage

(D) By an Order in the   County Court dated in proceedings between SP1 and SP2 bearing number the joint tenancy created by the transfer was severed and it was ordered that the Property be held upon the terms set out in this declaration with the SP1 being solely responsible for the monies due under the Mortgage
NOW IT IS HEREBY DECLARED:

1 Pursuant to the Order as from [*date of Court Order*] SP1 and SP2 shall hold the Property as trustees of land upon the terms of the Court Order Subject to the Mortgage and upon sale as to[ ] per cent of the net proceeds for SP1 and as to[ ]per cent of the net proceeds for SP2. For the purposes of this clause "net proceeds" shall mean the proceeds of sale less the amount required to discharge the Mortgage and all proper legal and estate agents charges and disbursements in connection with such sale [and after giving credit to the SPI for all repayments of capital made by him or her in respect of the Mortgage prior to the date of sale].

2 SP1 covenants with SP2 that with effect from [*usually a date specified in the Court Order*] and until the Property is sold that [he or she] will pay and discharge all principal monies interest costs and other monies secured by or to become payable under the Mortgage and will at all times indemnify and keep indemnified SP2 and [his or her] estate and effects against all proceedings costs claims and demands in respect thereof

3 [*Covenant to repair—Precedent 30, clause 2*]

IN WITNESS *etc*

THE SCHEDULE
[*brief description of property from title documents*]

E—Family home held by both parties as joint tenants to be held following court order or agreement by independent trustees for one party to reside until specified event, non-residing party to be responsible for major repairs (and receive credit) and both parties covenanting with the trustees

Transfer of whole of registered title(s)

PRECEDENT 33

Land Registry

TR1

If you need more room than is provided for in a panel, use continuation sheet CS and attach to this form.

1. **Stamp Duty**

    Place "X" in the appropriate box or boxes and complete the appropriate certificate.

    ☐ It is certified that this instrument falls within category ☐ in the Schedule to the Stamp Duty (Exempt Instruments) Regulations 1987

    ☐ It is certified that the transaction effected does not form part of a larger transaction or of a series of transactions in respect of which the amount or value or the aggregate amount or value of the consideration exceeds the sum of

    ☐ It is certified that this is an instrument on which stamp duty is not chargeable by virtue of the provisions of section 92 of the Finance Act 2001

2. **Title Number(s) of the Property** *Leave blank if not yet registered.*
    [TITLE NUMBER] [OR LEAVE BLANK IF APPLYING FOR FIRST REGISTRATION]

3. **Property**

    [ADDRESS]

4. **Date**

5. **Transferor** *Give full names and company's registered number if any.*
    [BOTH PARTIES]

6. **Transferee for entry on the register** *Give full name(s) and company's registered number, if any. For Scottish companies use an SC prefix and for limited liability partnerships use an OC prefix before the registered number, if any. For foreign companies give territory in which incorporated.*

    [INDEPENDENT TRUSTEES [X] AND [Y]]

    Unless otherwise arranged with Land Registry headquarters, a certified copy of the Transferee's constitution (in English or Welsh) will be required if it is a body corporate but is not a company registered in England and Wales or Scotland under the Companies Acts.

7. **Transferee's intended address(es) for service (including postcode) for entry on the register** *You may give up to three addresses for service one of which must be a postal address but does not have to be within the UK. The other addresses can be any combination of a postal address, a box number at a UK document exchange or an electronic address.*

    [ADDRESS OF INDEPENDENT TRUSTEES]

8. **The Transferor transfers the Property to the Transferee**

9. **Consideration** *Place "X" in the appropriate box. State clearly the currency unit if other than sterling. If none of the boxes applies, insert an appropriate memorandum in the additional provisions panel.*

    ☐ The Transferor has received from the Transferee for the Property the sum of *In words and figures.*

    ☒ *Insert other receipt as appropriate.* (See panel 12 below)

    ☐ The transfer is not for money or anything which has a monetary value

HOME TO BE HELD ON CERTAIN TERMS AND CONDITIONS 173

10. The Transferor transfers with *Place "X" in the appropriate box and add any modifications.*

☐ ☒ full title guarantee ☐ ☐ limited title guarantee

11. Declaration of trust *Where there is more than one Transferee, place "X" in the appropriate box.*

☐ The Transferees are to hold the Property on trust for themselves as joint tenants

☐ The Transferees are to hold the Property on trust for themselves as tenants in common in equal shares

☐ The Transferees are to hold the Property *Complete as necessary.*
UPON TRUST AS TENANTS IN COMMON PURSUANT TO THE TERMS OF A DECLARATION OF TRUST DATED [ ] AND MADE BETWEEN [X] AND [Y] etc ...
NB: An application to add an additional restriction must be made on form RX1 as stated on p.156–157 Para.6–09.

12. Additional provisions *Insert here any required or permitted statements, certificates or applications and any agreed covenants, declarations, etc.*

12.1 The transfer is made pursuant to an order of the [ ] County Court dated [ ] in proceedings between [*First spouse' name*] and [*Second spouse' name*] bearing number [ ].

12.2 The Transferee covenants with the Transferor to observe and perform the covenants and conditions referred to in the Charges Register so far as still subsisting and relating to the property and to keep the Transferor and their personal representatives effectually indemnified against all losses resulting from their non observance or breach.

Note to Clause 12.2-This clause is only necessary when the parties entered into the original restrictions affecting the property (if any) or, in the conveyance to them, covenanted to observe them. Otherwise the transferor is not entitled to them.

Refer to continuation sheet (CS)

13. Execution *The Transferor must execute this transfer as a deed using the space below. If there is more than one Transferor, all must execute. Forms of execution are given in Schedule 9 to the Land Registration Rules 2003. If the transfer contains Transferee's covenants or declarations or contains an application by the Transferee (e.g. for a restriction), it must also be executed by the Transferee (all of them, if there is more than one).*

SIGNED as a DEED by (enter full name of individual) in the presence of: [FIRST SPOUSE]

Signature of Witness ....
Name (in BLOCK CAPITALS) ....
Address ....

SIGNED as a DEED by (enter full name of individual) in the presence of: [SECOND SPOUSE]

Signature of Witness ....
Name (in BLOCK CAPITALS) ....
Address ....

Continuation sheet for use with application and disposition forms

Land Registry

CS

1. Continued from Form TR1   Title number(s) TITLE NUMBER

2. *Before each continuation, state panel to be continued, e.g. "Panel 12 continued".*

Panel 13 continued

SIGNED as a DEED by (enter full name of individual) in the presence of: [X]

SIGNED as a DEED by (enter full name of individual) in the presence of: [Y]

Continuation sheet 1 **of** 1
Insert sheet number and total number of continuation sheets e.g. "sheet 1 of 3".
© Crown copyright (ref: LR/HQ/CD-ROM) 6/03

Precedent 34—Declaration of Trust

THIS DECLARATION OF TRUST is made the   day of   200[ ] by (1) [X] of
and [Y] of
(l)("the Trustees" which expression shall include all other the trustee or trustees for the time being of this trust) and [*First party's name*] of (2) ("SP1") and [*Second party's name*] of (3) ("SP2")

WHEREAS

(A) By a Transfer bearing the same date as but executed before this Declaration the Property briefly described in the Schedule below was transferred to the Trustees

(B) The Trustees make this Declaration to set out the terms upon which the Property is held and SP1 and SP2 join in to give the covenants and agreements set out in this declaration

NOW IT IS HEREBY DECLARED as follows:—

1   The following expressions shall have the following meanings:—

    1.1   "The property" shall mean the property described in the Schedule below and any house bungalow flat or maisonette purchased by the Trustees in accordance with the provisions of this declaration in substitution for the Property

    1.2   "The specified events" shall mean:—

        1.2.1 the remarriage of SP2 [or entering into a registered civil partnership as appropriate]

        1.2.2 the death of SP2

        1.2.3 the cohabitation of SP2 for a period in excess of six months

        1.2.4 SP2 ceasing to occupy the dwelling for any period in the aggregate in excess of six calendar months in any period of one year

    whichever shall first occur

2   *Precedent 28, clause 2—trustees of land*

3   *Precedent 28, clause 3—SP2 to reside free of charge*

4   *Precedent 28, clause 4—change of dwelling*

    5.1   SP2 covenants with the Trustees and with SP1 that [he or she] will pay the rent (if any) and other outgoings in respect of the property and shall keep the property in good repair both externally and internally (subject to the provisions of sub-clause (5.2) of this clause) and keep the same insured comprehensively to its full value [*continue as Precedent 28, clause 5*]

    5.2   In the event that major repairs are required to the property to retain its value SP1 covenants with SP2 and the Trustees to pay the cost of them and to pay such sum to the Trustees before commencement of the necessary work. In the event of any dispute as to whether or not such repairs are major or are required such dispute shall be referred by the Trustees to a Chartered Surveyor whose decision shall be final and binding on the parties. The fees of the Surveyor shall be paid equally by SP1 and SP2

5.3 SP2 agrees that on the sale of the property under the provisions of clause 6 the cost of any repairs under clause 5.2 which shall have been paid by SP1 shall be reimbursed to SP1 before division of the net proceeds of sale as set out in clause 6. The Trustees shall only be bound to repay SPI as stated above if they receive a receipted account from SP1 showing the cost of such repairs.

5.4 In the event that SP2 shall improve the property at his or her own cost (as opposed to repairing or maintaining it in good repair) and provided he or she shall have first obtained the written consent of SP1 to such improvements the SP2 shall be repaid the cost of such improvements before division of the net proceeds of sale as set out in clause 6. The Trustees shall only be bound to repay SP2 stated above if they receive a receipted account from SP2 showing the cost of such improvements and written evidence of the consent of SP1 to them

6 *Precedent 28, clause 6—division of proceeds*

7 *Precedent 28, clause 7—indemnity of Trustees*

8 *Precedent 28, clause 8—power of Trustees to repair, etc.*

9 *Precedent 28, clause 9—appointment of Trustees*

10 *Precedent 28, clause 10—charging clause*

IN WITNESS whereof this declaration has been executed as a deed on the date appearing above.

SCHEDULE
[*brief description of property*]

Chapter 7

Deferred Charges and Adjustment between both Parties of their Interests

There are many adjustments that can be made to the interests of the parties in the family home. It can be transferred to one of them alone (*see* Chs 3 and 4) or the rights of one party can be postponed until the happening of a specified event (*see* Ch.6). Similarly, the interest of one party can be increased (for instance, where the parties hold the property as tenants in common and it is agreed, or ordered by the court, that one party's share should be increased). Agreement should be reached on responsibility for repairs and insurance. More commonly, the parties (or the court) may consider that the family home should stand in the sole name of one party but that the other party should be compensated by the payment of cash, or (if cash is not available) that the non-owning party should have a charge on the property for a fixed amount (as opposed to an interest in the equity—as to which *see* Ch.6), the calling in of the charge being deferred until a specific time or happening of a specified event (e.g. death or remarriage/new civil partnership of occupying party). Such an order, sometimes known as a *Browne v Pritchard* order (*Browne v Pritchard* [1975] 3 All E.R. 721), might look as follows:

7–01

> "It is ordered that the Respondent shall within 28 days transfer with full title guarantee to the Petitioner the property known as 1 Blackacre Drive, Blackacre and that the Petitioner shall thereupon execute a Legal Charge of the said property in favour of the Respondent in the form of the draft annexed to secure the sum of £25,000 and that the said charge shall provide that the statutory power of sale thereunder shall be deemed to arise on the death or remarriage of the Petitioner or upon January 10, 2015 whichever is the earlier."

The court has no specific power to order a charge to be given over a transferred property, but has assumed it has such power under Matrimonial Causes Act 1970, s.24(1)(b), which gives it power to settle property as between the parties. Judicial approval has been given to charges on property (*Knibb v Knibb* [1987] 2 F.L.R. 396 and *Ciutton v Clutton* [1991] 1 W.L.R. 359).

From the non-occupying party's point of view it is obviously more satisfactory to have repayment of the mortgage on a fixed date or on the happening of a specified event (such as remarriage of the other party) if earlier rather than have repayment of his or her charge postponed until sale of the property. In this latter event, unless the party concerned is to receive a reasonable rate of interest on the monies outstanding, the monies received on repayment of the charge could be worth very little in purchasing power by the time they are received. Recognising this, it is not unusual for the court to make an order that the property be transferred to one party, but with a charge in favour of the other equivalent to a percentage of the net proceeds of sale with the calling in of the charge deferred until the happening of one of the "specified events" (*see* Precedent 41).

While the house in one party's sole name with a fixed charge in favour of the other facilitates the owning party's control of the property, it does not offer that party the flexibility to move house that might be incorporated when the house is held by trustees until a specified event (*see* Ch.6). If it is desired to give the owning party the facility to sell the property and give a charge over the substituted property upon the same terms and conditions, these provisions should be contained in the court order (see *Encyclopaedia of Forms and Precedents* Vol.16(2) 1996 Butterworths, p.343). It is not appropriate to incorporate provisions to transfer the charge to another house in the original charge, as that charge relates to a specific property (and will remain with those title documents); such flexibility can raise difficulties particularly if the owning party wishes to move down market and release some funds (without repaying the other party) as this thereby reduces the security, especially if the non-owning party only has the security of a second charge (see Precedent 39).

Very few court orders, whereby one party is to take a charge over the former family home, contain details of the specific provisions to be contained in such charge. There is no reason why a consent order should not incorporate a draft legal charge. If the parties cannot agree on the terms of the mortgage, application can always be made to the court who will settle the terms of the mortgage or direct that conveyancing counsel be appointed by the court to do so.

In view of disadvantages of the non-occupying party having a fixed sum tied up in property at a time of depreciating money values, practitioners might be advised to consider including in the mortgage a provision to the effect that any capital sum received by the owning party during the currency of the mortgage (for example, by way of inheritance or lottery win) should be paid to the other party by way of reduction of the mortgage debt. It is suggested that such provision be specifically mentioned in the court order as it is unlikely to be accepted voluntarily.

Conversely, unless the charge so specifies, there is no limitation on the owning party redeeming the mortgage early (*Popat v Popat* [1991] 2 F.L.R. 163).

1 Conduct of the conveyancing

7–02 Unless any cash payment is passing between the parties for the purchase of another property, a contract would appear to be unnecessary and is certainly not required if the transaction is to be carried out following a court order (whether by consent or otherwise) as application can always be made to the court for the terms of the order to be carried out (*see* Ch.8).

It is appropriate that solicitors acting for the "acquiring party" should draw the appropriate transfer and the other party's solicitors should, therefore, provide official copies. As previously stated official copies can easily be obtained by the transferees solicitor by posting form OC1, by telephone or electronically from Land Registry Direct.

If the transferor is to take a mortgage over the former family home, then, following usual conveyancing practice, his or her solicitors should draft and submit this to the other party's solicitors.

If the house was formerly in the sole name of one party, it would be appropriate for the acquiring party's solicitors to insist on a full abstract of title commencing with a good root of title, although it seems to be accepted in practice that the title was properly investigated at the time of the other party's purchase. If the house is already in the joint names of the parties, it is usual to accept that the title was properly investigated at the time of purchase.

Once the documentation is complete, it is suggested that a "completion date" be agreed, so that the necessary searches can be made (*see* Ch.3, p.61) and monies requisitioned by reference to that date.

2 Covenants for title

(a) Transfer by one party to the other. As mentioned in Ch.1 (p.6) there seems no good reason why the transferor should not transfer to the transferee with full title guarantee.   7–03
(b) Leasehold. Practitioners attention is drawn to the position of leasehold property (*see* Ch.1, p.6).
(c) The Mortgage. In addition to those covenants implied by the "acquiring party" being expressed to charge the property with full title guarantee such words further imply:

   (i) where the disposition is a mortgage of property subject to a rentcharge, the mortgagor will fully and promptly observe and perform all the obligations under the instrument creating the rentcharge that are presently enforceable (Law of Property (Miscellaneous Provisions) Act 1995, s.5(1) and (2));

   (ii) where the disposition is a mortgage of leasehold land, the mortgagor will fully and promptly observe and perform all the obligations under the lease imposed on the tenant (s.5(3)).

Whilst these additional covenants are also implied where property is charged with limited title guarantee, there seems to be no good reason why full title guarantee should not be required.

3 Tax considerations

So far as the transfer of the property or the whole or part of the transferring party's share in it to the other party is concerned, the provisions set out in Ch.2 apply and for the reasons there mentioned there is unlikely to be a liability for capital gains tax or inheritance tax.   7–04

Similarly the creation of a charge for a fixed amount in favour of the transferring party, and the repayment of that charge, would not appear to involve any liability for capital gains tax (Taxation of Chargeable Gains Act 1992, s.251 provides that there is no charge to capital gains tax on repayment of a debt to a creditor) or inheritance tax.

If the charge on the property in favour of the transferring party is not for a fixed amount but is expressed to be equivalent, for example, to one third of the net proceeds of sale, then that party has acquired a chargeable asset (*Marren v Ingles* [1980] 1 W.L.R. 983) and payment of the capital sum by way of redemption of the charge would appear to be a chargeable disposal for capital gains tax purposes (TCGA 1992, s.22). One would deduct from the amount received the value of the charge at the date the charge was executed in order to arrive at the taxable gain and claim other reliefs (*see* Ch.2).

It is not thought that repayment of this type of charge would result in any charge to inheritance tax, as there is not a disposition intended to confer gratuitous benefit (Inheritance Tax Act 1984, s.10).

4 Form of transfer

(a) Unregistered land

7–05   If the house already stands in the joint names of the parties as beneficial joint tenants and one party is to have a specific interest in it, then the tenancy should be severed and a declaration of trust made (*see* Ch.6). If, however, the parties already hold as tenants in common, and there is to be an adjustment in the extent of their respective interests, then, so far as the legal title is concerned, no alteration needs to be made. Neither of these operations will give rise to compulsory registrations although an opportunity for voluntary registration arises and should, in the writer's view, be taken.

Any purchaser is already on notice that to get a good receipt he or she will have to pay purchase money to two trustees or a trust corporation (Law of Property Act 1925, s.27 as amended by Trusts of Land and Appointment of Trustees Act 1996). However, the change in the equitable interests must be evidenced. To lodge a copy of the court order with the title deeds may be sufficient, but to be strictly formal a deed of assignment should be made (*see* Precedent 35). It is suggested that copies (or duplicates) be held by both parties so as to evidence the extent of their respective interests.

On any assignment of an equitable interest, notice should be given to the trustees of the legal estate (*Deane v Hall* (1828) 3 Russ 1); but if the parties are the trustees this is academic. Notice should be given if the trustees of the legal estate are persons other than the parties.

For the reasons mentioned in Ch.6, the parties should be advised to agree how replacement trustees of the legal estate should be appointed, rather than the surviving trustee being left with this power (Trustee Act 1925, s.36). Such provision can be in a separate deed between the parties (to be lodged with the deeds). Agreement should also be reached as to responsibility for maintenance, repairs and insurance of the property (*see* Precedent 31).

So far as a transfer to one party coupled with a deferred charge in favour of the other is concerned, this should proceed by way of a transfer (*see* Chs 3 and 4) followed by a separate charge (*see* Precedent 39). Any transfer of title will require an application for first registration.

(b) Registered land

If the parties hold as tenants in common, a restriction will already be on the register to the effect that a disposition by a sole proprietor of land (not being a trust corporation) under which capital money arises will not be registered except under an order of the Registrar (Land Registration Act 2002, s.44; Land Registration Rules 2003, r.92). This restriction should be extended to protect the interest of the estate of either party by entering the further restriction set out in Precedent 30.

7–06

In addition, of course, there should be a Memorandum off the register or declaration of trust (*see* Precedent 31) as to the shares in the net proceeds of sale of each party, and obligations as to repair and maintenance.

(c) Property held by the parties and a third party

In circumstances where one party is to convey his or her interest in the house to the other, little needs to be done to the legal title other than for the transferor to retire as a trustee although a transfer should be made which has the same effect; the transferee and third party (possibly his or her mother) will be left holding the legal estate, the beneficial interests being "behind the curtain".

7–07

Section 39 of the Trustee Act 1925 provides that where a trustee desires to be discharged from the trust and where after his or her discharge there will be either a trust corporation or at least two individuals to act as trustees, then if the trustee by deed declares that he or she desires to be discharged and his or her co-trustees consent, he shall be deemed to have retired from the trust. The transferor's beneficial interest will be dealt with by an assignment (*see* Precedent 42).

5 Where the property is subject to a mortgage

If the family home is already subject to a mortgage then the requirements of the mortgagees will have to be ascertained prior to a transfer and if, although the house is to remain in joint names, liability for the mortgage payments is to be assumed by one party, an indemnity to the other party will have to be included in the declaration of trust (*see* Precedent 32).

7–08

If the property is subject to a first mortgage and is, for instance, to be transferred from one party to the other, subject to a charge being given in favour of the transferor to secure a fixed sum, the transferor will have to be satisfied with the security of a second charge, notice of which should be served on the first mortgagee (*see* Precedent 40).

Where the charge to be granted to the transferor or other party is to be a second charge then it is essential that the consent of the first mortgagee is obtained as they will invariably have the benefit of a restriction registered at HM Land Registry preventing any dealings with the property without their express consent. These matters should be checked at the stage when any agreement is being formulated by the parties in order to ensure that what is desired is achievable.

Where the property is to be transferred subject to a mortgage, or where a new mortgage is to be created, it will be necessary to obtain consents to such transactions from any occupants of the property aged 18 years or over (following the case of *Williams & Glyn's Bank Ltd v Boland* [1981] A.C. 487). (*see* Precedent 6).

6 Steps to be taken following the completion of the transfer

(a) Stamp duty land tax

7–09 The circumstances envisaged in this chapter fall within Sch.3 to the Finance Act 2003 (*see* Ch.2) and a self-certificate in form SDLT 60 can be given so that no stamp duty land tax is payable.

A mortgage is not subject to stamp duty land tax.

(b) Cancellation and registration at HM Land Registry: notices

7–10 If the former family home has been in the sole name of one party, then on completion of the various transactions the family home rights registrations should be cancelled. Similarly, any registration of a pending action or action should be cancelled.

A second mortgage will be registered automatically against the title on the lodging of the application for registration provided that the consent of the first mortgagee is obtained in order to circumvent the inevitable restriction registered in its favour. Pursuant to the Land Registry Act 2002, s.49 the party having the benefit of a deferred charge must serve notice of that charge on any prior mortgagee otherwise the first mortgagee can make further advances with priority over the second mortgagee, where the first charge was made for securing further advances (in addition to the original advance). Practitioners should remember to serve notice of the second charge on the first mortgagee (*see* Precedent 40).

(c) Court order and completion of the abstract

7–11 In the case of all transactions, a copy of the court order, marked as examined against the original, should be delivered with the application for registration of the transfer to HM Land Registry.

(d) HM Land Registry fees

7–12 The registration or modification of a restriction attracts no fee (Land Registration Fees Order 2006).

Unless the transfer is for a monetary consideration (in which case fees under Scale 1 of the Order are payable based on the consideration) fees will be charged on Scale 2 based on the value of the land the subject of the dealing after deduction therefrom of the amount of any charge to which the property remains subject. Where the transfer gives effect to the disposition of a share in registered land, the fee is based on the value of that share. The value of the land may be evidenced by a statement from the solicitors lodging the application (either by letter or on HM Land Registry Form AP1 or FR1).

Where a charge is given over land (e.g. Precedents 38 and 39), Scale 2 of the Fee Order will apply by reference to the amount of the charge. However, where a charge is delivered together with an application to register a transfer of title then a scale fee is payable on the transaction but no fee is payable for the registration of the charge.

(e) Insurance

If the property passes to one party alone, the insurance policy should be effected in that party's name. If the other party's name remained there, this could cause difficulties in respect of any claim as that party's receipt might be required.   **7–13**

If there is a mortgage granted in favour of the non-owning party, it is probably best either that the policy be in the names of the both parties, or (more properly) in the owning party's sole name, but with the other party's interest as mortgagee noted thereon.

(f) Leasehold

Notice of assignment of leasehold property should be given to the lessor who should also be given details of any mortgagee so that, in the event of non-payment of rent, the mortgagee can be approached for payment, thus avoiding forfeiture of the lease.   **7–14**

PRECEDENTS

A—Assignment by one party (tenant in common) of part of undivided share in sale proceeds of family home to other party (co-tenant in common) following court order. No sale until happening of specified event

Precedent 35—Applies to both registered and unregistered land

THIS ASSIGNMENT is made the   day of   200[ ] BETWEEN (1) [*Assignor's name*] of   ("A") and (2) [*Assignee's name*] of   ("B")

WHEREAS:

(A) A and B are respectively entitled to an equal half interest in the Property described in the Schedule free from incumbrances.

(B) By an Order in the   County Court dated   and in proceedings between A and B bearing number   it was ordered that A should transfer part of [his or her] interest to B so that A and B should hold the Property as to 75 per cent for B and as to the remaining 25 per cent for A and that no sale of the Property should take place until the happening of one of the events specified in the Order

NOW pursuant to the Order THIS DEED WITNESSES:

1 A assigns to B absolutely a sufficient part of [his or her] interest in the Property so that from the date of this assignment it shall be held by A and B as trustees of land as to 25 per cent for A and 75 per cent for B.

2 The assignment is made with full title guarantee

3 A and B agree with each other that no sale of the Property shall take place until the happening of one of the events specified in the Order and in accordance with the terms thereof unless both of them shall consent in writing

4 [*Covenant to repair and insure by B*]—*Precedent 31, clause 2*

IN WITNESS *etc*

THE SCHEDULE
Description of property [including title number if registered]

B—Family home in one party's name. Transfer to other subject to payment. Court order

Transfer of whole of registered title(s)

PRECEDENT 36

Land Registry

TR1

If you need more room than is provided for in a panel, use continuation sheet CS and attach to this form.

1. Stamp Duty

Place "X" in the appropriate box or boxes and complete the appropriate certificate.

☐ It is certified that this instrument falls within category ☐ in the Schedule to the Stamp Duty (Exempt Instruments) Regulations 1987

☐ It is certified that the transaction effected does not form part of a larger transaction or of a series of transactions in respect of which the amount or value or the aggregate amount or value of the consideration exceeds the sum of ☐

☐ It is certified that this is an instrument on which stamp duty is not chargeable by virtue of the provisions of section 92 of the Finance Act 2001

2. Title Number(s) of the Property *Leave blank if not yet registered.*
[TITLE NUMBER] [OR LEAVE BLANK IF APPLYING FOR FIRST REGISTRATION]

3. Property

[ADDRESS]

4. Date

5. Transferor *Give full names and company's registered number if any.*
[TRANSFEROR]

6. Transferee for entry on the register *Give full name(s) and company's registered number, if any. For Scottish companies use an SC prefix and for limited liability partnerships use an OC prefix before the registered number, if any. For foreign companies give territory in which incorporated.*

[TRANSFEREE]

Unless otherwise arranged with Land Registry headquarters, a certified copy of the Transferee's constitution (in English or Welsh) will be required if it is a body corporate but is not a company registered in England and Wales or Scotland under the Companies Acts.

7. Transferee's intended address(es) for service (including postcode) for entry on the register *You may give up to three addresses for service one of which must be a postal address but does not have to be within the UK. The other addresses can be any combination of a postal address, a box number at a UK document exchange or an electronic address.*

[TRANSFEREE'S ADDRESS] (this will usually be the address of the property)

8. The Transferor transfers the Property to the Transferee

9. Consideration *Place "X" in the appropriate box. State clearly the currency unit if other than sterling. If none of the boxes applies, insert an appropriate memorandum in the additional provisions panel.*

☐ The Transferor has received from the Transferee for the Property the sum of *In words and figures.*

(AMOUNT OF CONSIDERATION IN WORDS AND NUMBERS)

☐ *Insert other receipt as appropriate.*

☐ The transfer is not for money or anything which has a monetary value

10. The Transferor transfers with *Place "X" in the appropriate box and add any modifications.*

    ☐ ☒ full title guarantee ☐   ☐ limited title guarantee

11. Declaration of trust *Where there is more than one Transferee, place "X" in the appropriate box.*

    ☐ The Transferees are to hold the Property on trust for themselves as joint tenants

    ☐ The Transferees are to hold the Property on trust for themselves as tenants in common in equal shares

    ☐ The Transferees are to hold the Property *Complete as necessary.*

12. Additional provisions *Insert here any required or permitted statements, certificates or applications and any agreed covenants, declarations, etc.*

    12.1   The transfer is made pursuant to an order of the [   ] County Court dated [   ] in proceedings between the Transferor and Transferee bearing number [   ].

    12.2   The transferee covenants with the transferor to observe and perform the covenants and conditions referred to in the Charges Register so far as still subsisting and relating to the Property and will keep the Transferor and [his or her] personal representatives effectually indemnified against all losses resulting from their non observance or breach.

    Note to Clause 12.2—This clause is only necessary when the parties entered into the original restrictions affecting the property (if any) or, in the conveyance to them, covenanted to observe them. Otherwise the transferor is not entitled to them.

    12.3   The covenant by the Transferor implied by section 4(1)(b) Law of Property (Miscellaneous Provisions) Act 1994 by reason of the Transferor transferring with Full Title Guarantee shall be limited so as not to extend to any breach of the terms of the registered lease on the part of the Transferor relating to the condition of the property [Limitation of Transferor's liability in relation to repair: (see p.6)] [Only relevant if leasehold]

13. Execution *The Transferor must execute this transfer as a deed using the space below. If there is more than one Transferor, all must execute. Forms of execution are given in Schedule 9 to the Land Registration Rules 2003. If the transfer contains Transferee's covenants or declarations or contains an application by the Transferee (e.g. for a restriction), it must also be executed by the Transferee (all of them, if there is more than one).*

    SIGNED as a DEED by (enter full name of individual) in the presence of: [TRANSFEROR]

    Signature of Witness ....
    Name (in BLOCK CAPITALS) ....
    Address ....

    SIGNED as a DEED by (enter full name of individual) in the presence of: [TRANSFEREE]

    Signature of Witness ....
    Name (in BLOCK CAPITALS) ....
    Address ....

DEFERRED CHARGES AND ADJUSTMENT BETWEEN BOTH PARTIES 187

C—Family home in joint names of parties as joint tenants. Transfer of whole to one party by court order. Other party to have charge. Not to be called in until fixed date. Interest payable meantime. Leasehold

Transfer of whole of registered title(s)

PRECEDENT 37

Land Registry

TR1

If you need more room than is provided for in a panel, use continuation sheet CS and attach to this form.

1. **Stamp Duty**

   Place "X" in the appropriate box or boxes and complete the appropriate certificate.

   ☐ It is certified that this instrument falls within category ☐ in the Schedule to the Stamp Duty (Exempt Instruments) Regulations 1987

   ☐ It is certified that the transaction effected does not form part of a larger transaction or of a series of transactions in respect of which the amount or value or the aggregate amount or value of the consideration exceeds the sum of _____

   ☐ It is certified that this is an instrument on which stamp duty is not chargeable by virtue of the provisions of section 92 of the Finance Act 2001

2. **Title Number(s) of the Property** *Leave blank if not yet registered.*
   [TITLE NUMBER] [OR LEAVE BLANK IF APPLYING FOR FIRST REGISTRATION]

3. **Property**
   [ADDRESS]

4. **Date**

5. **Transferor** *Give full names and company's registered number if any.*
   [BOTH PARTIES]

6. **Transferee for entry on the register** *Give full name(s) and company's registered number, if any. For Scottish companies use an SC prefix and for limited liability partnerships use an OC prefix before the registered number, if any. For foreign companies give territory in which incorporated.*

   [TRANSFEREE]

   Unless otherwise arranged with Land Registry headquarters, a certified copy of the Transferee's constitution (in English or Welsh) will be required if it is a body corporate but is not a company registered in England and Wales or Scotland under the Companies Acts.

7. **Transferee's intended address(es) for service (including postcode) for entry on the register** *You may give up to three addresses for service one of which must be a postal address but does not have to be within the UK. The other addresses can be any combination of a postal address, a box number at a UK document exchange or an electronic address.*

   [TRANSFEREE'S ADDRESS] (this will usually be the address of the property)

8. The Transferor transfers the Property to the Transferee

9. **Consideration** *Place "X" in the appropriate box. State clearly the currency unit if other than sterling. If none of the boxes applies, insert an appropriate memorandum in the additional provisions panel.*

   ☐ The Transferor has received from the Transferee for the Property the sum of *In words and figures.*

   ☒ Insert other receipt as appropriate. (See panel 12 below)

   ☐ The transfer is not for money or anything which has a monetary value

10. The Transferor transfers with *Place "X" in the appropriate box and add any modifications.*

☐ ☒ full title guarantee ☐   ☐ limited title guarantee

11. Declaration of trust *Where there is more than one Transferee, place "X" in the appropriate box.*

☐ The Transferees are to hold the Property on trust for themselves as joint tenants

☐ The Transferees are to hold the Property on trust for themselves as tenants in common in equal shares

☐ The Transferees are to hold the Property *Complete as necessary.*

12. Additional provisions *Insert here any required or permitted statements, certificates or applications and any agreed covenants, declarations, etc.*

12.1 The transfer is made pursuant to an order of the [ ] County Court dated [ ] in proceedings between the Transferor and the Transferee bearing number [ ].

The transferee covenants with the transferor to observe and perform the covenants and conditions referred to in the Charges Register so far as still subsisting and relating to the property and will keep the Transferor and [his or her] personal representatives effectually indemnified against all losses resulting from their non observance or breach.

Note to Clause 12.2 – This clause is only necessary when the parties entered into the original restrictions affecting the property (if any) or, in the conveyance to them, covenanted to observe them. Otherwise the transferor is not entitled to them.

12.2 The covenant by the Transferor implied by section 4(1)(b) Law of Property (Miscellaneous Provisions) Act 1994 by reason of the Transferor transferring with Full Title Guarantee shall be limited so as not to extend to any breach of the terms of the registered lease on the part of the Transferor relating to the condition of the property [Limitation of Transferor's liability in relation to repair: (see p.6)] [Only relevant if leasehold]

13. Execution *The Transferor must execute this transfer as a deed using the space below. If there is more than one Transferor, all must execute. Forms of execution are given in Schedule 9 to the Land Registration Rules 2003. If the transfer contains Transferee's covenants or declarations or contains an application by the Transferee (e.g. for a restriction), it must also be executed by the Transferee (all of them, if there is more than one).*

SIGNED as a DEED by (enter full name of individual) in the presence of: [TRANSFEROR]

Signature of Witness ……………………………………………………..
Name (in BLOCK CAPITALS) ……………………………………………
Address ……………………………………………………………………

SIGNED as a DEED by (enter full name of individual) in the presence of: [TRANSFEREE]

Signature of Witness ……………………………………………………..
Name (in BLOCK CAPITALS) ……………………………………………
Address ……………………………………………………………………

Precedent 38—Legal Charge

HM LAND REGISTRY

Land Registration Act 2002

County and District or
London Borough:
Title Number: [leave blank if application for first registration]
Property: [Address of Family Home]
This LEGAL CHARGE is made the   day of 200 between [*transferee's name*] of ("the mortgagor") (1) and [*transferor's name*] of   ("the mortgagee")   (2) pursuant to an order of the [County Court] dated   in proceedings between the Mortgagor and the Mortgagee bearing number [no. of proceedings].

1. The Mortgagor covenants with the Mortgagee to pay to the Mortgagee [six] months from the date hereof [*this being the legal date for redemption*] the sum of £ [*20,000*] with interest thereon from today at the rate of [8] per cent per annum and if such sum shall not be paid on that day then so long as any part of it shall remain owing [he or she] will pay to the Mortgagee interest at the said rate on the principal money for the time being hereby secured by equal monthly payments on the last day of each calendar month

2. PROVIDED that if (a) the Mortgagor pays interest at the said rate and on the said date (or within seven days of the same) and (b) the power of sale applicable to this mortgage has not become exercisable and (c) the Mortgagor has complied with all [his or her] obligations hereunder then the Mortgagee will not call in the said sum of £[*20,000*] or any part thereof before [*January 1, 2015 or other specified date*]

3. The Mortgagor CHARGES by way of legal mortgage with full title guarantee the land comprised in the above title ("the Mortgaged Property") with payment to the Mortgagee of the principal money interest and any other monies hereby covenanted to be paid by the Mortgagor

4. THE Mortgagor covenants with the Mortgagee that the Mortgagor:

    4.1 will at all times during the continuance of this security keep the Mortgaged Property in good and sufficient repair and condition and insured against fire and other risks in accordance with the covenants in that behalf contained in the Registered Lease and if the Mortgagor shall be in default in the performance and observance of any of such covenants the Mortgagee shall be entitled to repair and keep in repair the Mortgaged Property and insure the same in accordance with the covenants and all money expended by the Mortgagee under this power shall be deemed to have been properly paid by him or her

    4.2 will not during the continuance of this security without the consent in writing of the Mortgagee register or cause to be registered under the Land Registration Acts 2002 or any amendment thereto for the time being in force any person or persons as proprietor of the Mortgaged Property

    4.3 will not without the written consent of the Mortgagee grant or agree to grant any lease or tenancy of the Mortgaged Property or any part thereof

4.4 will on demand repay to the Mortgagee all money properly paid and all charges costs and expenses properly incurred hereunder by the Mortgagee together with interest thereon from the time of paying or incurring the same until repayment at the rate specified in clause 1 and until so repaid such costs charges and expenses shall be chargeable on the Mortgaged Property and shall be added to the principal money hereby secured with interest chargeable thereon at the rate aforesaid

4.5 forthwith will produce to the Mortgagee any order direction requisition permission notice or other matter whatsoever affecting or likely to affect the Mortgaged Property and served upon the Mortgagor and allow the Mortgagee to make a copy of it

4.6 will pay to the Mortgagee within thirty days of the receipt of the same any capital sum received by the Mortgagor (whether by gift inheritance or otherwise howsoever) by way of reduction of the principal sum hereby secured and for the purposes of this clause "capital sum" shall be any sum in excess of £3,000

5 IT IS AGREED AND DECLARED that the statutory power of sale shall be applicable hereto with the extension following namely that the same shall become exercisable immediately by the Mortgagee without notice to the Mortgagor if the Mortgaged Property or any part thereof or any chattel thereon belonging to the Mortgagor is taken in execution or if any chattel in the Mortgaged Property is taken under a distress for the rent reserved by the Lease

SIGNED as a Deed
by [*mortgagor's name*] in the presence of:

SIGNED as a Deed
by [*mortgagee's name*] in the presence of:

D—Family home in sole name of one party. Court order. Transfer to other party subject to existing charge. Deferred charge (2nd mortgage) in favour of transferor for specific amount not to be enforced until certain events. No interest chargeable until happening of events

Precedent 39

HM LAND REGISTRY
Land Registration Act 2002

County and District or
London Borough:
Title Number: [leave blank if application for first registration]
Property: [Address of Family Home]

This LEGAL CHARGE is made the   day of   20 between [transferor] of   ("the Mortgagor") (1) and [transferee's name] of   ("the Mortgagee")   (2) pursuant to an order of the [County Court] dated in proceedings between the Mortgagor and the Mortgagee bearing number [no. of proceedings].

1 THE Mortgagor covenants with the Mortgagee to pay to the Mortgagee [six] months from the date hereof [*this being tile legal date for redemption and when the power of sale arises*] the sum of £20,000 with interest thereon at the rate of [8] per cent per annum such interest only to become chargeable with effect from the first of the dates below mentioned ("the Specified Dates"):

   1.1 the remarriage of the Mortgagor

   1.2 the death of the Mortgagor

   1.3 the eighteenth birthday of [*youngest child of the family*]

   1.4 [*a fixed date*]

   such interest to be payable on the principal money for the time being hereby secured by equal monthly payments on the last day of each calendar month

2 PROVIDED THAT if the power of sale applicable to this charge has not become exercisable then the Mortgagee will not before the first to happen of the Specified Dates call in the said sum of £20,000 or any part of it

3 PROVIDED ALWAYS that notwithstanding and without prejudice to the provisions of this charge the power of sale applicable to this charge shall for the protection of a purchaser be deemed to arise [six] months from the date hereof [*this will the same date as the legal date for redemption*]

4 The Mortgagor CHARGES by way of legal mortgage with full title guarantee the land comprised in the above title ("the Mortgaged Property") with payment to the Mortgagee of the principal money interest and other money hereby covenanted to be paid by the Mortgagor SUBJECT TO the Charge dated in favour of [Bank or Building Society] and registered on '"the First Mortgage")

5 The Mortgagor further COVENANTS with the Mortgagee that the Mortgagor:

5.1 will duly and punctually pay all interest payable in respect of the First Mortgage and will from time to time produce to the Mortgagee on demand evidence of every such payment

5.2 will at all times keep the Mortgaged Property insured in accordance with the covenant contained in the First Mortgage (whether or not the First Mortgage remains in force and effect) and produce on demand evidence of the terms of the policy and the receipt for the last payment of premium thereunder

5.3 will at all times keep the Mortgaged Property in good repair and condition in accordance with the covenant in that regard contained in the First Mortgage

5.4 will not charge the Mortgaged Property in favour of any person without the written consent of the Mortgagee

5.5 will not during the continuance of this security without the consent in writing of the Mortgagee register or cause to be registered under the Land Registration Act 2002 or any amendment thereto for the time being in force any person or persons as proprietor of the Mortgaged Property

5.6 will not without the written consent of the Mortgagee grant or agree to grant any lease or tenancy of the Mortgaged Property or any part thereof

5.7 will on demand repay to the Mortgagee all money properly paid and all charges costs and expenses properly incurred hereunder by the Mortgagee together with interest thereon from the time of paying or incurring the same until repayment at the rate specified in clause 1 and until so repaid such costs charges and expenses shall be chargeable on the Mortgaged Property and shall be added to the principal money hereby secured with interest chargeable thereon at the rate aforesaid

5.8 forthwith will produce to the Mortgagee any order direction requisition permission notice or other matter whatsoever affecting or likely to affect the Mortgaged Property and served upon the Mortgagor and allow the Mortgagee to make a copy thereof

5.9 will pay to the Mortgagee within thirty days of the receipt of the same any capital sum received by the Mortgagor (whether by gift inheritance or otherwise howsoever) by way of reduction of the principal sum hereby secured and for the purposes of this clause "capital sum" shall be any sum in excess of £3,000

5.10 will not borrow any further money on the security of the Mortgaged Property

6 IT IS AGREED AND DECLARED as follows:

6.1 The statutory power of sale shall be applicable hereto with the extension following namely that the same shall become exercisable immediately by the Mortgagee without notice to the Mortgagor

6.1.1 if the Mortgagor becomes bankrupt or has a Receiving Order made against [him or her] or enters into any arrangement or composition with [his or her]creditors;

6.1.2 if a Receiver of the Mortgaged Property or any part thereof is appointed under the First Mortgage;

6.1.3 if any step is taken or proceedings instituted by way of sale or otherwise for the purpose of enforcing the security constituted by the First Mortgage

6.2 The Mortgagee may settle and pass the accounts of any person in whom the First Mortgage is for the time being vested and all accounts so settled and passed shall as between the Mortgagee and [his or her] assigns and the Mortgagor be conclusive and binding on the Mortgagor

SIGNED as a Deed
by [mortgagor's name] in the presence of:

SIGNED as a Deed
by [mortagee's name] in the presence of:

Precedent 40

Notice of second charge to first mortgagee

To [name and address of First Mortgagee]
Re [Property]
Your Account/Roll no

As Solicitors for   [Mortgagee's name] we hereby give you NOTICE that by a Mortgage dated and made between (1) [Mortgagor's name] (2) [Mortgagee] the above property presently in Mortgage to you was charged by way of legal mortgage by [Mortgagor's name] to the [Mortgagee's name] to secure payment of the sum of £[   ] and interest

We request you to acknowledge receipt of this Notice by signing and returning the duplicate hereof

Date
[Name and address of Mortgagee's Solicitors]

E—Family home in sole name of one party (following court order) subject to existing charge. Deferred charge in favour of other party for percentage of sale proceeds on specified events. No interest chargeable meantime

Precedent 41

HM LAND REGISTRY
Land Registration Act 2002

County and District or
London Borough:
Title Number: [leave blank if application for first registration]
Property: [Address of Family Home]

This LEGAL CHARGE is made the   day of 20 between [*Transferee's name*] of ("the Mortgagor") (1) and *[Transferor's name]* of   ("the Mortgagee")   (2) pursuant to an order of the [County Court] dated   in proceedings between the Mortgagor and the Mortgagee bearing number [no. of proceedings].

 1 In this Deed the following expressions have the following meanings:

  1.1 "the Repayment Date" shall be the first of the dates below mentioned:

   1.1.1 the remarriage of the Mortgagor

   1.1.2 the death of the Mortgagor

   1.1.3 [*fixed date*]

   1.1.4 any disposition of a legal or equitable estate or interest in the Mortgaged Property

 2 "the Specified Sum" shall mean an amount equal to 25 per cent of the net proceeds of sale of the Mortgaged Property after deducting from the gross proceeds of sale:

  2.1 the amount outstanding on the Repayment Date in respect of the First Mortgage

  2.2 any amount due to the Mortgagee by reason of expenditure by [him or her] in accordance with clause 6.7 hereof

  2.3 the proper legal and estate agency charges and disbursements incurred in connection with the sale OR

 3 in the event that the Mortgaged Property is not sold "the Specified Sum" shall mean the amount arrived at by taking the open market value of the Mortgaged Property on the Repayment Date with vacant possession as certified by a qualified valuer appointed by the Mortgagee and deducting therefrom

  3.1 the amount outstanding on the Repayment Date in respect of the First Mortgage

3.2 any amount due to the Mortgagee by reason of the expenditure by [him or her] in accordance with clause 6.7 hereof and

taking 25 per cent of the resulting figure

4 The Mortgagor covenants with the Mortgagee to pay to the Mortgagee the Specified Sum on the Repayment Date with interest thereon at the rate of [ ] per cent per annum from the Repayment Date until the date of actual payment

5 The Mortgagor CHARGES by way of legal mortgage with full title guarantee the land comprised in the above title ("the Mortgaged Property") with payment to the Mortgagee of the Specified Sum interest and other money hereby covenanted to be paid by the Mortgagor SUBJECT to the Charge dated [date of charge] in favour of [Bank or Building Society] and registered on [date] ("the First Mortgage")

6 THE Mortgagor further COVENANTS with the Mortgagee that the Mortgagor:

6.1 will duly and punctually pay all interest payable in respect of the First Mortgage and will from time to time produce to the Mortgagee on demand evidence of every such payment

6.2 will at all times keep the Mortgaged Property insured in accordance with the covenant contained in the First Mortgage (whether or not the First Mortgage remains in force and effect) and produce on demand evidence of the terms of the policy and the receipt for the last payment of premium thereunder

6.3 will at all times keep the Mortgaged Property in good repair and condition in accordance with the covenant in that regard contained in the First Mortgage

6.4 will not charge the Mortgaged Property in favour of any person without the written consent of the Mortgagee

6.5 will not during the continuance of this security without the consent in writing of the Mortgagee register or cause to be registered under the Land Registration Act 2002 or any amendment thereto for the time being in force any person or persons as proprietor of the Mortgaged Property

6.6 will not without the written consent of the Mortgagee grant or agree to grant any lease of tenancy of the Mortgaged Property or any part thereof

6.7 will on demand repay to the Mortgagee all money properly paid and all charges costs and expenses properly incurred hereunder by the Mortgagee together with interest thereon from the time of paying or incurring the same until repayment at the rate specified in clause 1 and until so repaid such costs charges and expenses shall be chargeable on the Mortgaged Property and shall be added to the principal money hereby secured with interest chargeable thereon at the rate aforesaid

6.8 forthwith will produce to the Mortgagee any order direction requisition permission notice or other matter whatsoever affecting or likely to affect the Mortgaged Property and served upon the Mortgagor and allow the Mortgagee to make a copy thereof

6.9 will not borrow any further money on the security of the Mortgaged Property

7 IT IS AGREED AND DECLARED as follows:

7.1 The statutory power of sale shall be applicable hereto with the extension following namely that the same shall become exercisable immediately by the Mortgagee without notice to the Mortgagor

7.1.1 if the Mortgagor becomes bankrupt or has a Receiving Order made against [him or her] or enters into any arrangement or composition with [his or her] creditors;

7.1.2 if a Receiver of the Mortgaged Property or any part thereof is appointed under the First Mortgage;

7.1.3 if any step is taken or proceedings instituted by way of sale or otherwise for the purpose of enforcing the security constituted by the First Mortgage.

7.2 The Mortgagee may settle and pass the accounts of any person in whom the First Mortgage is for the time being vested and all accounts so settled and passed shall as between the Mortgagee and his or her assigns and the Mortgagor be conclusive and binding on the Mortgagor

8 The power of sale and all other statutory powers vested in the Mortgagee shall in favour of a purchaser arise [six] months from the date hereof

SIGNED as a Deed
by [*mortgagor's name*] in the presence of:

SIGNED as a Deed
by [*mortgagee's name*] in the presence of:

DEFERRED CHARGES AND ADJUSTMENT BETWEEN BOTH PARTIES   197

F—Family home held by both parties and one party's mother as to two thirds for the both parties as joint tenants and one third for the mother. Transfer by order of court of one party's interest to the other

Transfer of whole of registered title(s)
PRECEDENT 42

Land Registry

TR1

If you need more room than is provided for in a panel, use continuation sheet CS and attach to this form.

1.	**Stamp Duty**

Place "X" in the appropriate box or boxes and complete the appropriate certificate.

☐ It is certified that this instrument falls within category ☐ in the Schedule to the Stamp Duty (Exempt Instruments) Regulations 1987

☐ It is certified that the transaction effected does not form part of a larger transaction or of a series of transactions in respect of which the amount or value or the aggregate amount or value of the consideration exceeds the sum of ☐

☐ It is certified that this is an instrument on which stamp duty is not chargeable by virtue of the provisions of section 92 of the Finance Act 2001

2.	**Title Number(s) of the Property** *Leave blank if not yet registered.* [TITLE NUMBER] [OR LEAVE BLANK IF APPLYING FOR FIRST REGISTRATION]
3.	**Property** [ADDRESS]
4.	**Date**
5.	**Transferor** *Give full names and company's registered number if any.* [BOTH PARTIES AND MOTHER-IN-LAW]
6.	**Transferee for entry on the register** *Give full name(s) and company's registered number, if any. For Scottish companies use an SC prefix and for limited liability partnerships use an OC prefix before the registered number, if any. For foreign companies give territory in which incorporated.* [TRANSFEREE AND MOTHER-IN-LAW] *Unless otherwise arranged with Land Registry headquarters, a certified copy of the Transferee's constitution (in English or Welsh) will be required if it is a body corporate but is not a company registered in England and Wales or Scotland under the Companies Acts.*
7.	**Transferee's intended address(es) for service (including postcode) for entry on the register** *You may give up to three addresses for service one of which must be a postal address but does not have to be within the UK. The other addresses can be any combination of a postal address, a box number at a UK document exchange or an electronic address.* [ADDRESS OF TRANSFEREE AND MOTHER-IN-LAW] (this will usually be the address of the property)
8.	**The Transferor transfers the Property to the Transferee**
9.	**Consideration** *Place "X" in the appropriate box. State clearly the currency unit if other than sterling. If none of the boxes applies, insert an appropriate memorandum in the additional provisions panel.* ☐ The Transferor has received from the Transferee for the Property the sum of *In words and figures.* ☐ *Insert other receipt as appropriate.* See panel 12 below ☐ The transfer is not for money or anything which has a monetary value

10. The Transferor transfers with *Place "X" in the appropriate box and add any modifications.*

    ☐ ☒   full title guarantee ☐   ☐   limited title guarantee

11. Declaration of trust *Where there is more than one Transferee, place "X" in the appropriate box.*

    ☐   The Transferees are to hold the Property on trust for themselves as joint tenants

    ☐   The Transferees are to hold the Property on trust for themselves as tenants in common in equal shares

    ☐   The Transferees are to hold the Property *Complete as necessary.*
ON TRUST AS TENANTS IN COMMON (AS APPROPRIATE – SPECIFY PERCENTAGE SHARES OR RECITE TRUST DEED).

NB: This will need to be discussed and instructions taken as to the client's wishes.

12. Additional provisions *Insert here any required or permitted statements, certificates or applications and any agreed covenants, declarations, etc.*

    12.1   The transferee covenants with the transferor to observe and perform the covenants and conditions referred to in the Charges Register so far as still subsisting and relating to the Property and will keep the Transferor and [his or her] personal representatives effectually indemnified against all losses resulting from their non observance or breach.

            Note to Clause 12.1 – This clause is only necessary when the parties entered into the original restrictions affecting the property (if any) or, in the conveyance to them, covenanted to observe them. Otherwise the transferor is not entitled to them.

    12.2   The Transferees declare that the survivor of them cannot give a valid receipt for capital money arising on a disposition of the land.

    12.3   The covenant by the Transferor implied by section 4(1)(b) Law of Property (Miscellaneous Provisions) Act 1994 by reason of the Transferor transferring with Full Title Guarantee shall be limited so as not to extend to any breach of the terms of the registered lease on the part of the Transferor relating to the condition of the property [Limitation of Transferor's liability in relation to repair: (see p.6)] [Only relevant if leasehold]

13. Execution *The Transferor must execute this transfer as a deed using the space below. If there is more than one Transferor, all must execute. Forms of execution are given in Schedule 9 to the Land Registration Rules 2003. If the transfer contains Transferee's covenants or declarations or contains an application by the Transferee (e.g. for a restriction), it must also be executed by the Transferee (all of them, if there is more than one).*

    SIGNED as a DEED by (enter full name of individual) in the presence of: [TRANSFEROR]

    Signature of Witness ....
Name (in BLOCK CAPITALS) ....
Address ....

    SIGNED as a DEED by (enter full name of individual) in the presence of: [TRANSFEREE]

    Signature of Witness ....
Name (in BLOCK CAPITALS) ....
Address ....

Chapter 8

Reluctance by Transferring Party to Execute Transfer or Mortgage

When the court has ordered that one party should transfer the family home to the other (if in the transferor's sole name) or his or her interest to the other alone or to trustees, the situation increasingly arises where the transferor either disappears without executing the transfer or refuses or merely fails to execute it because he or she disapproves of the court order. A similar position arises when the transferor refuses to execute a charge over the former family home ordered in favour of the transferee. We must consider how the transferee's solicitors proceed in these circumstances. (In most such cases the reluctant party will probably not have any solicitors acting for him or her, or if he or she has, those solicitors might find that they are unable to obtain meaningful instructions.) 8–01

If the family home is in the transferor's sole name the transferee's solicitors should in any event have taken steps to protect the transferee's position by lodging an application for a pending action land charge (unregistered title) or an application for registration of a unilateral notice (if registered land) (*see* pp.51–60) so that in effect the transferor cannot deal with the property.

Most court orders contain a time-limit (rarely, it must be admitted, adhered to) within which the transferor must execute the transfer or mortgage. If no such time-limit is imposed, then the order is defective; to avoid applying to the court asking it to make the order good by imposing a time-limit, it is suggested that a reasonable period of time be allowed to elapse. By then the transferee's solicitors should know if the transferor has executed the document. Faced with the transferor's reluctance or refusal to execute the document concerned, application can be made to the court for further help.

1 Execution of the transfer or mortgage by the court

The procedure outlined for asking the court to execute a transfer on behalf of a recalcitrant transferor can similarly be used where he or she refuses to execute a mortgage in favour of the transferee and what follows should be read and adapted accordingly. 8–02

The court's power to execute a transfer or mortgage on behalf of a reluctant signatory or someone who is untraceable is contained in the

Supreme Court Act 1981, s.39 and extended to county court jurisdiction by the County Courts Act 1984, s.38 (as substituted by the Courts and Legal Services Act 1990, s.3) provided there has been an order to execute. As there is always the possibility that the transferor will refuse to execute the transfer, to save time and further application to the court, one is tempted to couple the original application seeking the transfer of property to the transferee with a request that the court execute the relevant conveyance if the transferor does not do so within a specified time-limit.

Generally, the court will not make this latter order as it prefers to give the transferor the chance to execute the document. The court does not like to presume that someone will disobey its order; and it is only likely to make such an order if the transferor has shown by his or her past conduct that he or she certainly will not execute the document. Before the court gives its order as to execution it requires to be satisfied that the transferor has neglected or refused to comply with its order (*Savage v Norton* [1908] 1 Ch. 290).

In those cases where the court is satisfied that the transferor will not execute the transfer it may make an order further to the order for the transfer of property in the following terms:

> "And it is further ordered that if the Respondent shall not have duly executed and returned to the Petitioner's Solicitors a proper deed of transfer of [his or her] estate and interest prepared by the Petitioner's Solicitors within the said 28 days or within 21 days of delivery of such deed of transfer to the Respondent's last known address at [*insert last known address*] (whichever shall be the later) then a District Judge of the County Court be appointed and authorised to execute the deed of transfer of the Respondent's estate and interest in place of the Respondent."

Whether or not the court makes this above further order it is suggested that following the order for transfer the transferee's solicitors should send the engrossed transfer together with a copy of the court order to the transferor at his or her last known address by recorded delivery with acknowledgement of delivery being requested from the Post Office. If the transfer is not received back from the transferor duly executed within a reasonable time (or in the case of the court order above within the time-limit specified) application should be made to the court for the court to execute the transfer.

In the usual case where the court had not anticipated that the transferor would refuse to sign the transfer, the order sought would be on the following lines:

> 1 An Order under the Supreme Court Act 1981, s.39 and the County Courts Act 1984, s.38 that a Transfer to the Petitioner of the Respondents estate and interest in [freehold]—1 Blackacre Drive, Blackacre shall be executed by such person as the Court may nominate for that purpose, the above named Respondent having failed or neglected to do so.

2 Such further or other Orders as may be just.

[3 *Costs*].

A copy of the above application should be sent to the transferor as before giving him or her details of the date, place and time of the hearing of the application.

The application should be supported by an affidavit giving evidence of the service of the court order directing the transfer upon the transferor or to his or her last known address and evidence of the neglect of the transferor to execute the same (*see* Precedent 43). Even if the court anticipated the transferor's refusal to execute the transfer it would want an affidavit showing that the transferor had the opportunity to execute it and the affidavit should therefore show that the transfer was sent to the transferor for execution together with a copy of the court order, or that both were served upon him.

The expected form of court order, following the transferor's lack of response or refusal to execute the transfer, would be as follows:

"The Court directs that the Transfer to the Petitioner of the Respondent's estate and interest in 1 Blackacre Drive, Blackacre, be executed by a District Judge of the [   ] County Court."

The court order as to execution having been issued, or the court being satisfied in the case of anticipated refusal that the transferor will not execute the transfer, it will be necessary to re-engross the transfer (as the transferor will presumably still have this if his address is known or may have sent it back unsigned).

Whilst there is no reason why the transfer should not be re-engrossed following the form of the document submitted to the transferor for execution (but this time containing the attestation clause set out in Precedent 45), it is strongly recommended that the practice of the relevant district judge first be ascertained. Although there can be no legal reason, owing to the overriding power of the court to execute the transfer, it is known for a district judge to require a recital to the effect that the transfer was served on the respondent transferor who refused to sign the same. Similarly, it has been known for a district judge to refuse to execute a transfer containing covenants for title on the grounds that this was not a requirement set out in the original court order. To ascertain the individual requirements of the relevant district judge before re-engrossing the transfer could save considerable time.

Following re-engrossment and subject to any particular requirements of the district judge, the transfer can be lodged (by letter) with the clerk of the court with the request that it be placed before the district judge for his signature. On return of the transfer duly executed by the court on behalf of the transferor and steps following completion set out in previous chapters can be followed (as appropriate).

2 Vesting orders

8–03 All transfers of land or of any interest therein are void for the purposes of conveyancing or creating a legal estate unless made by deed (Law of Property Act 1925, s.52(1)). However, this section does not apply to vesting orders of the court (s.52(2)(f)).

There have, from time to time, been ingenious court orders which have been put forward as vesting orders, for instance, by declaring one of the joint proprietors to be deemed to be dead (see *Jones v Jones* [1972] 1 W.L.R. 1269 where the Chief Land Registrar refused to register the wife as proprietor of the family home) or that "the interest of the Respondent in the family home be extinguished". Such attempts to "telescope" conveyancing do not work as these are not vesting orders, quite apart from the fact that it is thought that a person can only be presumed dead after proper judicial process (see Matrimonial Causes Act 1973, s.19) and a district judge only has power to extinguish an interest in an ante or post nuptial settlement (s.24(1)(d)).

The circumstances where a vesting order can be made are set out in Trustee Act 1925, s.44. The essence of the section is that there should be a trustee who fails to make a transfer (and for these purposes it is considered that once a court orders a party to transfer he or she is in effect constituted as a trustee for this purpose).

The county court can make a vesting order (Trustee Act 1925, s.63A as inserted by the County Court Acts 1984, s.l48(1) and Sch.2, Pt 1) but its powers appear to be limited to cases where the total value of the property involved does not exceed the relevant monetary limits for proceedings in the county courts from time to time. Where the value exceeds this figure there would have to be a transfer to High Court jurisdiction and while this is procedural it is another item of procedure that can go wrong.

While the court can make a vesting order ab initio, it prefers not to do so where there is a party who has the opportunity of executing a transfer. If there is refusal then s.44(vi) provides that an application can be made if:

(a) there is evidence of wilful refusal or neglect by the transferor to execute the transfer (*see* Precedent 42); or

(b) 28 days have elapsed since the requirement should have been met.

In practice therefore, this is a similar procedure to that dealt with in the county court in the form set out in the earlier section of this chapter. There seems no advantage in utilising the provisions relating to vesting orders contained in the Trustee Act 1925.

HM Land Registry has power to give effect to vesting orders (Land Registration Act 2002) but these should contain a direction to the Chief Land Registrar that is clear and unequivocal. Sometimes the Land Registrar is unable to read into the court order an implied vesting order (*see* generally Ruoff & Roper, *Registered Conveyancing* looseleaf edition, para.35.008). Sometimes an order under the Supreme Court Act 1981, s.39 or the County Courts Acts 1984, s.38 (above) is put forward as a vesting order when it should be put into effect by a transfer.

Unless the scope of vesting orders is extended it is better to apply to the county court in those circumstances where the transferor refuses to execute a transfer, or where he cannot be found, as the procedure is well tried and tested in that arena.

3 The lack of title documents

We should consider the position where the title documents are not handed over or made available by the recalcitrant transferor. **8–04**

If the property is subject to a mortgage debt, no problem should arise, for the title documents will be under the control of the mortgagee and can be produced. If the property is not subject to a mortgage debt the situation is as explained below.

(a) Unregistered land

If it is known where, within the jurisdiction, the title deeds are, a court order would compel their production. A court order could be made (preferably at the same time as the order for transfer) that the documents of title be delivered up by the transferor. The order should specify to whom the deeds must be delivered up. **8–05**

If, however, the transferor is outside the jurisdiction and the whereabouts of the deeds unknown, the transferee's solicitors will have to proceed to prepare the transfer on the basis that the title deeds are lost; the solicitors who acted on the purchase should be contacted to see if they have retained any relevant papers; statutory declarations should be made by the transferee and previous owners (if available); and adjoining owners' solicitors should be contacted to see if any information can be given concerning covenants and the title generally built up so far as possible. Indemnity insurance should be considered.

Registration of title must, in any event, be applied for; if the transferor at a later date tries to sell or charge the property by producing the deeds it is to be hoped that a prospective purchaser/mortgagee would make an Index Map search at HM Land Registry which would reveal registered title—thus preventing the transferor's fraud. HM Land Registry will require a statutory declaration, proof of identity of the applicant and a fee will be payable. Practitioners who need to make an application for first registration where the deeds have been lost should, in order to ensure that the correct procedure is followed, obtain from HM Land Registry Practice Guide No. 2 entitled "First Registration of Title where deeds have been lost or destroyed". As with all other Land Registry documents this can be obtained from the HM Land Registry website (*www.landregistry.gov.uk*)

(b) Registered land

Since the abolition of Land and Charge Certificates by the Land Registration Act 2002 official copies of the entries at HM Land Registry are all that is required and these can be obtained by completing and posting form OC1, **8–06** by telephone or electronically from Land Registry Direct. If the title number is not known by the transferee's solicitor then an application can be made using the property address only.

PRECEDENTS

Precedent 43—Affidavit of petitioner's solicitors where transferor fails to execute transfer. Mortgage

[Order 20 Rule 10 County Court Rules 1981 (as amended by County Court (Amendment) Rules 1991 (SI 1991/525)) extending the practice direction dated July 21, 1983 ([1983] 3 All E.R. 33 relating to the Court of Appeal and the High Court to the county court requires affidavits to be marked in the top right-hand corner, on the backsheet and on the front of any exhibit with details of (1) the party on whose behalf the affidavit is filed (2) the initials and surname of the deponent (3) the number of the affidavit in relation to the deponent (4) the date sworn (5) the date on which it is filed.

Affidavits must not be bound with thick plastic strips or anything else which would hamper filing.

    (1) Petitioner
    (2) S R Harker
    (3) 1st
    (4) 29.09.06
    (5) [Date of Filing]

IN THE [   ] COUNTY COURT

    No of Matter

BETWEEN:

    [Name of Petitioner]   Petitioner
    and
    [Name of Respondent]   Respondent

AFFIDAVIT BY PETITIONER'S SOLICITORS IN SUPPORT OF APPLICATION FOR AN ORDER DIRECTING THE EXECUTION OF AN INSTRUMENT

I,   of
Solicitor, MAKE OATH and say as follows:
OR I,   of   solicitor, do solemnly and sincerely affirm and say as follows:

1 I am a Partner in the firm of   and that, as such, I have the conduct of this cause on behalf of the Petitioner.

2 The Petitioner made application in [his or her] Petition for Orders, *inter alia*, transferring to [him or her]:
"Such interest if any as the Respondent has in the property, 1 Blackacre Drive, Blackacre in the County of Blackacre".

3 Notice of Intention to Proceed with the application was duly given to the Respondent by post on [*date*] and, in due course the application came for

hearing before [Deputy] District Judge [   ] on [date] when [he or she] made the following Order:

> "IT IS ORDERED that the Respondent shall transfer to the Petitioner absolutely within 28 days from the date of this Order all [his or her] estate and interest in the property at 1 Blackacre Drive, Blackacre subject to the existing mortgage to the Blackacre Building Society, the Petitioner indemnifying the Respondent against all claims in respect thereof."

4   I have in my possession, the [title deeds] [official copies of the entries at HM Land Registry] relating to the property which disclose that the property is freehold and registered in the joint names of the Petitioner and the Respondent as beneficial joint tenants subject to a Mortgage in favour of [name of lender]. Accordingly the only way in which the Respondent could properly and legally give effect to the Order of the [Deputy] District Judge would be for [him or her] to execute a Transfer of [his or her] interest in the property to the Petitioner subject to the said Mortgage.

5   My firm has drafted a Transfer and the engrossment of this Deed is now produced and shown to me marked "SRHI".

6   By letter dated   and sent by first class post, I wrote to the Respondent at [his or her] address as given to the Court at the previous hearing, enquiring whether I should send the Transfer to [him or her] directly or to Solicitors on [his or her] behalf. I received no reply to my letter.

7   On the [date] my firm sent to the Respondent at [his or her] address a letter by Recorded Delivery enclosing an engrossment of the Transfer and asking that the Respondent should execute it and return it to me. That letter, a copy of which will be produced at the hearing of this Application, also enclosed a copy of the Order made by [Deputy] District Judge [   ] My firm was notified by the Post Office that the letter was delivered to the Respondent's address on the [date]. The Transfer has not been returned to me by the Respondent, nor has any reply to, or other acknowledgement of, the letter been received [or if process server has delivered the transfer].

[OR That on the [date] my firm instructed [process server] to serve on the Respondent a copy of the Order made by [Deputy] District Judge [   ] together with an engrossment of the transfer and a letter from my firm requesting the Respondent to execute the transfer and return it to me. The transfer has not been returned to me by the Respondent nor has any reply to, or other acknowledgement of, the letter been received.]

8   In the circumstances the Respondent has failed or refused to execute the transfer which the Order of the [Deputy] District Judge [   ] directed [him or her] to execute and I therefore ask the Court to make an Order appointing some other person to execute the transfer "SRHI" in place of the Respondent.

SWORN by the above-named
at this   day of   200
[OR Affirmed at   this   day of   200   ]
Before me,
Solicitor
of the Supreme Court

This Affidavit is filed on behalf of the Petitioner
this   day of   200   by
                            Petitioner's Solicitors

Precedent 44—Affidavit by process server as to delivery of engrossed transfer to respondent and service of court order

[*For details of markings to be contained on Affidavits, backsheet and exhibits see head note to Precedent 43*]

                        (1) Petitioner
                        (2) J. Jones
                        (3) 1st
                        (4) 29.09.06
                        (5) [Date of Filing]

IN THE [   ] COUNTY COURT
                                      No of Matter

BETWEEN:
               [*Name of Petitioner*]   Petitioner
                       and
              [*Name of Respondent*]   Respondent
            AFFIDAVIT OF SERVICE

I,   of
Process Server, MAKE OATH and say as follows:
OR I,   of   Process Server, do solemnly and sincerely affirm and say as follows:

    1 That I am instructed in this matter by [Name of Solicitors]
                                                      of

    Solicitors acting for the Petitioner.

    2 That on instructions received from [name of Solicitors] I personally served the Respondent at o'clock on [*date*] at [place of service] with the following papers:

        (a) a sealed copy of an Order of the Court dated [   ]a copy of which is now shown to me and marked "JJ1";

        (b) a Transfer, a copy of which is now shown to me and marked "JJ2";

        (c) a letter addressed to the Respondent from [name of solicitors] a copy of which is now shown to me and marked "JJ3".

    3 I know the person upon whom I served the above papers to be the said Respondent because [I have previously served papers upon [him or her] for [name of solicitors] and I refer to my Affidavit sworn on the [date] as to the identity of the person upon whom I served the papers].

SWORN *etc* [*see previous Precedent*]

Precedent 45—Attestation clause on transfer to be executed by the court
(*see* **Execution of documents, p.19**)

SIGNED as a Deed

by

a [Deputy] District Judge of the [   ]

County Court on behalf of [*full names of Transferor*] pursuant to an Order dated [date] and made under Section 39 of the Supreme Court Act 1981 and Section 38 of the County Courts Act 1984 in the presence of:

Chapter 9

Life Policy Collateral to the Mortgage on the Home

1 Introduction

Although tax relief on life assurance premiums was abolished in respect of policies taken out after March 13, 1984 (Finance Act 1984, s.72(1)), on occasion one will still come across mortgages on the family home which are secured not only by a charge on that property but also by a charge on a life assurance policy which is assigned to the mortgage lender by way of collateral security. Most mortgage lenders no longer insist on formal assignments, and are content with the deposit of the policy with them (by way of equitable charge) and the service of a notice of deposit on the assurance company. When the mortgage is repaid no formal re-assignment of the policy needs therefore to take place; a notice of release of deposit is served on the assurance company and the receipted notice is placed with the policy. Many mortgage lenders have now gone one step further: no assignment or deposit of the life policy is required, but if the policy is not kept up, then there is a breach of the terms of the mortgage. 9–01

The purpose of this chapter is not only to draw to the attention of the family practitioner that such policies may be in existence and should therefore be covered in the settlement between the parties in relation to the family home, but also to provide precedents as to how such policies may be dealt with.

It may be appropriate for instance that if the one party is to receive the family home (previously in joint names) subject to mortgage, that party should also receive the benefit of the life policy collateral to the mortgage or otherwise.

It had previously been thought that the court had power to order the transfer of a policy, or one spouse's interest in it under Matrimonial Causes Act 1973, s.24 but some doubt has now been expressed on this (*see Encyclopaedia of Forms and Precedents* Vol.16(2) [p.1324] Butterworths 1996 and the ruling of some district judges). It is accepted that the court does not have power to order a party to surrender the policy or to pay premiums; those matters would have to be dealt with by way of undertaking. It would seem appropriate to cover all these matters by way of undertaking which may be as follows:

"UPON the Respondent undertaking to the Court and agreeing with the Petitioner that he will:

(a) assign to the Petitioner within 28 days from the date hereof all his legal and beneficial interest in policy number (number) ('the Policy') with Insurance Company [subject to the charge thereon in favour
of Building Society].

(b) promptly pay all premiums in respect of the Policy as they fall due BY CONSENT etc."

2 Procedure

9–02 It is appropriate that the solicitor acting for the party who is to have the benefit of the policy should draw the deed of assignment and very often following the court order, the original policy is sent by the transferor's solicitors to the transferee's solicitors for them to draw the relevant assignment (unless the policy is subject to charge).

The original policy (or full copy) should be inspected so that:

(i) it can be checked that the terms of the policy are exactly as the parties thought and that the policy contains no unusual conditions or endorsements and is capable of assignment;

(ii) it can be ascertained that the age of the life assured has been "admitted" (i.e. the assurance company has seen the birth certificate of the life assured, lack of which can cause delay at the time of a claim).

The draft assignment can be submitted to the assignor's solicitors for acceptance together with a copy of the policy unless they retain the original until "completion".

It will be apparent that if the grantee of the policy is the transferor alone and the agreement or order is that after repayment of the mortgage (i.e. the policy is to remain charged to the mortgagee) the transferor is to have any surplus proceeds, then whether or not the family home is in the sole name of the one party (and is being transferred to the other) or in the joint names of the parties (and is being transferred to the one alone), no deed of assignment of the surplus equity of the policy is necessary; once the mortgagee has repaid itself, it must account for the surplus policy proceeds to the policy-holder or his or her estate.

As most life policies charged to a mortgagee are collateral to a mortgage of the family home, it is not considered necessary for the mortgagee to join in any assignment of life policy to release the transferor from the charge affecting it if he or she is being released from the mortgage affecting the family home.

3 The different policies

(a) Policy on life of one party alone

9–03 Such a policy with the transferor as the life assured and usually the grantee of the policy can be subject to an absolute assignment in favour of the other (Law of Property Act 1925, s.136). Provided notice of assignment is properly given (*see* Precedent 48) the transferee would be able to claim the policy proceeds on the death of the transferor (producing the death certificate, the policy, the assignment and receipted notice thereof).

(b) Policies on lives of both parties

Such a policy will usually be written on the basis that both parties are the grantees of the policy with the monies payable on the death of the first of them to die, the surviving spouse (as surviving trustee) claiming the policy proceeds. This is in contrast to policies arranged for inheritance tax purposes which usually pay out on the second death and where additional trustees should be appointed.

9–04

Under the Policies of Assurance Act 1867, s.1 it would appear that an assignee of an equitable assignment is put in the same position as a legal assignee and thus in a position to claim the policy proceeds. The third edition of this book provided a precedent accordingly.

Leading insurance companies, however, take the view that they are not prepared to recognise such assignments, and assignments should accordingly be not only of the transferring party's equitable interest but of the legal interest of both parties.

The transferee should consider whether or not he or she should appoint another trustee of the policy; if he or she were to die first, his or her surviving trustee could claim the policy proceeds without having to wait for a grant of representation to his or her estate (although such proceeds would be an asset of his or her estate).

(c) Policy under MWPA 1882 on husband's life for wife

A policy may have been taken out by the husband on his own life but written under the Married Women's Property Act 1882 for the benefit of his wife (often pre-1974 for estate duty reasons).

9–05

If the wife is to have the benefit of the policy, obviously no assignment need take place but there should be a change of trustee (*see* Precedent 51) to avoid contact with the husband, should for instance the wife wish to surrender the policy. Under most trusts, the power of appointing new trustees is vested in the trustees for the time being (Trustee Act 1925, s.36). In the case of MWPA trusts, the power of appointing new trustees is vested in the life assured (MWPA 1882, s.11). Whilst in most cases this will be of little import, it could mean difficulty in appointing new trustees at a later date.

4 Covenants contained in the assignment

The covenants for title introduced by the Law of Property (Miscellaneous Provisions) Act 1994 apply on any disposition of property (s.1(4)) and are not merely limited to transactions in land. The key statutory words must be used. Chapter 1 deals more fully with the implied covenants and for the

9–06

reasons there stated it is appropriate that the husband should give a covenant for full title guarantee.

In the precedents that follow other covenants are incorporated; the covenant contained in clause 2 should bring to the attention of the assignor that he or she should not undertake activities (such as motor racing) contrary to the terms of the policy; whether or not the assurance company would invoke the strict wording of the policy at the time of a claim is a matter of practice at that time.

5 Payment of premiums

9–07 Who is to pay the premiums is really a matter for agreement between the parties which can be dealt with in the preamble to the court order by way of undertaking. For a pre-March 13, 1984 policy, the insured will continue to obtain tax relief on the payment of the premiums made (Finance Act 1984, s.72(1)). If the benefit of the policy on the life of one party (subject to the existing charge) is to pass to the other, then it is preferable that he or she should (subject to the question of tax relief—*see* above) have control of the payment of premiums. The payment of maintenance could be structured accordingly.

6 Steps to be taken following completion of the assignment

(a) Stamp duty land tax

9–08 All the assignments in this book fall outside the scope of stamp duty land tax.

(b) Notice of Assignment

9–09 Except in those cases where the Assignor is the grantee of the policy and is to remain entitled to the surplus proceeds, a notice of the assignment should be given to the assurance company and also to the building society/ mortgagee so that surplus monies over and above those required to redeem the mortgage will be paid to the assignee (*Crossley v City of Glasgow Life Assurance Co* [1876] 4 Ch. 421). No assignee of a life policy can sue the insurance company for the policy monies until notice of assignment has been given and such notice should specify the date and purpose of the assignment (Policies of Assurance Act 1867, s.3).

As insurance companies are required to enquire whether an assignment has been made as a gift or for value (Income and Corporation Taxes Act 1988, s.552) and notify HMRC, it does save difficulty if a copy of the deed is submitted to the insurance company at the same time as the notice of assignment, so that the insurance company can comply with its obligations.

PRECEDENTS

Precedent 46—Policy on life of one party to be assigned to other party by order of court

THIS DEED OF ASSIGNMENT is made this day of 200 BETWEEN (1) [*Insured's name*] of ("the Assignor") and (2) [*Beneficiary's name*] of ("the Assignee")

WHEREAS:

(A) The Assignor is entitled to the policy ("the Policy") details of which are set out in the schedule hereto
(B) By an Order of District Judge [ ] in the [ ] County Court dated [ ] in proceedings between the Assignor and the Assignee bearing number [ ] the Assignor was ordered to assign the policy to the Assignee

NOW THIS DEED WITNESSES:

1. The Assignee ASSIGNS to the Assignee ALL THAT the Policy and all monies assured by or to become payable thereunder and all benefit and advantages thereof TO HOLD the same to the Assignee absolutely free from any estate or interest of the Assignor therein.

2. The Assignor covenants with the Assignee that the Policy is valid and in full force and effect and that [he or she] will not do or omit or knowingly suffer anything to be done as a result of which the Policy may become void or voidable or whereby the Assignee or anyone claiming title through [him or her] may be prevented from receiving the monies thereby assured and all benefit and advantages thereof.

[3 The Assignor covenants with the Assignee to continue to pay each and every premium due in respect of the Policy.]

[3 The Assignee hereby releases the Assignor from any obligation to pay any further premiums in respect of the policy.]

4. This assignment is made with full title guarantee.

IN WITNESS whereof this deed has been executed on the date hereof

THE SCHEDULE

Assurance Company

Policy No
Life Assured   [*the Assignor*]

Sum Assured

When payable

Commencement of policy

Premium

SIGNED as a Deed
by the Assignor in the presence of:

SIGNED as a Deed
by the Assignee in the presence of:

Precedent 47—Policy on life of one party charged to bank or building society to be assigned to other party (subject to charge) by order of court

THIS DEED OF ASSIGNMENT etc *[parties as Precedent 46]*

WHEREAS:

(A) The Assignor is entitled to the policy ("the Policy") details of which are set out in the schedule hereto subject to a charge ("the Charge") thereon in favour of [*bank or building society*] by an assignment dated [   ] and between (1) the Assignor and (2) [*bank or building society*] [OR where policy is merely deposited by way of charge with building society (A) the Assignor is entitled to the policy ("the Policy") details of which are set out in the schedule hereto subject to charge by way of deposit ("the Charge") in favour of [*bank or building society*].

(B) By an Order of District Judge [   ] in the [   ] County Court dated in proceedings between the Assignor and the Assignee bearing number [   ] the Assignor was ordered to assign the policy to the Assignee:

NOW THIS DEED WITNESSES:

    1 [Assignment—Precedent 46, clause 1] adding "SUBJECT to the Charge"

    2 [Covenant that Policy valid etc—Precedent 46, clause 2]

    3 [Covenant by Assignor to pay premiums—if appropriate—Precedent 46, clause 3 *or* if Assignee to pay premiums—Precedent 49, clause 3]

    4 This assignment is made with full title guarantee

IN WITNESS etc [*see Precedent 46*]

THE SCHEDULE—[see Precedent 46]

(Execution by both parties)

Precedent 48—Notice of assignment to assurance company given on behalf of assignee

TO [*Assurance Company—name and address*]

Policy No

Life Assured

As Solicitors for and on behalf of [*Assignee's name*] we hereby give you notice that by as Assignment dated made between (1) [*Assignor's name*] and (2) [Assignee's name] the Policy above mentioned and all monies assured by or to become payable thereunder was assigned by the said [*Assignor's name*] to the said [*Assignee's name*] absolutely to give effect to an Order of District Judge [   ] in the [   ] County Court dated 200 in proceedings bearing No [Subject to the existing charge in favour of [*Mortgagee*]

Please acknowledge receipt of this notice by signing and returning the duplicate attached

Dated

SIGNED
[name and address of solicitors]

Precedent 49—Policy on lives of both parties charged to bank or building society. Benefit of policy (subject to charge) by order of court to be assigned to one party. Assignee to pay premiums

THIS DEED OF ASSIGNMENT is made this   day of   200   BETWEEN (1) [*Assignor's name*] of   ("the Assignor") and [*Assignee's name*] of   ("the Assignee") and (2) the Assignee

WHEREAS:

(A) The Assignor and the Assignee are entitled to the policy ("the Policy") details of which are set out in the schedule hereto subject to a charge ("the Charge") thereon in favour of [*bank or building society*] by an assignment dated   made between (1) the Assignor and the Assignee and (2) [*bank or building society*]

[OR where the policy is merely deposited by way of charge with building society

(A) The Assignor and the Assignee are entitled to the policy ("the Policy") details of which are set out in the schedule hereto subject to charge by way of deposit ("the Charge") in favour of [*bank or building society*]]
(B) By an order of District Judge [   ] in the [   ] County Court dated [   ] in proceedings between the Assignor and the Assignee bearing number [   ] the Assignor was ordered to assign all his rights and interest in the policy to the Assignee

NOW THIS DEED WITNESSES:

1 The Assignor and the Assignee as owners of the Policy and the Assignor directing as to all his right title and interest therein ASSIGN to the Assignee ALL THAT the Policy and all monies assured by or to become payable thereunder and all benefit and advantages thereof TO HOLD the same to the Assignee absolutely free from any estate or interest of the Assignor therein SUBJECT to the Charge

2 The Assignor covenants with the Assignee that [he or she] will not do omit or knowingly suffer anything to be done as a result of which the Policy may become void or voidable or whereby the Assignee or anyone claiming title through [him or her] may be prevented from receiving the monies thereby assured and all benefit and advantages thereof

3 The Assignee hereby releases the Assignor from any obligation to pay any further premiums in respect of the Policy and covenants to indemnify [him or her] from any liability under the Charge

4 This assignment is made with full title guarantee

IN WITNESS etc

THE SCHEDULE [see Precedent 46]

(Execution by both parties)

[Note Precedent 48 Notice of Assignment can easily be adapted to cover the notice required following the above assignment]

Precedent 50—Policy on life of husband written under MWPA 1882 for benefit of wife. Husband as trustee. Benefit to be held for Assignor

THIS DEED OF ASSIGNMENT is made this   day of   20   BETWEEN (1) [Wife's name] of ("the Wife")

and (2) [Husband's name] of   ("the Husband")

WHEREAS:

(A) The Wife is entitled to the benefit of the Policy details of which are set out in the schedule hereto which Policy is held by the Husband as trustee for the Wife under the provisions of the Married Women's Property Act 1882

(B) This assignment is made pursuant an Order of District Judge [   ] in the [   ] County Court dated proceedings between the Husband and the Wife bearing number [   ]

NOW THIS DEED WITNESSES:

1 The Wife HEREBY ASSIGNS to the Husband the benefit of the Policy and all monies assured by or to become payable thereunder and all benefit and advantages thereof TO HOLD the same unto the Husband absolutely

IN WITNESS etc

SCHEDULE [see Precedent 46]

Note: No notice of assignment to the Assurance Company is necessary as the Assignor is already the legal owner of the policy as trustee

Precedent 51—Deed of appointment of new trustees where MWPA policy on life of husband held for benefit of wife by husband and another who now retire as trustees

THIS DEED OF APPOINTMENT is made this   day of 200   BETWEEN (1) [Husband's name] of   ("the Appointor") (2)

the [*Husband's name*] and XY of Trustees") and (3) [*Wife's name*] of Trustees') (together called "the Retiring and AB of ("the New

WHEREAS:

(A) The Retiring Trustees are the trustees of the policy ("the Policy") details of which are set out in the schedule hereto effected by the Appointor under the Married Women's Property Act 1882 for the benefit of the Wife

(B) The Retiring Trustees being desirous of retiring as trustees of the Policy the Appointor has determined to appoint the New Trustees to be trustees thereof

NOW THIS DEED WITNESSES that in exercise of the statutory power in that behalf and of every other power enabling him the Appointor hereby APPOINTS the New Trustees to be trustees of the Policy in place of the Retiring Trustees who hereby retire

IN WITNESS whereof this deed has been executed on the date hereof

THE SCHEDULE—[See Precedent 45]

(Execution by all parties)

SIGNED as a deed *etc*

Precedent 52—Notice of assignment on appointment of new trustees of a policy of assurance

TO [Assurance Company—name and address]

Policy No

Life Assured

As Solicitors for and on behalf of the trustees of the above Policy we hereby give you notice that by a Deed of Appointment dated   and made between (1) (2) and (3) [*as appropriate*] the said (3) were appointed as trustees of the Policy in place of (2) who retired as trustees thereof

Please acknowledge receipt of this notice by signing and returning the duplicate attached

Dated

SIGNED

[name and address of solicitors]

Chapter 10

The Insolvent Transferor

1 Introduction

The purpose of this chapter is to highlight a number of points relating to the family home, where there is potential or actual insolvency.   10–01

The possibility of the transfer to the one party being set aside in the event of the other's insolvency within five years of the date of the transfer has already been mentioned (*see* Ch.1, p.15). Such possibility should not of course discourage the court from making the order (*Mullard v Mullard* [1982] 12 F.L.R. 63).

Of course, if the transferee has notice of an act of bankruptcy on the part of the transferor before any order is made, the transferee must expect the transfer to be set aside.

The intermediate step could be a charging order (*see* Charging Orders Act 1979) against the transferor's interest in the family home. That is almost a topic on its own and is not covered here; if the house is in the transferor's sole name, the transferee's right of occupation should be protected by the registration of home rights (*see* Ch.3) and if the house is in joint names, the transferee should receive notice and any objection to the charging order application may well be adjourned so that it can be dealt with at the same time as the transferee's application for a property adjustment order (see *Austin-Fell v Austin-Fell* [1990] 3 W.L.R. 33).

2 Insurance

It has already been mentioned (*see* Ch.1) that the transferee may be advised, at the time of the transfer of the family home, to obtain a declaration of solvency from the transferor; a purchaser from the transferee within five years from the date of the transfer may be concerned about the risk of the transfer being put aside in the event of the transferor's insolvency, and the declaration may help to allay the purchaser's concern.   10–02

Insurers would not appear to be providing insurance cover at the time of the transfer to the transferee against the risk of a transferor becoming insolvent within five years, but they do issue policies for a single premium providing cover to a purchaser from the transferee. The policy is usually written for the benefit of the purchaser, their mortgagees and successors in title (see for instance policies issued by Norwich Union or Legal and Insurance Services Limited).

Most insurance companies when providing insurance in favour of a purchaser or mortgagee in such circumstances require:

(i) a copy of the transfer between the parties;

(ii) an up-to-date bankruptcy search against the transferor;

(iii) a copy of the transfer to the third party purchaser;

(iv) a statutory declaration from the transferor confirming solvency at the time of the transfer to the transferee *and* at the date the declaration is sworn.

Obviously if the transferor has disappeared or refuses to co-operate insurance cover may not be available, and the purchaser (and his or her mortgagees) will have to take a view on whether or not the transfer to the transferee could be liable to be set aside. It is to be hoped that the statutory declaration referred to above taken at the time of the transfer will in such circumstances be of persuasive effect.

3 The effect of the transferor's insolvency on the ownership of the family home

(a) House in solvent party's sole name

10–03 One would assume that the solvent party's position as absolute owner of the family home was relatively unassailable if the other party becomes insolvent, unless of course there has been a transfer to him or her without consideration or at an under value within the last five years (*see* Ch.1) and above.

A trustee in bankruptcy may well however try to lay claim to an interest in the house (particularly if the insolvent party has been paying the mortgage) and may either register a land charge at HM Land Charge Registry or lodge a notice at HM Land Registry which will not only stop the solvent party from disposing of the property but prevent him or her from raising monies on the security of it (Land Registration Act 2003, s.86). The solvent party will receive notice of the notice and (if appropriate) should be prepared to oppose its registration (*see* Ruoff and Roper, *Registered Conveyancing*, looseleaf para.42.011).

(b) House in insolvent party's sole name

10–04 On the party's insolvency title to the property automatically vests in the insolvent party's trustee in bankruptcy without transfer (Insolvency Act 1986, s.306) subject to the interest of any mortgagee.

Prior to the enactment of the Insolvency Act 1986, the trustee could petition for sale of the house in the normal way and would not be bound by any rights that the bankrupt's partner or ex-partner had registered under the Matrimonial Homes Act 1983 now Family Law Act 1996 (as amended by CPA 2004). The Insolvency Act 1986, s.336(2) changes this and provides that where a party's rights of occupation under the Family Law Act 1996 are a charge on the bankrupt's estate, the charge continues to subsist notwithstanding the bankruptcy.

Registration of home rights does mean that the registering party is in a stronger position to negotiate for the purchase of the property from the trustee in bankruptcy. However, such rights will only subsist until such time as the solvent party obtains an order pursuant to the Family Law Act 1996, ss.34 and 35 (as amended by CPA 2004).

(c) Joint Names

Where the family home is in the joint names of the parties, legal title does not on the insolvency of one party pass to the trustee in bankruptcy, because the property is already held on trust (Insolvency Act 1986, s.283(3)); the beneficial interest of the insolvent party does of course vest in the trustee who, having a statutory duty to realise the bankrupt's estate, will invariably apply to the court having jurisdiction in relation to the bankruptcy for an order for sale under Trusts of Land and Appointment of Trustees Act 1996, s.14 (Insolvency Act 1986, s.335A) of the family home, unless an arrangement can be reached with the solvent party. 10–05

The beneficial joint tenancy of the family home is severed by operation of law where one party becomes bankrupt (*see Re Turner* [1974] 1 W.L.R. 1556). Thereafter, the parties will hold as tenants in common in equal shares subject to any equitable accounting (*see Re Gorman* [1990] 1 All E.R. 717); where the trustee was entitled to an order for sale under Law of Property Act 1925, s.30 (now repealed—Trusts of Land and Appointment of Trustees Act 1996 and Land Registration Act 2002) but the court deferred such order to give the wife a chance to purchase the trustee's share). If of course the property is held as tenants in common with the interests defined by a declaration of Trust, or similar, that is conclusive unless there can be rectification by reason of fraud or mistake (*Pettitt v Pettitt* [1970] A.C. 777; *Goodman v Gallant* [1986] 1 All E.R. 311).

Precedent 53 is designed to cover a situation where another member of the family provides money to buy out the bankrupt party's equitable share.

If the insolvent party dies and their estate is subsequently the subject of an insolvency administration order, that order which dates back to the date of death does not sever the joint tenancy thus making the insolvent's interest in the property available to the trustee in bankruptcy: the interest has already accrued by right of survivorship to the solvent party at the moment of death (*Re Palmer* [1994] 3 W.L.R. 420).

A word of warning: sometimes the court is asked to make an order (where the house is in the joint names of the parties) to transfer one party's legal interest in the family home to the other so that the transferee can have sole conduct of a sale, from which the transferor would receive something, sole conduct for the transferee being necessary because of the transferor's unwillingness to co-operate. Apart from the risk to the transferor of the transferee in such circumstances decamping with all the money, there is the possibility of the purchaser raising objection to the transferee's title under the Insolvency Act 1986, s.339. To avoid both difficulties, it is suggested that the transferor retires as a trustee of the transfer title in favour of a new trustee (possibly his solicitor) so that the purchaser gets a good receipt for purchase monies (Law of Property Act 1925, s.27) from two trustees.

4 Steps to be taken following completion of the transfer from the insolvent party's trustee

(a) Stamp duty land tax

10–06 There will have been a transfer on sale so that form SDLT 1 will need to be completed and submitted to HMRC with a cheque (where the consideration exceeds £125,000) for the appropriate duty payable.

(b) Completion of the title

10–07 A marked copy of the court order appointing the trustee in bankruptcy will be required to complete the unregistered title or for the purposes of HM Land Registry and a certified copy should be sent to HM Land Registry with the application for transfer to the solvent party if already registered.

(c) HM Land Registry fees

10–08 The purchase of the insolvent party's share from the trustee in bankruptcy is a dealing for value within the Land Registration Fees Order 2006. Fees under Scale 1 will be payable, based upon the amount of the consideration.

(d) Insurance

10–09 The appropriate changes should be made to delete the insolvent party name from the policy and add that of the purchaser.

PRECEDENTS

A—Declaration of solvency at time of transfer to solvent party

Precedent 53

I, [*Insolvent party's name*] of   [*occupation*] and previously of [*address of family home*] do solemnly and sincerely declare as follows:

1 By a Transfer dated today's date I have transferred the property known as [*address of former family home*] to my former partner [*Solvent party's name*] following an Order of District Judge [   ] on the [   ] County Court datedproceedings bearing No [   ]

2 From an examination of my financial position at this date I have ascertained

    2.1 that I have an excess of assets over liabilities and

    2.2 that I am able to meet my debts and liabilities as they fall due

And as such I am solvent within the meaning of the Insolvency Act 1986

3 I have never been adjudicated bankrupt and that to the best of my knowledge no bankruptcy proceedings are to be or have been commenced against me

And I make this solemn declaration conscientiously believing the same to be true and by virtue of the provisions of the Statutory Declarations Act 1835

DECLARED at
this   day of   20

Before me

Solicitor

B—Transfer of insolvent party's share of former jointly owned property (held as Beneficial Joint Tenants) to solvent party's sister who has provided the purchase price, the property being subject to mortgage

Note: Covenant for title: it is very unlikely that a trustee in bankruptcy will give any title guarantee covenants, and these precedents have been drawn on that basis.

Transfer of whole of registered title(s)

PRECEDENT 54

Land Registry

TR1

If you need more room than is provided for in a panel, use continuation sheet CS and attach to this form.

1. Stamp Duty

Place "X" in the appropriate box or boxes and complete the appropriate certificate.

☐ It is certified that this instrument falls within category ☐ in the Schedule to the Stamp Duty (Exempt Instruments) Regulations 1987

☐ It is certified that the transaction effected does not form part of a larger transaction or of a series of transactions in respect of which the amount or value or the aggregate amount or value of the consideration exceeds the sum of ☐ as appropriate

☐ It is certified that this is an instrument on which stamp duty is not chargeable by virtue of the provisions of section 92 of the Finance Act 2001

2. Title Number(s) of the Property *Leave blank if not yet registered.*
[TITLE NUMBER] [OR LEAVE BLANK IF APPLYING FOR FIRST REGISTRATION]

3. Property

[ADDRESS]

4. Date

5. Transferor *Give full names and company's registered number if any.*
[BOTH PARTIES]

6. Transferee for entry on the register *Give full name(s) and company's registered number, if any. For Scottish companies use an SC prefix and for limited liability partnerships use an OC prefix before the registered number, if any. For foreign companies give territory in which incorporated.*

[TRANSFEREE and TRANSFEREE'S SISTER]

Unless otherwise arranged with Land Registry headquarters, a certified copy of the Transferee's constitution (in English or Welsh) will be required if it is a body corporate but is not a company registered in England and Wales or Scotland under the Companies Acts.

7. Transferee's intended address(es) for service (including postcode) for entry on the register *You may give up to three addresses for service one of which must be a postal address but does not have to be within the UK. The other addresses can be any combination of a postal address, a box number at a UK document exchange or an electronic address.*

[ADDRESS OF TRANSFEREE AND TRANSFEREE'S SISTER]

8. The Transferor transfers the Property to the Transferee

9. Consideration *Place "X" in the appropriate box. State clearly the currency unit if other than sterling. If none of the boxes applies, insert an appropriate memorandum in the additional provisions panel.*

☐ The Transferor has received from the Transferee for the Property the sum of *In words and figures.*

☐ [AMOUNT OF CONSIDERATION IN WORDS AND NUMBERS]

☐ *Insert other receipt as appropriate.* (See panel 12 below)

☐ The transfer is not for money or anything which has a monetary value

THE INSOLVENT TRANSFEROR

10. The Transferor transfers with *Place "X" in the appropriate box and add any modifications.*

☐ ☒ full title guarantee ☐ ☐ limited title guarantee

11. Declaration of trust *Where there is more than one Transferee, place "X" in the appropriate box.*

☐ The Transferees are to hold the Property on trust for themselves as joint tenants

☐ The Transferees are to hold the Property on trust for themselves as tenants in common in equal shares

(OR AS APPROPRIATE)

☐ The Transferees are to hold the Property *Complete as necessary.*

12. Additional provisions *Insert here any required or permitted statements, certificates or applications and any agreed covenants, declarations, etc.*

12.1   The Property is transferred subject to the charge ("the registered charge") dated [ ] and registered on [ ] [under which there is now owing the sum of £   ].

12.2   The [BANK OR BUILDING SOCIETY] ("the lender") being the proprietor of the registered charge hereby relieves and discharges [*Insolvent party's name*] and [his or her] estate from all obligations under the registered charge.

Refer to continuation sheet [CS]

13. Execution *The Transferor must execute this transfer as a deed using the space below. If there is more than one Transferor, all must execute. Forms of execution are given in Schedule 9 to the Land Registration Rules 2003. If the transfer contains Transferee's covenants or declarations or contains an application by the Transferee (e.g. for a restriction), it must also be executed by the Transferee (all of them, if there is more than one).*

SIGNED as a DEED by (enter full name of individual) in the presence of: [INSOLVENT PARTY]

Signature of Witness …………………………………………………..
Name (in BLOCK CAPITALS) ………………………………………….
Address ……………………………………………………………..

SIGNED as a DEED by (enter full name of individual) in the presence of: [SOLVENT PARTY]

Signature of Witness …………………………………………………..
Name (in BLOCK CAPITALS) ………………………………………….
Address ……………………………………………………………..

Continuation sheet for use with application and disposition forms

Land Registry

CS

1. Continued from Form [TR1]   Title number(s) [TITLE NUMBER]
2. *Before each continuation, state panel to be continued, e.g. "Panel 12 continued".*

Panel 12 continued

12.3 [SOLVENT PARTY'S SISTER] hereby covenants with the lender that [he or she] will at all times observe and be bound by the covenants and provisions of the registered charge as if [he or she] had been a party and executed the registered charge as "the borrower" defined in the registered charge.

12.4 [TRUSTEE IN BANKRUPTCY] being the trustee of the estate in bankruptcy of [INSOLVENT PARTY'S NAME] hereby acknowledges receipt of the consideration referred to in Panel 9 of this Transfer as Trustee in Bankruptcy.

12.5 The [SOLVENT PARTY] and [SOLVENT PARTY'S SISTER] covenant with [INSOLVENT PARTY] to observe and perform the covenants and conditions referred to in the Charges Register so far as still subsisting and relating to the Property and will keep [INSOLVENT PARTY'S NAME] and [his or her] estate effectually indemnified against all losses resulting from their non-observance or breach.

Note to Clause 12.5 – This clause is only necessary when the parties entered into the original restrictions affecting the property (if any) or, in the conveyance to them, covenanted to observe them. Otherwise the transferor is not entitled to them.

Panel 13 continued

SIGNED as a DEED by (enter full name of individual) in the presence of: [SOLVENT PARTY'S SISTER]

SIGNED as a DEED by (enter full name of individual) in the presence of: [TRUSTEE IN BANKRUPTCY]

Chapter 11

Transfer to Surviving Party from Deceased Party's Estate

From time to time, agreement is reached between the parties to the effect that if the family home is transferred absolutely to the one party, he or she will seek no further financial provision from the other, whether by way of capital or income, nor will he or she seek provision from out of the other party's estate in the event of death. Where agreement has been reached on this basis between the parties, it has been known for a transfer to be made and expressed to be in full and final settlement of the transferee's claims as indicated already. Naturally, when circumstances change, the parties seek advice as to whether or not this agreement can be upset. **11–01**

It has long been held that the parties cannot by agreement oust the jurisdiction of the court. *Hyman v Hyman* [1929] A.C. 601 established that a party cannot by agreement give up the right to apply for financial provision in family proceedings and *Re M* [1968] P 174 held that an agreement between husband and wife that the wife would not make application for provision out of the husband's estate did not oust the jurisdiction of the court to make such provision.

In short, therefore, any agreement between the parties to the extent mentioned above will be ineffective in barring the jurisdiction of the court.

It is worth noting that a dissolution or annulment of marriage or civil partnership does not revoke a will, but by virtue of Wills Act 1837, s.18A (as amended by Law Reform (Succession) Act 1995):

(a) it revokes the appointment of the former spouse or civil partner as an executor of the other spouse;

(b) it revokes any gift under the will in favour of the former spouse or civil partner;

(c) by virtue of the Children Act 1989, s.6. It revokes the appointment of the former spouse or civil partner as guardian of the children unless a contrary intention appears.

1 Avoiding further claims against the one party during his or her lifetime

The case of *L v L* [1962] P 101 established that an agreement between the parties that the wife would not seek further financial provision in family proceedings from the husband could only be effective if sanctioned by the court (*see* further *Minton v Minton* [1979] 2 W.L.R. 31). **11–02**

The advantages of a court order, where final agreement is reached between the parties. has been mentioned earlier (*see* p.2). In view of the encouragement now given to the principle of the "clean break" by the provisions of the Matrimonial and Family Proceedings Act 1984, it is certainly in the passing party's interest (in the context of this book) to seek a court order where financial matters between the parties are settled by agreement and the aim must be to achieve a recital to the court order as follows:

> "that the parties intend this order to be in full and final settlement of all claims which each party may have against the other or the estate of the other, whether pursuant to the Matrimonial Causes Act 1973, the Married Women's Property Act 1882, the Inheritance (Provision for Family and Dependants) Act 1975 or otherwise howsoever."

A transfer expressed to be in full and final settlement of a party's claim in the absence of a court order does not, as seen above, bar future application to the court, and at best such expression can only be evidentiary.

2 Avoiding a claim against the deceased's estate after his or her death

11–03 Just as the transfer of the family home to the one party may, with the consent of the court, stop further applications by that party against the other during that party's lifetime, so too, with the consent of the court, can applications by one party against the other party's estate after death be avoided.

The Inheritance (Provision for Family and Dependants) Act 1975 which came into operation in respect of deaths occurring after April 1, 1976, allows any member of a specified class of persons (as extended by Law Reform (Succession) Act 1995) to apply to the court on the grounds that the disposition of the deceased's estate is not such as to make reasonable financial provision for the applicant (s.1(1)) provided the deceased died domiciled in England or Wales.

Amongst the specified class are a spouse or civil partner and a former spouse or civil partner of the deceased who has not remarried (s.1(1)(b)). But even if the former partner has remarried or entered into a subsequent civil partnership a claim can be made under the provisions of s.1(1)(e) if immediately before the death the applicant was being maintained either wholly or partly by the deceased.

One party, therefore, in making financial settlement with the other, will wish to ensure that he or she cannot claim against his or her estate. Section 15 of the Act, as amended by the Family Law Act 1996, s.66(l), Sch.8, Pt 1, para.27(1), (5) and (6) (as amended by CPA 2004), provides that, on the granting of a decree of divorce nullity or juriced separation or equivalent order, the court, if it considers it just to do so, can order that either party be precluded from applying against the estate of the other under the provisions of this Act.

A court order, under s.15 may be as follows:

> "Pursuant to Section 15(1) of the Inheritance (Provisions for Family and Dependants) Act 1975 neither party shall upon the death of the other be entitled to make a claim for an order under Section 2 of that Act the court considering it just so to order."

Section 2 sets out the type of orders that the court may make in respect of the deceased's estate.

It is suggested that a copy of such court order be placed with the will of the party in whose benefit it is made so that his or her executors are in a position quickly to rebut a claim of a former partner.

3 Transfer to the surviving party following proceedings under Inheritance (Provision for Family and Dependants) Act 1975

If, however, the surviving party is not barred from claiming against the estate of the deceased party, he or she may bring proceedings against that estate under this Act. By virtue of s.2(1)(c) the court has power to make an order for the transfer to the applicant of property comprised in the estate.

11–04

In deciding what provision is reasonable for the surviving party, the court must ask itself the question "what would a family judge have ordered for this couple if divorce instead of death had divided them?" (*Moody v Stevenson* [1991] *The Times*, July 30).

It is worth noting that a transfer of a dwelling-house pursuant to an order under s.2 does not trigger the repayment of any discount granted in respect of a house purchased by the deceased under the provisions of the Housing Acts 1985, 1988 and 1996 from a provider of social housing.

In the case of unregistered or registered land, covenants for title will have to be considered (*see* Ch.1). It would be unreasonable to expect the personal representatives to transfer with full title guarantee; limited title guarantee implies covenants limited to acts and omissions since the last disposition for value (Law of Property (Miscellaneous Provisions) Act 1994, s.3(3)). Even this may be felt to be too wide as the executors may have had no connection with the property prior to the deceased's death. A narrower limit may therefore be prudent:

> "The covenant implied into this transfer by Law of Property (Miscellaneous Provisions) Act 1994, s.3(3) shall apply so far as it relates to the actions or omissions of the Executors/Transferors only to the period since the death of [deceased's name]."

The court may direct an outright transfer to the surviving party of the deceased's interest in the family home, whether it be in the sole name of the deceased or in the names of both parties as tenants in common.

Alternatively, it may direct that the house be held upon certain trusts; for instance, for the surviving party for life and after his or her death upon the terms of the deceased's will. In such a case, the house should be transferred to trustees to hold the same upon the terms of the court order (Precedent 26 can be adapted to this).

If the house is already in the joint names of the parties, who held as tenants in common, then strictly all the surviving party need do is appoint another trustee of the transfer (Trustee Act 1925, s.36) to act with him or her. On any sale a purchaser would get a good receipt if the purchase monies were paid to either two trustees or a trust corporation (Law of Property Act 2002); such purchaser need not concern himself or herself with the trusts upon which the monies are held. It is obviously advisable, from the point of view of the deceased's estate for the other trustee of the transfer to be one of the deceased's personal representatives, and in any proceedings under the inheritance provisions this should be requested, coupled with a request for a direction that future replacements for the "deceased's trustee" be appointed by his or her personal representatives (see, pp.156–157, para.6–09). Any transfer of title will give rise to an application for first registration as previously described.

(a) Registered land

11–05 If the parties held the land as tenants in common there will already be a restriction on the register to the effect that no disposition by a sole proprietor of land (not being a trust corporation) under which capital money arises will be registered except under an order of the registrar (Land Registration Act 2002, s.44 and Land Registration Rules 2003, r.91). If this is the only restriction, then the surviving proprietor can appoint an additional trustee. If, however, the further restriction referred to on pp.156 and 157, para.6–09 is entered, then although the surviving proprietor, can appoint an additional trustee the consent of the deceased's personal representatives will be required.

The appointment of a new trustee takes the form of a transfer from the surviving proprietor to himself or herself and the new trustee. The restriction previously entered on the register will remain unless application is lodged for its withdrawal. A declaration of trust or memorandum off the register should be made by the registered proprietors so that it is clear how the net proceeds of sale are to be dealt with following the termination of the trust (usually the death, remarriage or entering into a subsequent civil partnership of the surviving party).

(b) Steps to be taken following completion

11–06 (i) *Stamp duty land tax* Any transfer envisaged by this chapter of the book will be a transfer for no chargeable consideration and governed by Sch.3 to the Finance Act 2003 the transferee therefore can complete self-certificate SDLT 60 which should accompany the application for transfer to HM Land Registry. No SDLT will be payable.

(ii) *Memorandum* A memorandum of any court order will be endorsed on the original grant of representation to the deceased's estate by the court. A memorandum of a transfer to trustees, or to the surviving party, should also be endorsed on the grant.

(iii) *Court order* A certified copy of the court order will need to be lodged at the HM Land Registry when lodging the other documentation.

(iv) *HM Land Registry* fees Where the personal representatives of a deceased person are registered as proprietors on death (i.e. when HM Land Registry fees, according to the capital value of the land affected under Scale 2 Land Registration Fees Order 2006 are payable), a fee is not subsequently chargeable for registering any disposition of the land by them unless the disposition is for valuable consideration. If the personal representatives are not registered as proprietors the transfer from them to the surviving party is a dealing not for value, so that fees are payable in accordance with Scale 2 based on the value of the land which was the subject of the dealing less any charge secured thereon (e.g. by way of mortgage) or the value of the interest transferred. So far as an appointment of an additional trustee of the title is concerned, fees are payable on Scale 2, based on the value of the land.

A letter from the solicitor lodging the application certifying the value of the land, will be required, although such certificate seems to be acceptable by completing Form AP1 or FR1 accordingly.

PRECEDENTS

A—Transfer of house in deceased's sole name to surviving party (or former spouse or civil partner, not remarried or having entered into a new civil partnership) following court order under Inheritance (Provision for Family and Dependants) Act 1975. No mortgage

Transfer of whole of registered title(s)

Land Registry

TR1

PRECEDENT 55

If you need more room than is provided for in a panel, use continuation sheet CS and attach to this form.

1. **Stamp Duty**

   Place "X" in the appropriate box or boxes and complete the appropriate certificate.

   ☒ It is certified that this instrument falls within category ☐ in the Schedule to the Stamp Duty (Exempt Instruments) Regulations 1987

   ☐ It is certified that the transaction effected does not form part of a larger transaction or of a series of transactions in respect of which the amount or value or the aggregate amount or value of the consideration exceeds the sum of £ _____

   ☐ It is certified that this is an instrument on which stamp duty is not chargeable by virtue of the provisions of section 92 of the Finance Act 2001

2. **Title Number(s) of the Property** *Leave blank if not yet registered.*
   [TITLE NUMBER] [OR LEAVE BLANK IF APPLYING FOR FIRST REGISTRATION]

3. **Property**

   [ADDRESS]

4. **Date**

5. **Transferor** *Give full names and company's registered number if any.*

   [X] AND [Y] THE PERSONAL REPRESENTATIVES OF [DECEASED'S NAME] DECEASED

6. **Transferee for entry on the register** *Give full name(s) and company's registered number, if any. For Scottish companies use an SC prefix and for limited liability partnerships use an OC prefix before the registered number, if any. For foreign companies give territory in which incorporated.*

   [TRANSFEREE]

   Unless otherwise arranged with Land Registry headquarters, a certified copy of the Transferee's constitution (in English or Welsh) will be required if it is a body corporate but is not a company registered in England and Wales or Scotland under the Companies Acts.

7. **Transferee's intended address(es) for service (including postcode) for entry on the register** *You may give up to three addresses for service one of which must be a postal address but does not have to be within the UK. The other addresses can be any combination of a postal address, a box number at a UK document exchange or an electronic address.*

   [TRANSFEREE'S ADDRESS]

8. **The Transferor transfers the Property to the Transferee**

9. **Consideration** *Place "X" in the appropriate box. State clearly the currency unit if other than sterling. If none of the boxes applies, insert an appropriate memorandum in the additional provisions panel.*

   ☐ The Transferor has received from the Transferee for the Property the sum of *In words and figures.*

   ☐ *Insert other receipt as appropriate.* (See panel 12 below)

   ☐ The transfer is not for money or anything which has a monetary value

TRANSFER TO SURVIVING PARTY FROM DECEASED PARTY'S ESTATE   233

10. The Transferor transfers with *Place "X" in the appropriate box and add any modifications.*

    ☐   ☒   full title guarantee ☐   ☐   limited title guarantee

11. Declaration of trust *Where there is more than one Transferee, place "X" in the appropriate box.*

    ☐ The Transferees are to hold the Property on trust for themselves as joint tenants

    ☐ The Transferees are to hold the Property on trust for themselves as tenants in common in equal shares

    ☐ The Transferees are to hold the Property *Complete as necessary.*

12. Additional provisions *Insert here any required or permitted statements, certificates or applications and any agreed covenants, declarations, etc.*

    12.1   See Precedent 36 [recital of Court Order]

    12.2   The Transferee covenants with the Transferor and each of them that the Transferee will observe and perform the covenants and conditions referred to in the change register so far as still subsisting and relate to the property and will keep the Transferor and each of them and their respective estates and effects and the estate and effects of [*Deceased's name*] effectively indemnified against all losses resulting from their non observance or breach.

    Note to Clause 12.2 – This clause is only necessary when the parties entered into the original restrictions affecting the property (if any) or, in the conveyance to them, covenanted to observe them. Otherwise the transferor is not entitled to them.

    Refer to continuation sheet (CS)

13. Execution *The Transferor must execute this transfer as a deed using the space below. If there is more than one Transferor, all must execute. Forms of execution are given in Schedule 9 to the Land Registration Rules 2003. If the transfer contains Transferee's covenants or declarations or contains an application by the Transferee (e.g. for a restriction), it must also be executed by the Transferee (all of them, if there is more than one).*

    SIGNED as a DEED by (enter full name of individual) in the presence of: [X]

    Signature of Witness ....
    Name (in BLOCK CAPITALS) ....
    Address ....

    SIGNED as a DEED by (enter full name of individual) in the presence of: [Y]

    Signature of Witness ....
    Name (in BLOCK CAPITALS) ....
    Address ....

Continuation sheet for use with application and disposition forms

Land Registry

CS

1. Continued from Form TR1   Title number(s) TITLE NUMBER

2. *Before each continuation, state panel to be continued, e.g. "Panel 12 continued".*

Panel 13 continued

SIGNED as a DEED by (enter full name of individual) in the presence of: TRANSFEREE

Continuation sheet 1 of 1
Insert sheet number and total number of continuation sheets e.g. "sheet 1 of 3".
© Crown copyright (ref: LR/HQ/CD-ROM) 6/03

B—Appointment of new trustee of transfer, one of two tenants in common having died

Transfer of whole of registered title(s)

PRECEDENT 56

Land Registry

TR1

If you need more room than is provided for in a panel, use continuation sheet CS and attach to this form.

1. Stamp Duty

   Place "X" in the appropriate box or boxes and complete the appropriate certificate.

   ☐ It is certified that this instrument falls within category ☐ in the Schedule to the Stamp Duty (Exempt Instruments) Regulations 1987

   ☐ It is certified that the transaction effected does not form part of a larger transaction or of a series of transactions in respect of which the amount or value or the aggregate amount or value of the consideration exceeds the sum of £ _____

   ☐ It is certified that this is an instrument on which stamp duty is not chargeable by virtue of the provisions of section 92 of the Finance Act 2001

2. Title Number(s) of the Property *Leave blank if not yet registered.*
   [TITLE NUMBER] [OR LEAVE BLANK IF APPLYING FOR FIRST REGISTRATION]

3. Property

   [ADDRESS]

4. Date

5. Transferor *Give full names and company's registered number if any.*

   [TRANSFEREE] AND [X] AND [Y] X AND Y BEING THE PERSONAL REPRESENTATIVES OF [DECEASED'S NAME] DECEASED

6. Transferee **for entry on the register** *Give full name(s) and company's registered number, if any. For Scottish companies use an SC prefix and for limited liability partnerships use an OC prefix before the registered number, if any. For foreign companies give territory in which incorporated.*

   [TRANSFEREE AND A]

   Unless otherwise arranged with Land Registry headquarters, a certified copy of the Transferee's constitution (in English or Welsh) will be required if it is a body corporate but is not a company registered in England and Wales or Scotland under the Companies Acts.

7. Transferee's intended **address(es) for service (including postcode) for entry on the register** *You may give up to three addresses for service one of which **must** be a postal address but does not have to be within the UK. The other addresses can be any combination of a postal address, a box number at a UK document exchange or an electronic address.*

   [TRANSFEREE'S ADDRESS]

8. **The Transferor transfers the Property to the Transferee**

9. Consideration *Place "X" in the appropriate box. State clearly the currency unit if other than sterling. If none of the boxes applies, insert an appropriate memorandum in the additional provisions panel.*

   ☐ The Transferor has received from the Transferee for the Property the sum of *In words and figures.*

   ☐ *Insert other receipt as appropriate.* (See panel 12 below)

   ☐ The transfer is not for money or anything which has a monetary value

10. The Transferor transfers with *Place "X" in the appropriate box and add any modifications.*

☐ ☒ full title guarantee ☐ ☐ limited title guarantee

11. Declaration of trust *Where there is more than one Transferee, place "X" in the appropriate box.*

☐ The Transferees are to hold the Property on trust for themselves as joint tenants

☐ The Transferees are to hold the Property on trust for themselves as tenants in common in equal shares (OR AS APPROPRIATE)

☐ The Transferees are to hold the Property *Complete as necessary.*

12. Additional provisions *Insert here any required or permitted statements, certificates or applications and any agreed covenants, declarations, etc.*

12.1 [X] and [Y] hereby consent to this transfer as personal representatives of [*Deceased's name*] deceased

12.2 This transfer is entered into by the parties for the purposes of appointing a new trustee [*Deceased's name*] being one of the trustees having died

Refer to continuation sheet (CS)

13. Execution *The Transferor must execute this transfer as a deed using the space below. If there is more than one Transferor, all must execute. Forms of execution are given in Schedule 9 to the Land Registration Rules 2003. If the transfer contains Transferee's covenants or declarations or contains an application by the Transferee (e.g. for a restriction), it must also be executed by the Transferee (all of them, if there is more than one).*

SIGNED as a DEED by (enter full name of individual) in the presence of: [TRANSFEREE]

Signature of Witness ....
Name (in BLOCK CAPITALS) ....
Address ....

SIGNED as a DEED by (enter full name of individual) in the presence of: [X]

Signature of Witness ....
Name (in BLOCK CAPITALS) ....
Address ....

Continuation sheet for use with application and disposition forms

Land Registry

CS

| 1. Continued from Form | TR1 | Title number(s) | TITLE NUMBER |

2. *Before each continuation, state panel to be continued, e.g. "Panel 12 continued".*

Panel 13 continued

SIGNED as a DEED by (enter full name of individual) in the presence of: [Y]

Continuation sheet 1 of 1
Insert sheet number and total number of continuation sheets e.g. "sheet 1 of 3".
© Crown copyright (ref: LR/HQ/CD-ROM) 6/03

Index

1. Forms are included in the body of the text and are identified in the index by a bold entry for the preceding paragraph.
2. Precedents are included at the end of some of the chapters and are identified in the index by a bold entry for the chapter number followed by the precedent number, e.g. **6–P29**.

Assignments
  life policies
    covenants, 9–06
    notice of assignment, 9–09
    stamp duty land tax, 9–08
  steps following leasehold transfers
    declarations of trusts, 6–18
    deferred charges, 7–14
    transfers from joint names, 4–14
    transfers from sole name, 3–19

Bankruptcy. *see* **Insolvency**

Capital gains tax
  deferred charges, 7–04
  exemptions
    extra-statutory concession, 2–05
    parties living together, 2–03
    principle residence, 2–04
  general principles, 2–02
  other reliefs, 2–06
  settlements
    creation, 6–06
    termination, 6–07
Cautions against registration
  general principles, 3–07
  land registry application (CT1), 3–07
Children
  declarations of trusts, 6–11
Civil partnerships
  statutory reform, 1–04
  tax effects, 2–01
Class F Land Charges. *see* **Notice of home rights**
Compulsory first registration, 1–14
Conveyancing procedure
  deferred charges, 7–02
  land registry
    compulsory first registration, 1–14
    forms, 1–12
    property descriptions, 1–13
  life policies, 9–02
  special terms and conditions, 6–03

Conveyancing procedure—cont.
  transfers from ex-partner to new partner
    agreement or order, 5–02
    contracts, 5–03
    solicitors, 5–04
  transfers from sole name, 3–09
Costs
  legal service funding, 1–23
Council houses, 1–20
Council tax, 1–16
Court orders
  advantages, 1–05
  declarations of trusts
    cancellation of Class F registration, 6–14
    completion of abstracts, 6–15
    general principles, 6–11
    insurance, 6–17
    mortgages, 6–12
    registration of leasehold assignments, 6–18
    registration of title, 6–16
    stamp duty land tax, 6–13
  execution of documents, 8–02
  precedents
    deferred charges, **7–P35—7–P42**
    mortgage interest provisions, **6–P32**
    repairing and insuring provisions, **6–P29**
    residence conditions, **6–P33**
    simple transfers, **6–P26**
  registration of title, 3–16
  special terms and conditions
    appointment of trustees, 6–10
    conveyancing procedure, 6–03
    covenants for title, 6–04
    forms of transfer, 6–08—6–09
    Mesher orders, 6–02
    tax effects, 6–05—6–07
    typical provisions, 6–01
  transfers from ex-partner to new partner, 5–02

Court orders—cont.
  transfers from joint names, 4–01, 4–12
  transfers from sole name, 3–01
  vesting orders, 8–03
Covenants for title
  deferred charges, 7–03
  freeholds
    full title guarantees, 1–07
    general points, 1–06
    limited title guarantees, 1–08
    transfers from ex-partner to new partner, 5–05
    transfers from joint names, 4–07
    transfers from sole name, 3–10
  leaseholds
    full title guarantees, 1–09
    new and old tenancies distinguished, 1–10
    transfers from ex-partner to new partner, 5–06
    transfers from joint names, 4–08
    transfers from sole name, 3–11
  special terms and conditions, 6–04

Death. *see* **Transfers from deceased partner's estate**
Declarations of trusts. *see* **Trusts**
Deferred charges
  conveyancing procedure, 7–02
  covenants for title, 7–03
  forms of transfer
    general principles, 7–05
    registered land, 7–06
    third parties, 7–07
  general principles, 7–01
  mortgages, 7–08
  precedents
    family interests, **7–P42**
    interest payable pending fixed date, **7–P37**
    legal charge, **7–P38**
    notice of second charge, **7–P40**
    percentage sale proceeds, **7–P41**
    specified second mortgage, **7–P39**
    subject to payment, **7–P36**
    transfer between joint owners, **7–P35**
  steps following completion
    cancellation of entries, 7–10
    completion of abstracts, 7–11
    insurance, 7–13
    registration of leasehold assignments, 7–14
    registration of title, 7–12
    stamp duty land tax, 7–09
  tax effects, 7–04
Documents. *see* **Lack of documents**

Electronic conveyancing, 1–03
Execution of documents
  by the court, 8–02
  general practice, 8–01
  precedents
    attestation clauses, **8–P45**
    process server's affidavit, **8–P44**
    solicitor's affidavit, **8–P43**
  statutory provisions, 1–21
  vesting orders, 8–03

Forms
  land registry procedure, 1–12
  notice of home rights
    application for office copies (OC1), **3–04**
    application for registration (K2), **3–04**
    application (HR1), **3–05**
    application to register pending action (K3), **3–05**
    cancellation (HR4), **3–05**
    cancellation (K11), **3–15**
    cancellation of Class F, **3–05**
    index map search (SIM), **3–04**
  protection before registration
    cautions against registration (CT1), **3–07**
    unilateral notice (UN1), **3–07**
  registration of title
    first registration (FR1), **1–14**
    general application (AP1), **1–14**
Freeholds
  full title guarantees, 1–07
  general points, 1–06
  limited title guarantees, 1–08
  transfers from ex-partner to new partner, 5–05
  transfers from joint names, 4–07
  transfers from sole name, 3–10
Full title guarantees
  freeholds, 1–07
  leaseholds, 1–09

Home rights. *see* **Notice of home rights**

Indemnity covenants
  transfers from ex-partner to new partner, **5–P25**
  transfers from joint names
    leasehold assignment with mortgage transferred (court order), **4–P13**
    mortgage transferred (court order), **4–P12**

INDEX

Indemnity covenants—cont.
transfers from sole name
first and second mortgage liabilities shared, **3–P5**
leaseholds, **3–P2**
mortgage not transferred, **3–P4**
mortgage transferred, **3–P3**
Inheritance claims
after death, 11–03
during party's lifetime, 11–02
transfers following proceedings
general principles, 11–04
registered land, 11–05
steps following completion, 11–06
Inheritance tax
deferred charges, 7–04
general principles, 2–07
settlements
creation, 6–06
termination, 6–07
Insolvency
effect on ownership
insolvent party's sole name, 10–04
joint names, 10–05
solvent party's sole name, 10–03
insurance, 10–02
precedents
declaration of solvency, **10–P53**
transfer for full consideration subject to mortgage, **10–P54**
steps following completion
completion of title, 10–07
stamp duty land tax, 10–06
undervalue transactions
difficulties on resale, 1–19
setting aside, 1–18
statutory provisions, 1–17
Insurance
see also Life policies
declarations of trusts, 6–17
deferred charges, 7–13
insolvency, 10–02
transfers from ex-partner to new partner, 5–14
transfers from joint names, 4–13
transfers from sole name, 3–18

Joint names. *see* **Transfers from joint names**
Joint tenancies
see also **Severance of joint tenancies**
transfers from ex-partner to new partner
legal advice, 5–09
precedent, *5–P20*

Lack of documents
registration of title, 8–05
unregistered land, 8–04
Land registry procedure
compulsory first registration, 1–14
forms, 1–12
property descriptions, 1–13
Leaseholds
covenants for title
full title guarantees, 1–09
new and old tenancies distinguished, 1–10
transfers from ex-partner to new partner, 5–06
transfers from joint names, 4–08
transfers from sole name, 3–11
steps following completion
declarations of trusts, 6–18
deferred charges, 7–14
transfers from joint names, 4–14
transfers from sole name, 3–19
transfers from joint names
court order, **4–P13**
transfers from sole name, **3–P3**
Legal service funding
conveyancing costs, 1–23
statutory charges, 1–22
Life policies
conveyancing procedure, 9–02
covenants on assignment, 9–06
different arrangements
joint lives, 9–04
MWPA 1882, 9–05
single life, 9–03
general principles, 9–01
precedents
appointment of new trustees, **9–P51**
deed of assignment, **9–P46**
deed of assignment subject to charge (1), **9–P47**
deed of assignment subject to charge (2), **9–P49**
MWPA 1882, **9–P50**
notice of assignment, **9–P48**, **9–P52**
premium payments, 9–07
steps following completion
notice of assignment, 9–09
stamp duty land tax, 9–08
Limited title guarantees, 1–08

Mesher **orders**, 6–02
Mortgages
see also **Deferred charges ; Second mortgages; Statutory charges**
declarations of trusts, **6–P32**
deferred charges, 7–08
execution by the court, 8–02

Mortgages—cont.
  general principles, 1–11
  stamp duty land tax
    examples, 2–13
    general principles, 2–11
    hybrid situations, 2–12
    release of debt, 2–10
  transfer from insolvent's trustee, **10–P54**
  transfers from ex-partner to new partner, 5–08
    party solely entitled, **5–P24**
    tenants in common, **5–P22**
  transfers from joint names, 4–09
    leasehold assignment with mortgage transferred (court order), **4–P13**
    mortgage transferred (court order), **4–P12**
  transfers from sole name
    first and second mortgage liabilities shared, **3–P5**, **3–P5**
    first mortgage only, 3–12
    mortgage liability not transferred, **3–P4**
    mortgage liability transferred, **3–P3**
    second mortgages, 3–13
  trusts, 6–12

Notice of home rights
  cancellation
    following completion, 3–15
    following declaration of trusts, 6–14
    procedure, 3–05
  forms
    application for Class F registration (K2), **3–04**
    application for office copies (OC1), **3–04**
    application (HR1), **3–05**
    application to register pending action (K3), **3–05**
    cancellation (HR4), **3–05**
    cancellation (K11), **3–15**
    cancellation of Class F, **3–05**
    index map search (SIM), **3–04**
  protection before registration, 3–06
  registered land, 3–04
  statutory provisions, 3–02
  unregistered land, 3–03

Orders. *see* **Court orders**
Pending actions
  application to register (K3), **3–05**
  general principles, 3–07
Precedents
  court orders
    deferred charges, **7–P35**—**7–P42**

Precedents—cont.
  court orders—cont.
    mortgage interest provisions, **6–P32**
    repairing and insuring provisions, **6–P29**
    residence conditions, **6–P33**
    simple transfers, **6–P26**
  declarations of trusts
    agreed terms, **6–P27**
    application to enter restriction, **6–P30**
    independent trustees, **6–P28**
    mortgage interest provisions, **6–P32**
    net proceeds, **6–P31**
    rent and repairs, **6–P34**
    repairing and insuring provisions, **6–P29**
    residence conditions, **6–P33**
  deferred charges
    court order, **7–P36**
    family interests, **7–P42**
    interest payable pending fixed date, **7–P37**
    legal charge, **7–P38**
    notice of second charge, **7–P40**
    percentage sale proceeds, **7–P41**
    specified second mortgage, **7–P39**
    subject to payment, **7–P36**
    transfer between joint owners, **7–P35**
  execution of documents
    attestation clauses, **8–P45**
    process server's affidavit, **8–P44**
    solicitor's affidavit, **8–P43**
  insolvency
    declaration of solvency, **10–P53**
    transfer for full consideration subject to mortgage, **10–P54**
  life policies
    appointment of new trustees, **9–P51**
    deed of assignment, **9–P46**
    deed of assignment subject to charge (1), **9–P47**
    deed of assignment subject to charge (2), **9–P49**
    MWPA 1882, **9–P50**
    notice of assignment, **9–P48**, **9–P52**
  transfers from deceased partner's estate
    appointment of new trustees, **11–P56**
    following inheritance claim proceedings, **11–P55**
  transfers from ex-partner to new partner
    joint tenants without mortgage, **5–P20**

Precedents—cont.
  transfers from ex-partner to new partner—cont.
    party solely entitled with mortgage, **5–P24**
    sale of half share, **5–P25**
    from sole name without mortgage, **5–P23**
    tenants in common with mortgage, **5–P22**
    tenants in common without mortgage, **5–P21**
  transfers from joint names
    court order and transferee's indemnity, **4–P16**
    court order without mortgage, **4–P18**
    leasehold assignment with mortgage transferred (by agreement), **4–P15**
    leasehold assignment with mortgage transferred (court order), **4–P13**
    memorandum of severance, **4–P8**
    mortgage transferred (agreed sale), **4–P14**
    mortgage transferred (court order), **4–P12**
    notice of severance (registered land), **4–P9**
    notice of severance (unregistered land), **4–P7**
    release from subsequent mortgage, **4–P19**
    sale without mortgage, **4–P17**
    transfer without mortgage, **4–P11**
    transfer without mortgage by court order, **4–P10**
  transfers from sole name
    consent to transfer, **3–P6**
    first and second mortgage liabilities shared, **3–P5**
    freehold without mortgage, **3–P1**
    leasehold without mortgage, **3–P2**
    mortgage liability not transferred, **3–P4**
    mortgage liability transferred, **3–P3**
Procedure. *see* **Conveyancing procedure**
Property adjustments. *see* **Court orders**

Registered land
  deferred charges, 7–06
  notice of home rights, 3–04
  special terms and conditions, 6–09
  transfers following inheritance claim proceedings, 11–05

Registered land—cont.
  transfers from joint names
    forms of transfer, 4–06
    severance of joint tenancies, 4–03
  unilateral notices, 3–08
Registration of title
  compulsory first registration, 1–14
  declarations of trusts, 6–16
  deferred charges, 7–12
  electronic conveyancing, 1–03
  forms
    first registration (FR1), **1–14**
    general application (AP1), **1–14**
  lack of documents, 8–05
  transfers following inheritance claim proceedings, 11–06
  transfers from ex-partner to new partner, 5–13
  transfers from joint names
    court orders, 4–11
    land registry fees, 4–12
  transfers from sole name
    copy court orders, 3–16
    land registry fees, 3–17

Second mortgages
  see also **Deferred charges**
  notice of deferred charge, **7–P40**
  transfers from sole name
    general principles, 3–13
    precedent, **3–P5**
Settlements
  creation, 6–06
  termination, 6–07
Severance of joint tenancies
  form of notice, **4–P7**
  general principles, 4–02
Sole name. *see* **Transfers from sole name**
Solicitors
  see also **Conveyancing procedure**
  affidavit regarding execution of documents, **8–P43**
  transfers from ex-partner to new partner
    advice on joint tenancies, 5–09
    conveyancing procedure, 5–04
Stamp duty land tax
  declarations of trusts, 6–13
  deferred charges, 7–09
  general principles, 2–08
  life policies, 9–08
  mortgage debts
    examples, 2–13
    general principles, 2–11
    hybrid situations, 2–12
    release of debt, 2–10

INDEX

Stamp duty land tax—cont.
  reliefs, 2–09
  transfer from insolvent's trustee, 10–06
  transfers following inheritance claim proceedings, 11–06
  transfers from ex-partner to new partner, 5–10
  transfers from joint names, 4–10
  transfers from sole name, 3–14
Statutory charges, 1–22

Tax effects
  see also **Council tax**
  capital gains tax
    extra-statutory concession, 2–05
    general principles, 2–02
    other reliefs, 2–06
    parties living together, 2–03
    principle residence, 2–04
  civil partnerships, 2–01
  deferred charges, 7–04
  importance, 1–15
  inheritance tax, 2–07
  special terms and conditions
    creation of settlements, 6–06
    general principles, 6–05
  stamp duty land tax
    general principles, 2–08
    mortgage debts, 2–10—2–13
    reliefs, 2–09
  termination
    termination of settlements, 6–07
Tenancies in common
  legal advice, 5–09
  transfer with mortgage, **5–P22**
  transfer without mortgage, **5–P21**
Title *see* **Covenants for title**
Transfers
  deferred charges
    general principles, 7–05
    registered land, 7–06
    third parties, 7–07
  ex-partner to new partner, 4–06
  execution by the court, 8–02
  from joint names, 4–06
  registered land, 4–06
  special terms and conditions, 6–08—6–09
  unregistered land, 4–05
Transfers from deceased partner's estate
  avoidance of claims
    after death, 11–03
    during party's lifetime, 11–02
  general principles, 11–01

Transfers from deceased partner's estate—cont.
  precedents
    appointment of new trustees, **11–P56**
    following inheritance claim proceedings, **11–P55**
  transfers following proceedings
    general principles, 11–04
    registered land, 11–05
    steps following completion, 11–06
Transfers from ex-partner to new partner
  advice on joint tenancies, 5–09
  conveyancing procedure
    agreement or order, 5–02
    contracts, 5–03
    solicitors, 5–04
  covenants for title
    freeholds, 5–05
    leaseholds, 5–06
  forms of transfer, 5–07
  general principles, 5–01
  mortgages, 5–08
  precedents
    joint tenants without mortgage, **5–P20**
    party solely entitled with mortgage, **5–P24**
    sale of half share, **5–P25**
    from sole name without mortgage, **5–P23**
    tenants in common with mortgage, **5–P22**
    tenants in common without mortgage, **5–P21**
  steps following completion
    cancellation of entries, 5–12
    completion of title, 5–11
    insurance, 5–14
    registration of title, 5–13
    stamp duty land tax, 5–10
Transfers from joint names
  court order, 3–01, 4–01
  covenants for title
    freeholds, 4–07
    leaseholds, 4–08
  forms of transfer
    unregistered land, 4–05
  mortgages, 4–09
  precedents
    court order and transferee's indemnity, **4–P16**
    court order without mortgage, **4–P18**
    leasehold assignment with mortgage transferred (by agreement), **4–P15**

Transfers from joint names—cont.
  precedents—cont.
    leasehold assignment with
      mortgage transferred (court
      order), **4–P13**
    memorandum of severance, **4–P8**
    mortgage transferred (agreed sale),
      4–P14
    mortgage transferred (court order),
      4–P12
    notice of severance (registered
      land), **4–P9**
    notice of severance (unregistered
      land), **4–P7**
    release from subsequent mortgage,
      4–P19
    sale without mortgage, **4–P17**
    transfer without mortgage, **4–P11**
    transfer without mortgage by court
      order, **4–P10**
  severance of joint tenancies
    general principles, 4–02
    notice, 4–03
  steps following completion
    insurance, 4–13
    registration of leasehold
      assignments, 4–14
    registration of title, 4–11—4–12
    stamp duty land tax, 4–10
Transfers from sole name
  conveyancing procedure, 3–09
  covenants for title
    freeholds, 3–10
    leaseholds, 3–11
  forms of transfer
    registered land, 4–06
  mortgages
    first mortgage only, 3–12
    second mortgages, 3–13
  notice of home rights
    cancellation, 3–05
    protection before registration, 3–06
    registered land, 3–04
    statutory provisions, 3–02
    unregistered land, 3–03
  precedents
    consent to transfer, **3–P6**
    first and second mortgage liabilities
      shared, **3–P5**
    freehold without mortgage, **3–P1**
    leasehold without mortgage, **3–P2**
    mortgage liability not transferred,
      3–P4
    mortgage liability transferred, **3–P3**
  registration of title
    copy court orders, 3–16
    land registry fees, 3–17

Transfers from sole name—cont.
  steps following completion
    cancellation of home rights, 3–15
    insurance, 3–18
    registration of leasehold
      assignments, 3–19
    registration of title, 3–16—3–17
    stamp duty land tax, 3–14
Trusts
  appointment of trustees, 6–10
  conveyancing procedure, 6–03
  covenants for title, 6–04
  forms of transfer, 6–08—6–09
  Mesher orders, 6–02
  mortgages, 6–12
  precedents
    agreed terms, **6–P27**
    application to enter restriction,
      6–P30
    independent trustees, **6–P28**
    mortgage interest provisions, **6–P32**
    net proceeds, **6–P31**
    rent and repairs, **6–P34**
    repairing and insuring provisions,
      6–P29
    residence conditions, **6–P33**
  steps following completion
    cancellation of Class F registration,
      6–14
    completion of abstracts, 6–15
    insurance, 6–17
    registration of leasehold
      assignments, 6–18
    registration of title, 6–16
    stamp duty land tax, 6–13
  tax effects, 6–05—6–07
  typical provisions, 6–01

Undervalue transactions
  difficulties on resale, 1–19
  setting aside, 1–18
  statutory provisions, 1–17
Unilateral notices
  general principles, 3–08
  land registry application (UN1), **3–07**
Unregistered land
  compulsory first registration, 1–14
  lack of documents, 8–04
  notice of home rights, 3–03
  registration of pending actions and
    cautions, 3–07
  special terms and conditions, 6–08
  transfers from joint names
    forms of transfer, 4–05
    severance of joint tenancies, 4–03

Vesting orders, 8–03

THE COMPANION CD-ROM
Instructions for Use

Introduction

These notes are provided for guidance only. They should be read and interpreted in the context of your own computer system and operational procedures. It is assumed that you have a basic knowledge of WINDOWS. However, if there is any problem please contact our help line on 020 7393 7266 who will be happy to help you.

CD Format and Contents

To run this CD you need at least:

- IBM compatible PC with Pentium processor
- 8mb RAM
- CD-ROM drive
- Microsoft Windows 95

The CD contains data files of Precedent material. It does not contain software or commentary.

Installation

The following instructions make the assumption that you will copy the data files to a single directory on your hard disk (e.g. C:\Harker).

Open your **CD ROM drive**, select and double click on **setup.exe** and follow the instructions. The files will be unzipped to your **C drive** and you will be able to open them up from the new **C:\Harker** folder there.